Readers praise Laszlo Gati:

"It read like a novel and I frequently had to ignore my wife's calls to bed to find out what happened next."

Robert Sunter, CBC Radio

"Your book is WONDERFUL!! I'm enjoying reading it from the beginning in a continuous flow. What a life you've had! I'm glad you put it out for people to share and enjoy. If any field in the music world is more difficult to survive in than jazz it's being a symphony conductor. My hat's off to you. "

Paul Horn - Flutist, Recording Artist

"Many interesting memories and notable collaborations are recalled during the reading of Gati's 'Les Preludes'

Steven Staryk violinist, former concertmaster of the Chicago Symphony, The Royal Philharmonic Orchestra, The Amsterdam Concertgebow Orchestra

" I am totally fascinated by "Les Preludes". I find it an EXTRAORDINARY book.

Fanny Zichlinsky profesor, Conservatorio Nacional de Musica, Mexico City

"I'm continuing to read your book, and I find it more and more interesting from a musical and human point of view. . . . it is helping me to have a better relationship with myself and music!"

Roberto Russo, Concert Pianist

Les Préludes

Mosaics of a Musician's Life

Laszlo Gati

Published by Hardcopys DPS Inc.
Vancouver, British Columbia, Canada

Second printing February, 2005

This book is published by arrangement with the author by Hardcopys Digital Publishing Solutions Incorporated, Vancou-ver, B.C. Canada

Reach the publisher on the Web at www.hardcopys.com

ISBN 0-9735820-2-2

*Dedicated to all of the women
and to all of the musicians in my life*

Acknowledgments

This book had such long gestation periods that by now its origins have receded beyond my memory bank. I think it is easier to start with the present and proceed backward into the past, and see how far the roots go that made this story possible.

First of all, I have to thank Guy Whitford and my editors, Philip Whitford and Gary Klinga, who felt that my story merited telling and helped me make it a reality. Pavla Polcarova initiated the whole process and, through her legal expertise, helped finalize the necessary arrangements.

Naturally, without my father's and mother's help, I would not have acquired the necessary knowledge to pursue a career in Music.

I have so many friends, members of my family, members of my musical family, and members of the medical profession who contributed to my life story, that I find it literally impossible to come up with a logical order of 'importance' without offending somebody, or everybody.

Forget the order of importance, as everybody who is a friend is a cherished member of my family. My daughters, Kathleen and Suzanne, were also on my tail to "finish that damned book".

Helena Tichy, my invaluable friend, helped with proofreading the book, along with Monique Bergamo and Jacqueline Langlois, among others. Myfanwy Pavelic, the great Canadian painter, is not only my great friend and a constant source of inspiration, but also made several paintings of me, including the collage on the front cover of the book. Olga Domansky in Chicago, another source of inspiration, and many other friends who not only patiently waited for my publishing 'debut', but tirelessly prodded me over the years to finish the project.

Although I 'wrote' this book on and off perhaps for the last thirty years or so, I consider myself more of a raconteur than a writer. (You will notice this pretty quickly.)

My best friend and tutor Gheorghe Rozsa, who was and remained my best friend all his life, and who inspired me to strive for social justice. My mother, my ex-wife, my daughters, and all my wonderful women friends who helped me in so many different ways.

Although I had and have some wonderful male friends too, the majority of my best friends were women, perhaps because they were and are more sensitive than men. Let me list some male friends before I offend them too! Paul Horn, the wonderful flutist and 'new age' musician. My good friend John Kozak, violist and lawyer, who was instrumental in me being invited to Bangkok, Thailand to conduct the Bangkok Philharmonic Orchestra. My good friend Eduardo Rahn, Music Director of the Maracaibo Symphony Orchestra. Dr. Riemer and Dr. Gergely of the Budapest Psychiatric Institute. And so on.

My brothers and I lived in separate countries for more than fifty years, but I could always count on their help and understanding.

The musicians and the music in my life! This book deals mainly with them, their influence on me as a child, as an adolescent, as a professional musician, and as a performing artist joining in making music with the greatest musicians of the last fifty years or so.

Saying THANK YOU! Is simply not sufficient. Perhaps the only way I can express my gratitude is through the non-verbal medium of music itself.

My hope is that through my life story, you will be able to share not just the difficult times we had to go through, but also some of the divine musical highlights which made it all worthwhile.

Laszlo Gati
September 2004

FOREWORD

"If music be the food of love, play on. . ."
William Shakespeare
Twelfth Night

A human life and a musical performance have much in common. Though we can record them, and even play them back in some way, they both have their highest existence in the present moment, in the actual instant of performance. Though they may be accompanied by words, life and music communicate thoughts, emotions and lessons primarily through non-verbal means. Life and music alike are terribly fragile threads; a misplaced note, or taking the wrong turn at a street corner can abruptly, unfairly, and catastrophically, cut off a performance of genius — or a life of great promise.

If we consider Laszlo Gati's life a mosaic, there are three things to describe. First, the substrate of music, that great truth and unifying thrust which binds and beds all of the shiny incidents which make up his seventy-nine years of experience on this earth. And there are the incidents and coincidences, the colourful shards which have fallen upon and been arranged upon this bed, each piece a moment to be described and treasured and learned from. Birth in a feudal kingdom. Survival through pogroms and mass-murder. Delectable experiences with Communism and Capitalism. An airplane crash. Playing the violin and the viola. Conducting. World travel. Depression. Divorce. The pieces of the mosaic.

And then there is the picture itself. What the mosaic looks like when viewed from afar. What all the pieces add up to. What shape, what form, what significance does it all have?

The reader is the only one who can answer this question. As each musical performance is experienced, filtered, and interpreted by each individual in an audience in their own unique language, no one can say what piece of music is "best", nor what it may "say". The dialogue between performer and listener is the most private in the world. What you will make of Laszlo's life is not what he makes of it — nor should it be.

Should he give you a trailer, a preview, a teaser? In short, he was born in semi-feudal Romania, survived World War II and the Nazi holocaust. He moved from Romania to Hungary after the war and lived through both the establishment of his musical career and an early construction of Communism. He left Hungary in 1956, survived an airplane crash in Germany, and settled in Montreal. Laszlo has spent the last 48 years of his life in Canada. Through his life he has been a musician, a Romanian, an Hungarian, a Jew, a conductor, an artistic director, an entrepreneur, a suicidal depressive, a son, a brother, a husband, a father, and a Canadian patriot, sometimes all simultaneously. His life is both personal incident and a history of the Twentieth Century. He has witnessed war and revolution and the worst atrocities of man against man, horrors deeply personal and terrifyingly indifferent. He has experienced directly the most sublime artistic achievements of human beings, playing and being uplifted by the greatest music ever composed, and performing with many of the most accomplished musical artists of the last century. He has lost and gained several lifetimes.

He has burnished this mosaic many times over the last 30 years, diarizing his life, writing articles both political and related to arts, striving always to achieve a balanced and coherent view of this, his life, the tree and all its branches and leaves. Sitting here in the sunset of his life, the last light flashing through the leaves of his experience, he still wonders at the beauty revealed and he is still blinded by new revelations.

If, by revealing himself to you, he lets light and maybe sound into your existence, he has done more than he intended, and succeeded more than he hoped.

Philip Whitford, editor
July, 2004

Contents

Contents (con't)

PROLOGUE

THE PRELUDES

We had a lovely movie house not far from where we lived, called the Forum, which had beautiful deep, red, velour seats and a sloping floor. This theater was also used as a concert hall. I remember hearing Ian Kipura and Martha Eggert, two famous singers of the 1930's, in concert there.

It happened during the showing of the original "King Kong" film. Around the end of the intermission I was late coming back to my seat. At the time, it was customary during the intermission of movies to play classical music.

As I entered the auditorium, the loudspeakers were blaring out the incredibly forceful sounds of the ending of "Les Preludes", Franz Lizt's symphonic poem.

Suddenly — under the influence of the music — I changed the rhythm of my steps to coincide with the rhythm of the music, a very slow, solemn march. I had the feeling that I was conducting this glorious music, and everybody was watching me!

I recognized instantly, that *this* — conducting — is exactly what I should be doing!

I realized, at that moment, that the little sounds produced by the four strings of the violin were not sufficient for me to produce the kind of sounds and feelings I wished to express through music. I needed the whole physical force and the whole palette of sound that only an orchestra can produce.

In 1995, sixty years after those transcendent steps down the cinema aisle, after an absence of 39 years from Hungary, I returned to the stage of the Great Hall of the Franz Liszt Academy of Music in Budapest. The final piece of my

Les Préludes

program was "Les Préludes" of Franz Liszt, the music that had set the course of my life for so many years.

#

Les Préludes
(After Lamartine - Meditations Poetiques)

Is our life aught but a series of preludes to that unknown chant, whereof death intones the first solemn note? Love forms the magical aurora of all life; but whose may be the lot wherein the first raptures of happiness are not interrupted by some storm of which the baleful breath dissipates his fair illusions, of which the fatal lighting's consume his altar, and what sorely wounded soul is there which, emerging from such a tempest, does not seek reposeful oblivion amid the soothing calm of pastoral retreats? Nevertheless, man but seldom resigns himself long to the enjoyment of the beneficent tepidity whose charm welcomed him to Nature's breast; and when the "trumpet-call to arms shall ring out," he rushes to the post of danger, whatever be the war which summons him to the ranks, that in and through the combat he may regain full self-consciousness and the full command of his power.

#

It was spring of 1985 when I checked in for the second time that week to the Psychiatric Ward of the Hotel Dieu Hospital in Windsor, Ontario, Canada. I was depressed. This time I had a definite plan. The conditions seemed to be ideal. My room was quite far from the nurse's desk. My roommate had gone home for the weekend, and everything seemed to be quiet. The ward settled down for a peaceful night.

The day before, I had asked my elder daughter Suzanne to bring in the hair-cutting gizmo I had bought in Nuremberg, West Germany, during our European trip in 1973. This was a double-sided comb that had two razor blades inside. Supposedly it was invented by another Hungarian. Suzanne didn't know my secret plan. I had stripped the razor blades from the comb that afternoon.

The nurse brought in my evening dose of sedatives, which included Halcion. Halcion was very popular at the time for depressives such as me; later on they discovered it had a number of side-effects, including ... suicidal urges. The nurse stayed around to make sure that I took all my pills. Finally, she left.

I realized that I could not wait too long to execute my plan. I had taken quite a heavy dose of sedatives and I had to hurry up before they took effect and put me safely asleep. I thought myself both rational and considerate, so I decided to cut my arteries over the toilet bowl and not make a bloody mess. I took the chair, which stood beside my bed, into the bathroom, sat on it, leaned over the toilet bowl and started to cut what I thought were the arteries in my arm, which I assumed to be the places my nurses took their blood samples from. Cio-Cio San's suicide aria from Madame Butterfly of Puccini sounded gloriously in my head; on the other hand, cutting myself was quite painful.

When I woke up the next morning everything was peaceful. I was lying in bed. The chair was back in its place near the table. I felt quite normal. I looked at my left arm and saw the sleeve of my green pajama crusted with dried blood. I realized immediately, that my suicide attempt had not been a dream. I got up and rang the bell for the nurse. When she came in I pointed to my bloody pajama sleeve. She must have realized instantly what happened. She hugged me and held me in her arms and I hugged her and held her in my arms.

I will never forget this moment, the feeling of her soft body in my arms, a feeling beyond personalities, beyond description.

I felt that I was embracing womanhood, life, peace, future, eternity.

Les Préludes

Chapter One

BIRTH AND BACKGROUND

I was born in Timisoara, Romania, on September 25, 1925; I was the second son of a Hungarian-Jewish couple who owned a bakery in the city. Ignacz, my father, was born in the same city in 1894, when it was called Temesvar, but located in a different country, the Austro-Hungarian Empire. This explains my family's Hungarian ethnicity in the midst of Romania. In 1919, after the First World War, the Austro-Hungarian Empire had been carved up by the Allies (Britain, France, and the U.S.).

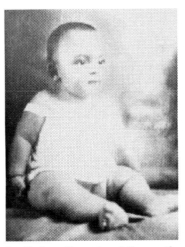

Ladislaus/Laszlo at 3 months - A real "bouncing baby boy."

One slice of that carving was the piece of Transylvania, including Temesvar, which was given to Romania. You could say that my family emigrated without having had to move! Maybe this is what caused my lifelong wandering, which was to include three citizenships on two continents, and decades of worldwide travel.

But that was all in the future.

For my first twenty years, I lived in Timisoara and celebrated my birthday on September 24th. We did so because that was the day when my mother, Vera, went into labour. She remembered clearly that it was Yom Kippur, the Day of Atonement, and she was happy not to have to fast. I was happy enough with this arrangement, and I thought, along with everyone else, that the 24th was the day of my birth.

In 1946, I needed my birth certificate to obtain my passport in order to go to Budapest to continue my musical studies. It turned out that my birthday was registered on the *25th* of September. Apparently, I was born after midnight and the date had turned, but my mother's happy memory of being able to eat on Yom Kippur, the day before, had become so strongly associated with her happiness at my birth, that we had been celebrating birthday parties a day early for 20 years! I hadn't missed anything, but it wasn't the first or the last time that things in my life were to change abruptly.

At the time of my birth, my father owned a small bakery. The bakery was in a basement, and customers had to descend twelve steps from the street to enter it. My father was a

This is the main square of Timisoara, about 1935. At the end of the street, facing the camera, is the Theatre and Opera House. In 1950, after the takeover of the Communists, my father was exhibited on the front steps, wrapped in chains, with a sign hanging off his neck, "I am a filthy Capitalist."

brilliant, practically self-taught baker and businessman. In spite of the obvious hindrance of his inconvenient location, through his excellent products and my mother's help in serving the customers, he developed the base of what was to become a little "conglomerate" in Timisoara.

Timisoara, in 1925, was a smallish town of about 60,000 with a multi-ethnic and multi-lingual makeup. It had Hungarian, Romanian, Schwab (German) and Serbian populations and accordingly, all four languages were spoken in the town; although, Romanian was the official language and French was the second language in education. The reason for French, the fifth language, was that Rumania belonged to the "Entente Cordiale" with France.

I was born in this building, which was the headquarters of Prince Eugene de Savoya during his 15th century campaign against the Turkish Occupation. I took this pictures during a trip to Romania in 1973. I had to be discreet, as the authorities of the time were deeply suspicious of any foreigner with a camera.

Timisoara/Temesvar is an old city with 2,000 years of history. It sits astride the Bega River, and has been an important transportation hub for nearly all that time. Previous occupiers of Romania left their ruins—the remains of Turkish and even Roman structures are found in different parts of the city. The British and American bombers of World War II left further ruins, but that was later on. Timisoara was and still is an important historical, industrial and cultural center. It has several universities and colleges, a municipal theater and opera house, a Greek-Orthodox cathedral, a large number of parks, and the aforementioned ruins, both early and late.

My childhood was spent playing, exploring, and growing up in the presence of deep history, an experience which many children in North America are deprived of.

My father, Ignacz Osterreicher, born 1894, prosperous businessman, at about 35 years of age.

My own shallower family history does not contain any Turkish or Roman ancestors, but it is interesting all the same.

My father, Ignacz (Ignatie in Romanian) Osterreicher was born in 1894. He was the son of Leopold (Lipot in Hungarian) Osterreicher, who had a bakery in Budapest. During the heyday of the Austro-Hungarian Empire it was, apparently, quite in vogue whether you were a Jew or not, to change your name to Osterreicher, which simply means "Austrian" in German. There is an unconfirmed rumor floating around our family that my great-grandfather's name was actually Lazarowitch.

After grandfather Leopold's first wife died of cancer of the colon, he remarried Malvin, a woman 44 years his junior. My father was the oldest of my grandfather's four children by his first wife. A brother and sister died when they were quite young and his brother Ferdinand, my uncle, who was instrumental in getting my parents to Canada after the war, died in Montreal in his fifties from prostate cancer.

My father spent some time on the front in Serbia during the First World War and told some of his stories repeatedly. When he started saying Csacsak (pronounced as Tchatchak) we continued almost silently "Obrenovatz, Zagreb." He was hard of hearing so he couldn't hear our whispers.

He lived in Budapest at the time and got married young and had a son when he was twenty years old. On his return from the war, he found his wife living with somebody else. Apparently, she thought that my father had died. He took his young son and returned to Temesvar.

All his life, my father was an extremely hard working man. He was also an excellent baker and a born businessman, who could see well in advance various business trends.

He started a little bakery in a basement and turned this little enterprise into a gold mine. Somehow, he managed to become the purveyor for the local army garrison. We really liked to eat the hot crispy crust of the dark bread we made for the army. After several years, my father was able to buy another fairly large property in Jozsefvaros (Joseph City).

Besides the bakery, he also established a pastry factory. He was always ahead of the competition and he gradually established franchises all over the city. By the time the fascists took away his business, he had twenty-five franchises in Timisoara.

During the Thirties he went to the Industrial Fair in Leipzig, Germany, every year. He always came back with innovations. For instance, while the competition was still kneading the bread manually, he bought a machine able to handle three-hundred kilos of bread dough at a time. The competition still used wood fired ovens — they made a bonfire in the oven with big slabs of wood and when the oven was hot enough they extricated the hot ashes and inserted the loaves of bread. But my father had two ovens heated by flame throwers and two ovens heated by steam. He also bought different machines for producing corn and buns, modern machines for the pastry factory to produce marzipan, and many other innovations.

He had an incredible business instinct. When he heard that the farmers expected a poor crop due to lack of rain, he bought ten boxcars of flour anticipating higher prices. His foresight paid off handsomely as the competition was forced to buy later smaller quantities at higher prices. In 1936, he went to Rome, Italy, for a World Congress of Bakers. We always had a great laugh when he told of his troubles due to his lack of Italian. One time, he had to go to the washroom. In Hungarian the washroom is called, "W.C." or "toilet". So he asked where the bathroom was — in Hungarian. The attendant did not understand, so he motioned to his tummy that he had to go. The attendant asked "Cabinetto?" My Father said "SI" "SI!" The attendant said, "Occupato" — which my father understood well enough to his discomfort. The point is that my father never let any lack of his stand in his way. Language, ethnicity, education, competition were things that other people used to excuse their lack of success. My father never made, nor did he accept any excuses.

My father had a dominant personality; competitive, intelligent, and self-centred in the way that successful businessmen need to be. These are not necessarily the traits; however, which enable one to get along with customers to schmooze and sell. This personality might have gotten in the way of his success, but for his wife, Vera.

My mother was in charge of serving the customers. She had excellent taste and during the holiday season (Easter, Christmas, and so on) made beautiful show windows. The children of Timisoara glued their noses to the windows to be as close as possible to those wonder worlds my mother created.

My mother Vera (Grosz) Osterreichter in her mid-forties.

In the mid-thirties, my father built a two story apartment building with four apartments and four stores. We moved up from our ground floor apartment to a spacious first floor apartment. My father knew how to make money and how to save it.

My mother Vera's maiden name was Grosz. She was born in Ciacova, a little village about 40 kilometers from Timisoara. Her father was an accountant. My maternal grandmother died in childbirth when Vera was two years old. She was a real beauty and my mother, at the age of 95, still hung an old tinted picture of her in her room in the old folks' home. Mother never got over the fact that she lost her own mother at such an early age.

Her father remarried and had a son and a daughter from this new marriage. Apparently, my mother's step-mother favoured her own children and mistreated Vera; at the very least, she was nicer to her own children than to my mother.

I don't know how my parents met. According to my

mother, it was my stepbrother who asked her to marry my father by telling her, "Vera, be my mother . . ."

On the one hand, my father could make money and on the other hand, my mother had wonderful taste and knew how to create beautiful surroundings for the family. How she managed to get the money from my father, directly or indirectly, remains a mystery to my brothers and me.

She had beautiful custom-built furniture in every room. The living room had beautiful display cases with inlaid woods of various kinds. The master bedroom was all white.

In our room (I shared my room with Dodi) the furniture was green. Very ingeniously, my Mother had two sets of built-in cupboards one on top of the other. In the summer the winter cloth was stored on the top cupboard and in the winter the summer cloth was stored on the top. We also had a washbasin in our room.

Beside the beautiful furniture, my mother procured Meissen Porcelain, Czech crystals, and other accessories of the highest quality. We had central steam heating. Some of the heaters were hidden in the furniture and you could open louvres to let the heat circulate freely.

While my father pretended not to know where the money came from to buy all this, he was very proud to show off our furniture, carpets, porcelains, crystals, and accoutrements to guests.

Our property had a glass-covered courtyard parallel to the bakery, so they were able to load the bread and pastries onto the horse-drawn carriages without being exposed to the elements. Behind the courtyard was the pastry factory, and behind the bakery and the ovens was storage for the boxcar loads of flour the bakery used.

In the back of the property there was another smaller courtyard where there was a stable for the horses. On the other side of the courtyard were quarters for our apprentices. We usually had four to six of them. We stabled four horses to deliver the bread and pastries to our various stores, but sometimes we also had a 'newcomer'.

At times it was a real zoo. Besides the four horses, there were always several dogs and cats and sometimes chicken,

The Three Musketeers, about 1928. left to right: Me Laci(Lotzi), Dodi, and Nandi

geese and turkeys. As an inevitable consequence of the business, we also had large number of mice and rats. Sometimes, I took part in extermination activities using rat poison on the roof of the bakery, and chasing the rats with our two ratting dogs.

I had two brothers. Nandi, whose given name was Ferdinand, was my half-brother from my father's first marriage. He was eleven years older than me. My full brother Dodi, (given name Jozsi or Joseph) was three and a half years older. As an infant he found it difficult to say his name Jozsi (pronounced "Yosi") correctly. He substituted a "D" and referred to himself as "Dodi". This stuck with him throughout his life. Dodi, now in his early eighties, lives in Tel Aviv, Israel. I was the last child, the baby of the family.

I would say I was a lonely child. By the time I awoke, my eleven-years-elder half-brother and my father had both been up for hours, baking and delivering bread to the city's stores and breakfast tables. My brother Dodi was only three years older than me; but when you are only three yourself, three years are a whole lot and in my infancy we were not together so much.

So there I was, a Hungarian Jewish kid, living in semi-feudal Romania between the wars, playing amongst ancient ruins of Muslim and pagan occupiers, while my father baked bread. Who could have predicted the life that followed?

Chapter Two

MUSICAL BEGINNINGS

I don't know if it was cheaper or what, but after I passed infancy, I ended up having to do whatever my brother Dodi did. His tonsils were taken out when he was seven years old. We went to the hospital together and they took out my tonsils at the same time, although I was only four years old and my tonsils were perfectly OK!

So when Dodi started to study violin at the age of eight I had to start at the same time when I was only five. We had a very strict German violin teacher who did not have much knowledge of human anatomy. I ended up getting scoliosis, a curvature of the spine, from practicing and playing the violin for almost 15 years with a totally incorrect posture. This was to provide one of the impetuses for my leaving Timisoara when I turned twenty-one.

The early thirties was the time of the "wunderkinders"— child prodigies; nine year old Yehudi Menuhin had already performed with the Philadelphia Orchestra, and nine and ten year old kids were conducting symphony orchestras. The dream of all mothers, especially Jewish mothers, was to turn their own children into prodigies.

"Study my son! Knowledge is the only thing they cannot take away from you!" was the regular admonition of a Jewish mother. Accordingly, Jewish kids had to study languages, musical instruments, and various sports.

Dodi and I received our violin lessons at home. Prior to

Herr Professor's arrival, my brother would march up and down the room imitating him. My brother would yell at the top of his voice: "FALSCH! (Out of tune!) YOU DIDN'T PRACTICE! BEETHOVEN MUST BE TURNING IN HIS GRAVE LIKE A PROPELLER!" and other such endearing critiques. It was forever the opinion of this teacher that my brother had no musical talent whatsoever; he did not know of Dodi's excellent impressions.

For the first couple of years, I hated the violin lessons and the noises I managed to produce. But then some miracles occurred.

First, we went to Bucharest, the capital of Romania, about five hundred kilometres from Timisoara, to hear Bronislaw Huberman, considered at the time to be one of the greatest living violinists.

This was one of the most significant musical experiences of my life.

The whole audience was spellbound! We were hanging at the tip of Huberman's bow. For the first time I realized that a great performer can control the breathing of the audience for the whole length of a concert and create an incredible array of emotions through music.

Contemporary readers must realize that in the 1920's the only way to hear classical music under decent conditions was to attend a concert in person, or to play an instrument yourself. Radio transmissions at the time were a novelty and consisted mainly of all kinds of background noises. The so called 'long play' records lasted about four minutes a side at seventy-eight rpms, so you had to stop and change the records frequently. It was virtually impossible to get the music flowing continuously and appreciate the full effect of a performance.

The second great experience was another live concert. This was given in Timisoara by the marvelous American violinist Nathan Milstein. Milstein was a dashing looking young man in full evening dress, tie and tails, who in my opinion played like a "god". Once again, I felt myself uplifted in ways I could not have imagined.

These two concerts gave me the inspiration to take my violin studies more seriously, and start to practice. I came to the conclusion that one day I too would walk onstage in full evening dress, make great music, and travel the world.

What really made me serious about the whole music business, and what gave me the most important impetus at that stage of my life, was the film *Intermezzo* with Ingrid Bergman and Leslie Howard. Upon watching the film I fell immediately in love with Ingrid Bergman! Suddenly, I thought that not only could I eventually make great music; wear full dress and travel the world, but eventually even have a gorgeous accompanist and lover by my side! I was quite young at the time; perhaps it is another example of my general precociousness.

Recently, I saw the original Swedish film version of the film with Ingrid Bergman. Bergman and the Swedish actor who played the violinist looked very plain, very "blah." There was none of the Hollywood gloss and glamour which made the first version I saw so magical. I think if I had seen the Swedish version first, I likely would not have fallen in love with Ingrid Bergman — and perhaps not shared such a passion with my instrument!

In any case, immediately after seeing the Hollywood version, I went out and bought the music for the Fruhlings Rauschen by Sinding (The Murmurs of Spring) and learned it by memory. I still play it from time to time more than sixty years later.

What is funny is that although my main instrument was the violin, by that time I also took piano lessons. So I went out and I also bought and learned the piano piece that Ingrid Bergman was 'playing' in the film, rather than *Intermezzo* which is what Leslie Howard was 'playing' on the violin.

Spurred by my dreams of Ingrid Bergman, my habits changed. Whenever I had the chance, I practiced the violin for as many hours as I could spare. My mother, who in earlier times had to regularly prod me to practice, didn't know what had happened. Sometimes she had to pull the violin from my hands around ten or even eleven o'clock at night! Luckily for me, this period did not last too long. Several months later, another major musical experience decided my fate.

I have already recounted this story in the foreword, but it bears repeating, both because it set the course of my life, and because many impatient readers may have skipped the Foreword.

We had a lovely movie house called the Forum not far from where I lived. A real movie palace, it had beautiful deep red velour seats, rich carpeting, and a sloping floor. This theater was also used at the time as a concert hall. I remember hearing Ian Kipura and Martha Eggert, two famous singers of the time, in concert there, along with the great Swedish saxophonist, Sigurd Rasher.

It happened during the showing of the original King Kong film. At around the end of the intermission, I was late coming back to my seat. At the time it was customary to play classical music over the sound system during the intermission. As I entered the theatre, the loudspeakers were blaring out the incredibly forceful sounds of the ending of Franz Liszt's symphonic poem, Les Preludes. Suddenly, (under the influence of the music) I changed the rhythm of my steps to coincide with the rhythm of the music, which is like a very slow solemn march. I had the feeling that I was conducting this glorious music and everybody was watching me.

At that moment, I instantly recognized that this is exactly what I should be doing!

I realized then that the little sounds produced by the four strings of the violin were not sufficient for me to produce the magnitude of sounds, and feelings I wished to express through music. I needed the whole physical force and the whole palette of sounds that only an orchestra can produce.

Later, I also came to the conclusion that to play the violin at a standard which would have the same degree of power and effect on an audience as a Milstein or a Huberman, would have meant eight to ten hours of practice every day of my life.

Being fairly lazy, I wasn't too keen on that.

Chapter Three

GROWING UP

If I were to analyze myself as a young child, I would conclude that I was a loner, very much into myself and my own thoughts. I remember that I could play for hours with miniature pieces of wood floating in the wash basin, which in my imagination represented various ships. I was fascinated by the fact that my index finger had some kind of 'magnetic' effect (due to differential pressure), because when I trailed it through the water, the 'ships' followed it wherever it went. If I had not become a musician, I believe I would have been reasonably happy to be an engineer of some kind, for I enjoyed observing and exercising logic and the scientific process.

During my childhood my mother was working in the store serving the customers. She was not only the cashier and sales representative, she was also the window-dresser, putting together stunning arrangements of the breads and pastries the bakery produced. She excelled at all of this, but it took a lot of her time. Because of this, from my birth, I was usually under the care of a nanny, a sitter, or later on, a tutor. My first nanny was from Vienna, so my first spoken language besides Hungarian was German.

Then I went to French kindergarten, so I naturally spoke French by the time I was about three years old. The kindergarten was run by Werner 'Neni'. Neni means something like "Mrs." in Hungarian. I find it incredible that I still remember her name after nearly eighty years. I still have a picture of her class, in which I am sitting cross-legged on the floor in the first row with my eyes wide open.

Opposite our house in the Jozsefvaros district of Timisoara was a convent that had another kindergarten. I went there when I was about four, and learned to speak Romanian, the fourth of the six languages I was to speak fluently in my life. I still remember the lovely gardens in that convent. There is a German made mouthwash called Odol, which was being sold (and still is!) in a white porcelain container with blue lettering. The nuns used these containers to line their flower beds, which also enhanced the lovely view of the garden.

The selective memory of human beings is amazing. Certain things from very early in my life, such as the blue-and-white bottles of Odol mouthwash, are still sharp in memory, and certain things that happened much later in my life have receded into the shadow of the past.

The Greek Orthodox Cathedral in Timisoara was built in the 1930's. While it was being constructed, my friends and I used to climb up the tower, about 85 metres high, and look out over the city.

From very early childhood I felt and acted as a 'leader', a habit that endures to this day. Already in the elementary school, I was the 'defender' of the weaker kids from the usual bullies, and I had my 'coterie' of weaker kids who sought my protection.

At home, being the smallest, my 'leadership qualities' were obviously ignored and I did not even try to show them. I just silently watched the proceedings around me, and evaluated my parents, my brothers or whomever I came in contact with, through my own scale of critical observation. Although I had an increasingly intense 'inner life,' basically I was a happy-go-lucky-child, quite content with my lot in life.

When I was about five years old, my mother engaged Pori Neni (Mrs. Pori), who became a kind of 'factotum'. She charmed my mother completely. Sometimes she followed Vera, kissing her footsteps as she walked up the few stairs in our apartment. Mother saw only Mrs. Pori's 'utter devotion'; she did not see the monstrous way she treated me.

Mrs. Pori was ultra religious, bordering on the fanatical, going every morning to mass in a neighboring catholic church. We found out only years later that she was

Here I am on my bicycle. I am posing in front of one of stockpiles of wood which fueled the ovens in my father's bakery. Later on, he moved to blowtorches and steam heat

gifting the bell ringer of the church with stolen jars of jams and marmalades, which she hid in secret pockets lining her wide peasant skirt. As well as being a thief, she was a nudist. Her 'hobby' was to sweep the courtyard of the bakery around four o'clock in the morning, stark naked. Once, one of the apprentices, one of the three or four who lived on the premises (our apartment and bakery were situated in the same building with a joint courtyard) surprised her by throwing a bucket of cold water on her. I think this stopped her nude morning cleanups for a while.

Mrs. Pori forced me to say the Lord's Prayer regularly; and I was a Jew! If I refused, she would hold my head under the cold water tap. She threatened me, telling me that the devil would take me to hell if I didn't obey her, and that I dare not tell anything to my mother! I remember one night I woke up and a furry hand was pulling on my leg. What terror! She tried to scare me into believing that the devil wanted to take me, using some kind of animal pelt on her hand. She took me regularly to the Catholic Church to attend Mass. This 'reign of terror' lasted a couple of years. I am sure that at least part of my jaundiced attitude towards religion rests with the misguided and sadistic actions of Mrs. Pori.

Finally my mother found out about Mrs. Pori's misdeeds and exiled her. Soon afterwards, a miracle occurred, which proved to be influential in shaping the rest of my life.

My parents engaged Rozsa Gyuri (George Rozsa) as my tutor. He was about eleven years older than me, in his late teens, extremely bright, with a wonderful sense of humor. Gyuri brightened not only my childhood, but my whole life. In view of the fact that my brothers left Timisoara in 1940 for Palestine, and I did not see Dodi for fourteen years and Nandi for twenty-two years, Gyuri became my older 'brother' and confidante. I will speak later about Gyuri's lifelong influence on me and our friendship.

In the first and second grades of elementary school, I wanted to excel more than anyone else in my classes. This urge did not last too long. In the third grade I ended up in the same class as the son of the Kantor of our Synagogue, whose name was Andrei Katz. In order to let the Kantor's son get the 'first prize' that year, they gave out a prize for the best calligrapher and not for the best overall student! I was outraged at the obvious injustice at the "fix". I had a great facility for absorbing knowledge, but thereafter, I could care less whether I was first or last in class, and I stopped exerting myself.

It was one of the first, but certainly not the last, of the lessons of injustice that I was to learn throughout my lifetime.

Chapter Four

LATER CHILDHOOD

Though Gyuri was born in 1914, eleven years earlier than I, he, and later his family, became my lifelong friends. He had a great sense of humor, and could act foolishly like a child. We had boxing 'matches' with real boxing gloves, and we would laugh at the silliest things for minutes. For all practical purposes, he became my 'older brother' for the rest of my life!

When Gyuri and I began to spend time together, Dodi, only three years older, started to emulate and associate more and more with our half-brother Nandi, who was eleven years older than I. As my tutor, Gyuri was in my company frequently all of the day, several days a week. Despite the age difference, we got along very well. I remember that I spent much more time with Gyuri than with either of my real brothers. One complicating factor was the war, which did impact and complicate relationships. (Owing to the dangerous anti-Semitism of the early war years, my older brothers both emigrated to the British Protectorate of Palestine in 1940.)

Gyuri was very intellectually inclined. I had finally found a kindred artistic soul, whom I could play with, have serious discussions with; in short, communicate on every level. He became a writer later in life.

I cannot overestimate his influence on my life, my political outlook, and my artistic development. He was the one person in my family, much more than my parents, brothers, uncles, or cousins, who understood me and with whom I could talk on any subject and who was always my best ally in any conflict — particularly family conflicts.

By the time I started high school in 1936, the anti-Semitic propaganda of the Third Reich started to take roots in the local Schwabian (German) community. In Romania, in the thirties, school children wore uniforms, including caps. The distinctive cap of the Jewish Lyceum I attended had a blue and white ribbon around it, the colors of the present Israeli flag. The kids in the German high school wore red caps. We Jewish kids called the Germans "Paradeis Kopf", or "Tomato Heads".

Here are Dodi and I, perfect targets in our Jewish school uniforms with the blue-and-white caps

The first signs of anti-Semitism were verbal. Some of the German kids started to yell at us on the way to and from school, calling us 'Schweine Juden' ('Jewish Pigs') and other similar epithets. This was replaced soon with actual physical harassment, which gradually became more and more violent.

For instance, in the early fall or late spring, we wore short trousers. It became a favorite pastime of the Schwabs to run by us and whip the bare skin of our legs with poison ivy. From that it progressed eventually to stone throwing. One day they managed to knock out an eye of one of the Jewish kids. That took things a bit too far; the adults got together and things cooled off for a couple of months. But it never got any better.

I need to emphasize that all the incidents of anti-Semitism, both before and during the war, originated from the local Schwabian community. In all of my contacts with the members of the regular German army, I never encountered any anti-Semitic behavior or verbal slurs. Our anti-Semitic problems were limited to our local anti-Semites: ethnic Germans and Romanians. (The SS were another matter.)

My father and mother bicycling in Timisoara. I am on the left of the picture, behind my father; you can see my shadow. Dodi is behind my mother.

In the meantime, our normal life and activities went on. My family and friends used to go on bicycle excursions to the countryside in the plains around Timisoara. They were interesting experiences in many ways. In the Romanian villages, we had trouble making them accept any money for anything, they were so willing to share whatever little they had. In the Hungarian villages we could buy certain things. In the Schwabian (German) communities we could not buy anything.

And these German villages were the most prosperous villages; clean, well laid out with nice houses, beautiful demonstrations of the German saying 'Ordnung must sein!' ('There must be order!'). The Hungarian villages were much more casual, with better houses alternating with those of cheaper and shoddier construction. And the houses in the Romanian villages were mainly constructed of mud bricks with the roofs made of straw, and earth floors inside the houses. They were, of course, the poorest communities we visited on our outings.

We had also a lot of fun most of the time. I remember holding a stretched out towel between two bikes and 'sailing,' having a strong wind in our back!

We used to have picnics on the road. Our group usually consisted of my brother Dodi, my tutor Gyuri, and friends— a group of five to eight youngsters. Once, one of the kids had the 'brilliant' idea of breaking the shell of a hard-boiled egg on the knee of my brother as he sat on the grass with his knees pulled up. It turned out that this hard-boiled egg was not so hard. In fact, it was a rotten egg, and the still-liquid yolk started to run down my brother's leg, emitting an unholy stench. He jumped up and soon they had an unholy fight. And after all that, he had a real clean-up problem. We weren't going to give up our outing and he wasn't going back home. So he stayed with us, surrounding himself and the group with a vile, and to us, humorous stench. It took him quite a while to get rid of the stench. We didn't stop laughing for the rest of the day.

As I approached my teens, my life was full. Along with my fun with Gyuri and sometimes my family and friends, I had various studies and activities. Besides school and my violin studies and the necessary hours of practice, I was also taking piano and composition lessons. I had even taken up studying English. My body was not ignored. I played sports all year long: skating and table tennis in the winter, regular tennis, biking, soccer, and swimming in the summer were all frequent fun activities for me.

Increasing age meant increasing maturity. My personality became more distinct. As a result, communicating with my father became more difficult for me. I think we functioned on different wavelengths and his concepts of discipline and especially parental authority clashed more and more frequently with my sense of fair play.

For example, it became a monthly routine to present my expenses to my father and ask for money to pay for them. Naturally, it was quite a long list, including my music and language lessons, my monthly fares for the streetcars, sports lessons, my pocket money, and so on. Father always put on a little scene. "Why do you need this? Why do you need that? This costs too much!" all in his loud and hectoring voice. It was clear that he expected me to beg or flatter him, as my smarter brother Dodi did. But I simply could not. My usual answer was, "I don't care." I would add, "You (my parents) want me to do all these things, so if you don't want to pay for it, it is fine with me!", and I would walk out and not speak to father for a while. Finally, my mother would have to play the intermediary and get the money for me, either from my father's hand, or from the cashier's drawer.

Dodi used to be all over my father, kissing him, even putting his arms around him, all the while secretly stealing cash out of his pocket. And of course, he accepted any money he could get father to give him voluntarily. That was not my style. Fair play or no play! Meanwhile, my mother kept begging me to act like my brother and be nicer to my father.

Dodi and I in the early 1930's. Every summer my father had our heads shaved. To be fair, he shaved his head too. He said it had something to do with "growing stronger hair."

During the thirties, before the war disrupted lives, careers, and business, my father planned everything for his sons. As the years passed and the business grew, one of my brothers was supposed to run the pastry factory, the other one the bakery and I was supposed to run the mill that would make flour from the grains grown on my father's farm where he planned to retire. This farm so far existed only in my father's imagination, but he was well on the way to creating a vertically-integrated business with profit made at every level.

My brothers were active in the bakery and pastry factory when they were young, but up until about the age of eleven, I managed to stay away. Father finally had the brilliant idea to give me a break from music and school and to introduce me to both institutions. My mother immediately commissioned six white jackets for me, with white aprons embossed with my monogram in blue.

My career as a baker and patissier only lasted a week.

I started first in the pastry factory. Naturally, having the boss's son playing the apprentice gave the other apprentices opportunities to play all kind of tricks on me. First, they gave me a knife and assigned me 'make finer' the oo white flour. oo white flour is considerably finer than face-powder, and naturally, I could not make it any finer with a knife. My

My father in Marienbad in about 1937. Every year my father went to a spa to lose weight. He lost 40 pounds every year, then gained it back. I once went with him. Exercise and a vegetarian diet. For a month, the cloeet I came to meat was mushrooms!

colleagues had a good laugh at my expense. I got tired of this pretty quickly.

I and my violin teacher, who taught my brother Dodi too.

Then I was in the bakery feeding hundreds of brioches on metal plates into the ovens. These metal plates were heavily oiled so the brioches would not stick. We had both steam ovens and ovens heated with industrial burners which blew flame.

I was working at the steam oven, baking brioches at very high temperatures. I had a flat wooden paddle with a very long handle to feed the raw loaves to the oven, and to remove the baked brioches. One of the extremely hot, oiled metal plates slid down as I was taking it out from the oven, and I caught it with both hands. My skin literally sizzled on contact with the plates and both my palms were covered with second-degree burn blisters. They were extremely painful.

The end of my bakery career came when they made me carry those extremely heavy, long wooden planks which supported about a dozen or more loaves of bread. After doing this for only a few hours, I developed fallen arches which have lasted until today. The pain in my feet was so great I couldn't even crawl on all fours, much less walk! Feet and hands: all of these injuries happened in only one week. This spelled the end of my career in baking.

Another profession that seemed to interest me was mechanical engineering. My father was not closed to this interest because a mechanical engineer would have been useful in running a mill to produce flour.

The closest I could get to this aim was when my father arranged with the head of the local Bosch Company that I could work there. I really loved it, and I was on very good terms with the German Meister, Herr Diestel, who came from Stuttgart, Germany. I think that Bosch made (and still makes) the finest electrical equipment. It was almost an aesthetic pleasure to work on starters, dynamos, and other electrical apparati. They were so beautifully built, all with different colour patterns. Master Herr Diestel was a real pro and I learned a lot from him.

Through my childhood my Jewishness was not significant. Certainly, anti-Semitism existed at many levels, but in a multi-ethnic society like the one in Timisoara, anti-Semitism wasn't good for business or social relations. So it was more an irritation, familiar and tolerated. Well, not really tolerated. While I was working at Bosch, one of the young Schwab apprentices started to taunt me, calling me "Jude" (Jew). I lifted up a heavy hammer and went after him. This was the last time that I had any problem with that individual.

But the time was soon to come when such individual action on my part would be no longer admirable, but foolish, and dangerous as well.

As a baby, I was very fat, and then from the age of one, I was quite skinny — until they took out my tonsils at the age of four. Then my weight started on the roller coaster ride it has been to this day. By the time I was thirteen years old I was quite well developed physically, in most respects.

Chapter Five

MATURITY

Maturity means different things to different people. "Maturity" is different for boys and girls, different for Jews and gentiles, different for Russians and Africans. For me, thirteen was my year of maturity.

One formal recognition of maturity I had plenty of warning for. It was my brother Dodi's Bar Mitzvah. For those who do not know it, all observant Jewish males should go through a Bar Mitzvah at the age of thirteen. First, they must receive instruction from a rabbi for a period of time. The rabbi emphasizes the most important aspects of the Jewish faith for the boy, and teaches him enough Hebrew to read from (or at least recite from memory) passages from the Torah. When the rabbi is sure the boy is prepared, the Bar Mitzvah is announced.

The proud parents invite all of their friends, and many others as well, to the ritual in the Synagogue. The thirteen-year-old boy, as often as not terrified by the pressure, reads the Torah to the congregation, and after more rituals, is declared a Jewish man. The tradition continues with the guests presenting the "Bar Mitzvah Boy" with gifts of various kinds — cash, items for his education, things for the family, and so on. The celebration can be quiet, but more often there is a big fuss made.

My brother Dodi had a huge Bar mitzvah celebration in 1935. After all, my father was a pillar of the Jewish community and an extremely successful businessman.

After the service at the synagogue, a lot of people came to our place and brought all kinds of gifts. I remember a beautiful edition on the life of Napoleon in a large white cover (five volumes) with coloured pictures, also several gold fountain pens (which disappeared by the time the guests left . . .) I found the whole thing not very religious at all, and more an opportunity for people to score social points off one another with the grandness of their gifts and the insincerity of their congratulations.

With this as my example, I was not looking forward to my own Bar Mitzvah three years hence.

My attitude wasn't helped when I attended synagogue a few times in the company of my father. Here was this place, a holy place supposedly, where my fellow Jews came to worship. And I saw my father and his friends go about making business transactions. I doubt he intended it so, but with these visits, my father gave me an early indoctrination into atheism.

As luck would have it, by 1938, when my Bar Mitzvah should have taken place, the political situation, the increased anti-Semitism and the imminent war were not conducive to ostentatious celebrations in the Jewish community. So I never had my Bar Mitzvah. I do not miss it, and I feel I came to maturity in my own way.

There is one type of maturity accepted almost universally by men throughout the world — sexual maturity. In Romania, and in my family at that time, sex was quite literally, "that thing about which we do not speak." So, at the age of thirteen, I was quite ignorant about sex, and without excessive stimulation from pornography or sexual advertisements, I was not overly concerned about it.

Until one hot summer's day when the family maid and I played a game of strip poker. I shall not name names, or give details beyond what is necessary. The maid and I commenced an affair. We made love frequently and happily until we were caught and my sexual activities ended for a long while.

What is important is that I learned about sex the way it should be learned. It was spontaneous, natural, unforced, uncomplicated, and extremely pleasurable. I was excited, but not guilty. I was enraptured, but not enslaved. I was not a virgin any longer, but I wasn't a husband either. I believe that this introduction to sex gave me the healthy attitude towards it that I have kept throughout my life.

And I must say that I learned some more about adult hypocrisy, too.

After I was caught, I was summoned to confront my father in the warehouse where we kept about fifteen box car loads of flour for the bakery. It was a dark and forbidding room, and I expected my straitlaced father to yell at me and maybe even smack me. To my great shock, he wanted to talk to me about it. He wanted to know the smallest details of our love making, what positions we used, where we made love, and so on. Of course telling him all of this was very embarrassing. I learned later that he needed this information in order to go all around town and gloat about his youngest son having reached sexual maturity in such a spectacular fashion!

Les Préludes

Chapter Six

MUSICAL FOUNDATIONS

I sat down to the second part of King Kong, having decided at the advanced age of nine to be a conductor. I had the 'long playing' records — four minutes on each side at seventy-eight rpms — of Toscanini conducting Beethoven's Symphonies number six and seven. So I bought the pocket scores for both symphonies and started to conduct while listening to the recordings. In movies such as *Sophie's Choice,* and television shows such as *Frasier,* only pompous fools and the mentally ill are shown conducting to recorded music. People seem to find it funny, or even childish to conduct along with a recording — in fact, such practice is extremely useful in learning the subtle tempo changes, phrasings, and musical emphases of great conductors. I am still using those pocket scores now, nearly seventy years later.

Family, 1938: from left, Nandi, Father, Laci (Lotzi), Dodi, and Mother.

Despite my decision to be a conductor, I still had a great deal of conventional music training and practice ahead of me. After three years of studying the violin, I joined Timisoara's amateur orchestra. The musicians were mainly professionals, such as doctors and pharmacists, plus a few music students such as myself. Even our conductor was an architect, not a full-time musician. There was a standing joke that the musicians said that hopefully he was a good architect, and the architects said that hopefully he was a good conductor.

This was also the time when I started to play chamber music with my friends, mainly string quartets, violin and violin-viola duos and violin-piano sonatas. This experience proved to be extremely useful in my later musical life, because I became an excellent sight reader.

And the life-lessons in music continued to accumulate. Earlier, I mentioned traveling by train five hundred kilometres to Bucharest to hear a violin recital by the great Russian violinist, Bronislaw Huberman. Huberman made me realize that a great artist can, and should control the breathing of the audience. We listeners were literally 'hanging' on the tip of Huberman's bow. To my shock, I realized that I was unable to breathe on my own, that the musician on the stage was totally in control of my breathing and that of the rest of the audience. Here was, literally, a spellbinding experience, and an illumination of one of the great, basic truths of musical performance.

I have spent the last fifty years of my career as a professional musician honing my ability to do just that in my performances. If a performer, soloist, or a conductor is not able to establish and control a uniform pattern of breathing in the audience, he or she will have no contact with the audience. He or she will have to deal with one to three thousand different rhythms, different breathing patterns emanating from the audience. The emotive power of the music, the interpretation of the musician, and the final effect on the listeners are all magnified synergistically when the audience's breathing is controlled.

In later years I shared my perception of this truth often, with anyone who would listen, in casual conversation, in my public lectures, and when I was interviewed. I remember the headline of an interview I gave for a local paper prior to my concert in Midland, Michigan, in the 1970's. "Come and breathe along with Gati!" I think that the reporter did not fully realize the importance of his statement.

Chapter Seven

THE WAR BEGINS

The political situation in Europe was rapidly worsening. Germany was re-arming, defiant in the face of the restrictions of the Treaty of 1919. And the Nazis were encouraging and exporting virulent anti-Semitism. In April of 1939, Great Britain and France guaranteed military aid to Greece and Romania, should they be attacked by Germany or Italy. Formal Anglo-French guarantees were presented to Poland. In May, Germany and Italy signed the "Pact of Steel". On August 23rd, much to the world's astonishment, the U.S.S.R. and Germany signed a mutual nonaggression treaty, which included secret provisions on their mutual spheres of influence in Eastern Europe.

Ignacz Osterreicher, as intelligent and far-seeing a businessman as he was, didn't need to be told to hedge his bets. My father sold an apartment house he owned in Timisoara, took the money out of Romania and deposited it in a London bank. As Romania was to enter World War II on the side of the Axis, this money ended up being frozen as the assets of a citizen of a hostile country, and he was not able to attain access to it until the 1950's, long after the end of the war.

For me, the summer of 1939 was ominous. I was thirteen and the war clouds were gathering on the horizon. The "Anschluss" of Austria into the Third Reich and the occupation of the Sudetenland in Czechoslovakia were already fait accompli. Britain's Prime Minister Neville Chamberlain's trip to Munich, his declaration of "peace in our time", and the imminent outbreak of the war were in the news every day.

Anti-Semitism in Romania was becoming more obvious and the actions of the Fascist Iron Guard (*Garda de Fier*) of Horia Sima were becoming more provocative.

My father was considering the idea of exchanging his business, the bakery and pastry factory, with a similar outfit in Sydney, Australia. Unfortunately, he weighed the pros and cons of the exchange with Sydney so long that the outbreak of the war made the decision for him.

In spite of the insecurities, my parents pretended that life was normal, and did not depart from their regular routines of business and family activities. My eldest brother, Nandi, who suffered from rheumatoid arthritis, went to Calimanesti, on the Black Sea for his holidays. They had some kind of mud treatment that was supposed to be good for this kind of ailment. I was sent to a boy's camp in Busteni in the Carpathian Mountains, between Predeal and Sinaia, where the King of Romania had his summer castle.

This was really the first time that I went all by myself to a camp with other teenage boys. There was military discipline in the camp buildings, which included disconnecting the electricity at 10 P.M. sharp, so the "good" little boys would have a good rest before the next day's activities.

Of course, the enforced darkness was the time when the "bad" little boys became very active, terrorizing and "initiating" the newcomers. This "initiation" or welcoming "ceremony" consisted mainly of spreading black shoe polish (I still remember the name "Schmoll Paszta", a German brand) all over us and our immaculate bed sheets and covers. This was no small matter, as each of us had to bring our own bed sheets and blankets to camp. I remember my mother sent me off with a brilliant white "pique" cover. I had hardly gone to sleep, when in the pitch dark night, all kind of ghosts materialized to "welcome" us, the new kids. In the dark we only felt their touch over our blankets and bodies; we did not realize until the morning that both were covered with black shoe polish. I was quite upset.

Mount Caraiman was an extremely imposing looking mountain with a forty-five foot-high cross on top of its summit, which was illuminated during the night. In the darkness, the mountain disappeared, and the illuminated cross floated in the air like a sign directly from heaven. At that particular spot, the Caraiman and the surrounding mountain range dropped almost perpendicularly to the valley floor, whereas the other side of the mountain range descended in a gentle slope.

Late in August, when Nandi was on his way home from the Black Sea, he came to see me at the camp, and proposed a hike up to the top of Mount Caraiman, which was close to 2450 metres

The infamous trip up Mount Caraiman. I am on the far right. The mountaineers are in the front.

high. At the time, I was an overfed Jewish kid, weighing about ninety-two kilos (about two hundred four pounds). If I had known the difficulties lying ahead of me, I would definitely not have accepted his suggestion.

Nandi had his own disability. My brother had broken his left leg as a child and because the doctors did a lousy job, the bone did not heal correctly. So they broke it again and it still didn't heal right. His left foot had remained stiff, and much smaller than his right foot. He had a limp all his life, and it led later on to his early death from another operation. I developed a limited respect for doctors early on in life.

We started on our journey at a very early hour. He was just wearing a regular pair of shoes, while at least I was wearing some boots with a backpack with a couple of changes of clothing. At first the hike was quite pleasant and not too steep. In a meadow we met with a group of "professional" hikers with huge backpacks and a proper mountain guide. They were also climbing up the Caraiman, so we decided to join them.

I did not realize what I was getting into. The guide set a quick pace that I was unable to follow, so I ended up trailing the pack at a gradually increasing distance. After making the group wait for me a couple of times, the guide had a brilliant idea, and put me right at the front of the whole pack. Perhaps from his point of view, psychologically this was brilliant, but from my point of view it turned the hike into a horrible experience.

The trail became narrower and narrower until it was hardly enough for one mule or even one person. It was also getting steeper by the minute. There was a steep rocky wall on my right and a crevasse two thousand feet deep on my immediate left! Added to all this, I was being followed by about thirteen experienced mountain climbers who were used to a pretty brisk tempo in climbing.

Here I was, hardly able to lift my 200 plus pounds one step at a time, being followed by this group of eager-beaver mountaineering enthusiasts. I thought that I would expire right then and there! To this day, I don't know how I was able to make it to the plateau near the top, where I literally collapsed on the ground. And I don't know how my limping brother in his regular street shoes managed to keep up with them, or how he kept from skidding on the pebbles we were climbing on. I remember that my little fatty thighs were all bloodied and painful for days from the friction of this forced march.

Once on the plateau, it was a cakewalk by comparison. Actually, we ended up behind the Caraiman in a large hut, where we spent the next few days. We slept on bunk beds, about twelve of us in one room, with a roaring fire, talk and jokes going on all night long. The fresh mountain air in the morning was invigorating. We spent the day collecting various kinds of mushrooms. I never realized that there were so many edible varieties of mushrooms and the fact that there were so many different ways you could prepare them.

While we were in the woods searching for mushrooms, somebody brought a lamb from somewhere, and when we returned, loaded with edible fungi, the others were busy preparing it to be roasted on an open fire. After it was killed, cut open and the inside cleaned, they added various herbs, salt and milk to the inside of the lamb. Then it was sewn up and put on a skewer over a large roaring fire that was set in a trench that they had dug out that afternoon.

The fur of the lamb gradually burnt off, emitting a pungent smell which the prevailing breeze carried some distance. The hours passed and the air became quite cool. Finally, the lamb made a sound like a big sigh, when the gases that built up from the boiling milk inside the lamb made themselves an opening in the carcass. Apparently, this was the sign that the lamb was all cooked and ready to be eaten. The remains of the fur were taken off with a wooden scraper and the meat carved and put on our plates. It turned out to be extremely tender and delicious. The lamb was accompanied by the different kinds of mushroom and with "muraturi de la pope" (various sour peppers, small watermelons, etc.), which were bought from the monks who lived in a nearby monastery, and who specialized in making these kinds of sour vegetables. After such a day of torture in getting to the top of the mountain, the camaraderie and excellent food were indeed wonderful.

After nearly a week it was time to return. My brother and I left the group and joined a train of pack-mules and mule-skinners, which had earlier brought up a load of short concrete tubing to be used for some kind of water works. The mules had wooden saddles for carrying their cargo, and I was proudly riding on one of them. While we were on the plateau this was actually quite pleasurable and comfortable, but when we hit the trail, which had caused me so much pain on the way up, this idyllic, peaceful scene turned into one of the most frightening experiences of my life.

The mule was suddenly descending at a forty-five degree angle, and I felt that I was going to slip down any moment, pitch over its head and tumble into the cavernous crevasse below. This was the same 2,000-foot drop I had been terrified of on the way up; going down, the terror was revisited and turned into real horror. The trail was so narrow and steep that there was no way for me to dismount from the mule. On top of everything, these dumb mules had the habit of walking right at the edge of the precipice. Finally, we reached a spot where I was able to get off that crazy mule. My legs were trembling as badly as they had done on the way up. Believe me, this was the last time in my life that I wanted to ride a mule going down a mountain — or even a little hill.

After a good ten-hour descent, we reached the valley floor in Sinaia, where Nandi and I parted company. We had spent nearly a week on the mountain. It was now the 1st of September 1939, and much to our horror, the town was buzzing with the news that Germany had invaded Poland and that war had been declared by Britain and France against Germany and its allies. My brother decided to take the train back home from Sinaia while I took a bus back to Busteni. Or so I thought.

The evening was pitch dark and moonless when the bus driver let me off. In absence of light I had made a mistake and gotten off a couple of stops before Busteni. When the bus left, I stood there in complete darkness beside the highway, lost in unfamiliar territory, crying in desperation and fear. After such a strenuous day I was physically drained and the dread of this new war sapped my emotional reserves. I did not know what to do and I was very much in despair.

At this very moment, a luxury limousine with a uniformed driver pulled up and stopped in front of me. A beautiful, very elegantly dressed lady asked me what I am waiting for and where did I want to go. I told them that the bus driver had mistakenly left me off at the wrong stop, and that I wanted to go back to Busteni to my boy's camp.

You can imagine how disheveled, sweaty, and dirty I must have looked after that all- day descent from the Caraiman. She offered me the seat beside her, and I rode back in great style to my "home base" in Busteni. I felt almost rejuvenated by the time I got back. Though I never knew this woman's name or nationality, I still consider the apparition of that lady and that limousine at that particularly black moment as some kind of divine act of fate, an act which delivered me out of one of my (literally) darkest hours.

Chapter Eight

THE SECRET OF MUSIC

It took a non-musician to describe the most important element in music.

In his book, "The Doors of Perception", Aldous Huxley tries to describe God. He writes: "The Blue of the Sky, the Expanse of the Ocean, THE SPACE BETWEEN TWO MUSICAL NOTES!" (My emphasis).

Some other people speak of the "silence between the notes." Whatever we call it, the 'secret' is indeed in that space between two notes, and very few performers realize this.

Even fewer are able to master this secret and use it in their performances.

The young violinist before the War. I am about fourteen.

The 'bridge' between two notes is an 'elastic space' which is always different, because it depends on the given circumstances of performance: the volume of sound, the tempo, the tension of the moment, the performer's (or conductor's) sensitivity, and so on. Acknowledging the importance of and using the space between two notes, gives a talented musician the means to express inspiration and beauty.

This is why there is such a difference between the performers who have mere technical mastery of their instrument, and the true artists who have mastery over the music itself-
and by extension, their audiences. The great performing artists have the ability to use this space appropriately as requested by the music itself: the given moment, the sonority, tempo, and so on. Can one describe in words the music of Mozart, Schubert, or Beethoven? This is impossible. In the same way it is impossible to describe verbally the subtle details that only music itself, through the performance of a great master, can express.

The secret of music ultimately remains a secret, which is revealed only at the moment of a great performance.

Chapter Nine

THE WAR YEARS

When I returned home from the boy's camp at the beginning of September 1939, the Germans had already overrun a substantial part of Poland. Naturally, everybody was greatly affected by the news. Some were concerned, but others were emboldened. Timisoara had a substantial Schwab, or ethnic German population. Many of them, especially the younger generation, were more and more openly anti-Semitic. The Romanian Fascists, under the leadership of Horia Sima, also acted more and more aggressively.

As I mentioned earlier, my father had built up a little conglomerate in our town. The bakery and pastry factory employed about seventy people and we had twenty-five stores all over Timisoara. As the level of Fascistic and anti-Semitic activities increased, the authorities started to harass my family and other Jews more and more.

I will never forget a peculiar incident that took place at this time. I had studied accounting for a few months and among other things, we did exercises involving some mocha-java coffee. One day our apartment and the bakery office were suddenly searched by the Fascist authorities. Somebody had denounced my father and had claimed he was keeping a secret set of books. When they found my accounting journals containing my bookkeeping exercises, they seized them, and carted them away in great triumph, thinking that these were proofs of embezzlement, smuggling, or other Jewish perfidy.

As the Fascist government stepped up the harassment of the Jewish businesses, they appointed a 'supervisor' to the bakery. This guy was a complete alcoholic who spent most of his time sleeping in our office. When he woke up, he would put on a sudden burst of activity. He would sign every paper in sight, to show that 'he was on the job', then would get his liquor and go back to sleep. We joked that he signed everything, even the toilet paper.

Officially, all Jewish properties were seized — first by the wartime Romanian Fascist government, and after the war by the peacetime Romanian Communist government; but through it all my father somehow managed to do some work in the pastry shop and bakery by taking advantage of the endemic corruption.

In the spring of 1940, the Fascists arrested my father and my older brother Nandi on some trumped-up charges, and locked them up in separate jails.

The Three Musketeers, 1940, just before Dodi and Nandi emigrated. We didn't hear from them for nearly a year, a terrible trial.

I remember visiting both of them in the different jails and taking them food in a basket. They were in jail for a whole month. While in jail, father got an infection in his nose that almost led to blood poisoning. These were the days before penicillin, and blood poisoning was frequently fatal. After this episode, Dodi and Nandi decided to leave for the British Protectorate of Palestine. I begged them to let me go with them, but they used the argument that I was too young to face the hazards of the trip and that somebody should remain with my parents. Late in 1940 my brothers left illegally, buying passage on a small ship called the "Transylvania." We did not have any news from them for more than a year, during which time we heard rumors that the boat had sunk. The uncertainty of their safety and well-being caused us all terrible anguish.

We later found out that upon arrival to Palestine, the British put my brothers in a concentration camp — the first and only members of my family to be in a concentration camp in the Second World War! And it was a British camp! My family was terribly split by the war and its aftermath. I did not see Dodi for fourteen years, or Nandi for twenty-two years.

How strange our concept of time is! During the war, time seemed to be stationary. It just didn't move. It looked like the war would never end. And as time passed, it looked more and more like we would not survive the war anyway.

In 1940, the Germans were already preparing for Operation Barbarossa, their attack on the Soviet Union, which would eventually lose the war for them. In order to get the Hungarians to join their campaign against the Soviet Union, the Nazis gave back to Hungary that part of Transylvania which up to the end of World War I had been a part of Austro-Hungary. I remember how excited everybody was at the prospect of becoming a part of Hungary again and then how disappointed we were when we learned that our

This is a passport photo, about 1940. It is clear that my father was looking for ways to get us out of the country, but we never managed to leave.

area, the province of Banat and the city of Timisoara would stay in Romania.

Little did we know at the time that this fluke in German politics actually saved our lives. Practically all Jews who ended up under Hungarian jurisdiction were systematically exterminated.

News of deportations of Jews and political prisoners to forced labour camps had slipped out from other parts of Europe under the Nazi heel, but few people were actually deported from Romania. We had not heard about the death camps, but "resettlement" and forced labour was a looming reality every single day. Our whole family had our backpacks all prepared in the living room several times, anticipating the ring of the bell or the knock on the door which would mean our time to go.

As the war progressed, and our local Fascists and anti-Semites became more and more vocal, the whole atmosphere of tension ratcheted higher and higher. We started to see more and more German troops, culminating in the spring of 1941, with the arrival of whole columns of German tanks prior to the invasion of Yugoslavia. The phalanx of the German tanks, motorized artillery, armored vehicles, troops in trucks, cars and motorcycles was very impressive.

Just before the invasion of Yugoslavia in April of 1941, the Germans sequestered our bakery in order to make bread for their troops. The Germans started the attack with a heavy bombing campaign against Belgrade. I remember delivering some pastries and bread that early morning and hearing the drone of hundreds of warplanes. Looking up into the sky to see the source of this tremendous noise, I saw very small planes—the Stukas,—flying very high in perfect formation. It was at once an aesthetic and horrible experience.

The Yugoslavs were quite outmatched at the time by the ultramodern German army, but one Yugoslav plane managed to drop a bomb on our local airfield. The crater left by the bomb became a kind of local tourist attraction.

By the very first night after the attack on Yugoslavia, we had Yugoslav P.O.W.'s working in the bakery for the German Army.

The period after the invasion of Yugoslavia was used by the Germans to prepare for their surprise invasion of Russia. This period coincided with increased activity of the Romanian "Iron Guard" of Horia Sima, the Romanian Fascists. In the spring of 1941, the Iron Guard had committed a pogrom in Bucharest, murdering, with disturbing appropriateness, three hundred Jews in the slaughterhouse.

A few hundred of the Fascists gathered on Dom Tér (The Dome Square) in Timisoara, armed with machine guns, swords, axes, and other murderous implements, apparently planning to stage another pogrom. We locked the doors of the building and waited in trembling expectation for whatever was going to happen.

We were saved — by the German Army!

Apparently, some German tanks pulled up at the square and one officer read out an announcement saying that "If you do not disperse in the next five minutes, we will start shooting!" Perhaps this was the only instance during the war where the German army saved the lives of Jews.

This was no merciful act on the part of the Germans. Their main desire was to get rid of these unreliable and disorganized hooligans, and to establish a reliable and organized military dictatorship under General Antonescu prior to the attack on the Soviet Union. The Germans certainly intended to exterminate the Romanian Jews, but were determined that it would not be done in a haphazard and inefficient manner.

On June 22 1941, Hitler's armies attacked the Soviet Union. Just as with the action against Yugoslavia, a few days later we had Russian P.O.W.'s working in the bakery, which was still run by the German Army. This led at the end of the war to some interesting developments.

We followed the events of the war day by day. It was forbidden to listen to the BBC (British Broadcasting Corporation) or any foreign radio. The penalties were severe; you could be shot if you were caught listening. So, of course, I listened to the BBC news, but in Italian, so the soldiers and the spies and the collaborators would not know what I was listening to. There were certain advantages to being multilingual. I had started to learn Italian both from the

BBC broadcasts themselves and from Italian films. Up to this day I can quote the BBC news in Italian, but now that I speak Spanish more often than I do Italian, my Italian has deteriorated.

We followed with great concern the dramatic early German gains in their war against the Soviet Union. After they so easily overran virtually all of Europe, it looked as if they would finish off the Soviet Union in no time. Except for their lend-lease agreements under which they sent trucks, jeeps, and other materiel to the British and Soviet war efforts, an actual intervention of the US in the war looked unlikely.

As I was working at Bosch, and also at another garage, I continued my school studies in private, and from time to time I even practiced the violin. At Bosch, I was regularly working on trucks and cars made by Ford and General Motors for the German army. GM marketed their cars under the Opel trade name and militaristic names like Opel Kadett, Kapitan and Admiral. The trucks were called Opel 'Blitz'. Blitz is the German word for lightning. Do you remember the Blitzkrieg of Hitler? The Lightning War! One day the role of these giant corporations building cars, trucks, and tank engines for both sides will see the light of day. Henry Ford's anti-Semitism and his admiration of Hitler are well documented. The profit Ford and GM made on both sides of the war is less well-known. The terrible irony of two armies confronting each other, wreaking human and material destruction on each other, with both sides providing profits to American corporations is one of the unheralded atrocities of World War II.

After the attack on Pearl Harbor on December 7, 1941, Americans finally joined the Allies in their war effort. It took us quite a while to realize that the Americans were not in a hurry to establish a second front in Europe. The Americans hoped that the Germans and the Russians would bleed each other to death, and then the United States could become the new and undisputed superpower. This position changed when they realized that the Soviet Union was not only able to liberate Eastern Europe by itself, but might be able to liberate all of Europe, with the danger to the capitalist powers that all of

Europe might come under Stalin's Communist rule.

By 1943 we started to have air-raid alarms. The American B-17 Flying Fortresses had the habit of not flying directly towards their bombing target, but flying more or less over our town, then changing direction and going northwest to bomb the industrial centers of Budapest, Hungary, or turned southeast in order to bomb the Romanian oil fields near Ploesti. This went on for months, and we Timisoarans became quite complacent and blasé about the danger.

I will never forget what happened in the following scene. I was attending a performance of Shakespeare's Hamlet. Right after Hamlet's monologue: "To be or not to be", we heard the air-raid alarm. The management lowered the curtain and Hamlet came out in front and asked the audience whether the performance should continue or if we should all go into the air-raid shelter? The overwhelming answer was to continue! This was one of the most memorable Hamlet performances that I attended in my life.

After the heroic resistance at Leningrad and especially the German surrender later at Stalingrad, our mindset changed for the better. Although there was no guarantee at all that we would survive, at least the eventual defeat of the Nazis started to look like a possibility. One day we heard news that some Jews were taken to Transnistria in subzero temperatures in open box cars. They were sprayed with water and left to freeze to death. This, and similar stories, circulated among the Jews and led us to a very pessimistic view.

I mentioned earlier that I continued my schooling in private. A group of boys and girls, (young teenagers), used to congregate at the home of our French teacher, Professor Déznai. These get-togethers had an air of conspiracy, as naturally any gathering of people would have raised the suspicion of the Fascist vigilantes.

Officially, the professor taught us the history of the arts. Here I heard for the first time the names of Le Corbusier, Picasso, and others. But our discussions covered much more than that. In retrospect, I am quite sure that he was a Marxist or at least a social democrat, as questions of social justice were frequently the subject of our discussions. These get-togethers represented a little island of serenity and civilized discourse in our increasingly tumultuous lives.

I then began to have some romantic liaisons of a very naive and nonsexual nature. At the time, the prevailing Jewish morals were such that one did not have sexual relationships with Jewish girls, only social relationships. For sex, you masturbated, went to prostitutes or made love to the housekeeper or to a 'Shiksa' (non Jewish girl). The definition of sex was still literally "That thing about which we do not talk".

When I reached eighteen, in 1943, I had to report for forced labour, or as the Romanian authorities called it, "Obligatory Labour".

My first job started in a funny way. I was told to report to Scudier Park and tell them that I was to be the archivist. In Hungarian, "letter" and "leaf" are the same word: "levél." I had no idea what kind of archives they could have at a park, but I reported dutifully for work as the future archivist. They didn't blink an eye; just gave me a rake and told me to start raking up the leaves!

Later, I worked at a tree farm. We were collecting seeds from mature trees for planting. My next job was harvesting ripe tomatoes in a field near our local forest, the 'Vadász Erdö' (Hunter's Forest). A large part of the forest was set aside for the King of Romania, who came to hunt there quite regularly.

The summer got quite hot, and we had a large number of pheasants who 'specialized' in taking a bite or two from the ripe tomatoes and then let the rest rot in the sun. These rotten tomatoes gave out quite a stench, but we teenagers also managed to have some fun chasing the pheasants off. We had to pick up these tomatoes, rotten or not, and make 'prune jam' out of them.

All this time I was still living at home, and after work I still had a chance to take part in some social activities, attend sessions with professor Déznai, even go to plays, opera and concerts. And every time I left the house I walked past the packed rucksacks which symbolized the complete lack of stability or security in our lives.

We followed the news from the various fronts in Russia,

Africa, and the Mediterranean, watching how the tide of the war started to gradually change, even as our hopes for our own personal survival remained gloomy.

In the spring of 1944, my new job consisted of working with a group of about 50 other Jewish kids for the Romanian Army. They wanted to fortify an old Turkish fortress against potential air raids, and to use it as a depository for their important archives. We built supporting beams inside, consisting of bricks and concrete. We were moving fairly large rocks that had to be delivered to our workplace. After carrying up the rocks in wheelbarrows, and placing them in some kind of orderly fashion, we covered up each layer with concrete. This location was directly adjacent to a military hospital and not far from the railway tracks.

I recall once watching some Russian lady doctors dissect corpses. The doctors were quite tall and good looking. I asked somebody who spoke Russian to teach me a few words that I could say to them. He taught me: "Ya lublyu tieba." When next day one of the doctors passed by me, I told her my 'magic' phrase, but all I got was a decent slap in my face from her! It turned out that what I said meant: "I love you!" During the war my Russian vocabulary expanded substantially.

The most detested job at this workplace was to go to the quarry to get the rocks. There, we would load the rocks on a horse-drawn flatbed carriage and bring the rocks back to our workplace and unload them. So far, I managed somehow to wiggle out from this task. Unfortunately, one day I could not wiggle out of it and I had to go to get the rocks.

We were close to the quarry when the air-raid alarm sounded. There was an ominous deep murmur emanating above from hundreds of plane engines. We stopped near some open trenches and hurriedly jumped in. I looked up and saw a big white circle in the sky. The murmur grew to a huge roar and finally, I saw some tiny planes (the Flying Fortresses) were coursing in beautiful formation at high altitude, sparkling in the sunshine. Actually, I exclaimed, "How beautiful!"

In that moment, we heard a series of huge explosions that shook even our trench, several kilometres from the city. Then we saw the clouds of the explosions rising over the city.

This was my first, and luckily the last chance to witness this US specialty: 'carpet bombing.' First, the spotter plane made a nice smoke circle where the bombers were supposed to lay down their bomb carpet, and then the bomber planes dropped all their bombs simultaneously, so the explosions sounded like a continuous roar and not like a series of separate explosions.

The smoke cloud over Timisoara kept growing and it was obvious that some major fires were burning. We decided to return to our workplace. When we got back, a horrible sight greeted us. Several of my friends and colleagues were lying dead near an open trench where they had tried to find shelter from the bombs. A bomb had landed by the trench and pushed in the side. Some were crushed to death by the earth, some suffocated and only one remained alive in that trench, as his head ended up somehow in an air-pocket so he was able to breathe until they dug him out.

Timisoara was an important railway junction. Obviously the focus of the bombing was the railway station, but the carpet bombing covered a large area. Besides the station and some industrial sites, many residential districts were also hit, both with explosive bombs as well as incendiary bombs. Our own house was hit by three incendiary bombs. Two got embedded in the thick dirt floor of the attic of our building but did not ignite. One came in through a window in the staircase, nicked one of the steps in the staircase and finally stopped on a landing without exploding.

These incendiary bombs were of two types, one that contained explosives along with the incendiary, and one containing only phosphorus. They were about three feet long and looked like a large hexagonal pencil. Apparently, a couple of dozen were included in a larger bomb container that opened up in the air at a certain height, and released the incendiary bombs to fall down like an evil rain.

After the bomb attack we were first busy giving first aid and bandaging people hurt in the attack. Later, we had to dig graves and help with the burial of those who were killed. Our next job was to collect unexploded bombs. Armed

Romanian soldiers kept a nice distance from us, just in case any of the bombs went off.

By D-day and the allied invasion of Normandy, the Soviet Army had already liberated all of the Soviet Union and was advancing towards the border of Germany.

We began to hope.

Les Préludes

Chapter Ten

AUGUST 23, 1944

As I wrote already, Timisoara (my city) was an important railway junction. Our house was only a few blocks from the train station. During the earlier carpet bombing of the station and surrounding districts by the Americans, three incendiary bombs fell on our house. Luckily, they failed to explode and caused just minor damage.

Realizing that the chances of our house being hit again were quite substantial, my parents rented couple of rooms about four-five blocks north from our house. I dug a makeshift trench for other potential bombing raids. I remember using the top of my table tennis table to cover part of the trench. I put some logs on top and covered it with dirt.

Naturally this 'bomb shelter' would have been totally useless in case of a direct hit, but could have given some protection against flying shrapnel. I dug out stairs to go down the shelter so my parents didn't have to jump in and climb out.

At the time we knew that the Soviet troops were approaching our city but we had no idea how far they were from our city or when they would reach us. The Soviet Military always announced with several days of delay the liberation of another city, when perhaps they were already few hundred kilometers further west.

In the evening of August 23 1944, around ten o'clock at night the air raid sirens sounded the alarm. Although we had perhaps hundreds of false alarms, after the American carpet bombing we didn't take any chances, so we descended into my air raid shelter. I was sitting on the stairs at the uncovered end of the trench to see what is going on.

The British specialized in night time bombings while the Americans specialized in day time carpet bombings. Gradually, we started to hear the engine noises of approaching planes. As I mentioned earlier, one plane made a huge red circle over our head and a few minutes later other planes dropped hundreds of light flares which were slowly descending on their parachutes turning the night into bright midday!

I still remember how I was shaking from fear. You felt totally helpless, except having some slight hope that perhaps you will not be hit by a bomb. By that time we were 'experts'. We knew that the bomb you hear will not hit you because the speed of sound was slower than the speed of the bomb!

In the middle of this 'scene' with the rumbling noise of the planes overhead, waiting any moment that the bombs will start falling, we heard some yelling on the street getting louder and louder. A man was running down the street yelling on the top of his voice THE WAR HAS ENDED!!! THE WAR HAS ENDED!!!

While we learned later that this was not exactly true, I will always remember the contrast between our situation and this fellow announcing in such a dramatic way the 'end of the war'. We found out little later, that they were reading the declaration of King Mihai on the Radio that Rumania changed sides and instead of fighting with Hitler's Germany against the Allies, from now on, Rumania will fight with the Allies against the Fascists!

How the approaching bombers learned about this sudden change in the very last moment before they started dropping their bombs will remain an eternal mystery! The fact remains that in spite of dropping those hundreds of light flares the bombers turned around and we were saved!

After we had waited five seemingly endless years (September 1, 1939 to August 23, 1944) for the War to end, we could not have anticipated a more sudden and more dramatic end. Although this 'end' just lasted a few days, as we had some more military adventures before us, still this was the 'official' end of our war . . .

AFTERWARDS

After the historic "END OF THE WAR" evening and night when Romania changed sides in the Second World War, life seemed to be suspended. On the morning of August 24, the local German Garrison surrendered to the local military.

I will never forget watching through the blinds this interesting procession. About two hundred German soldiers and officers in uniform (but without helmets or hats), walking in front of our house guarded by eight Romanian soldiers in their decrepit uniforms and First World War guns with mounted bayonets,

Behind this sorry procession, there were several horse drawn flatbed carts with the machine guns, hand guns, pistols, helmets, etc. of the 'prisoners' thrown into baskets. The sight, situation and the whole scene were totally surreal. All kinds of wild rumors were circulating.

"The German Army was retreating from Yugoslavia and was headed toward our City." The Soviet troops were nowhere in sight, so we (and several hundred other Jews) decided to leave town and head toward Lugoj, which was about fifty kilometres southwest from Timisoara in the direction from where we expected the Soviet troops to be advancing.

We used one of our horse drawn carts normally delivering bread. Our 'horse power' was provided by Bela, our favourite strong horse. Our family doctor, Dr. Lampel decided to join us. The passengers were my father, my mother and Dr. Lampel. I acted as the driver.

On the highway we encountered an incredible sight. Hundreds and hundreds of men, women, and children were walking on the highway to escape another possible horror story and toward the expected liberation. There were only a few cars and few horse drawn buggies in this procession.

About fifteen kilometres from Timisoara, we were approaching a train station which had some freight trains stationed there. Suddenly, several Stuka dive-bombers came in at low level and started strafing the station and the trains with their machine guns.

You can imagine the panic! People, who were walking on

the road threw themselves and their children in the trenches on both sides of the highway. We tried to do likewise, except one of the planks broke under the weight of my Mother and she was stuck up to her thigh in the opening.

We tried desperately to pull her out while the German planes returned on their strafing runs two or three times. By the time we managed to pull her out (all bloodied) the planes had left.

It was good to have a doctor with us to administer some medical help for my Mother. After all this excitement, we continued our journey. Several hours later we arrived in Lugos. We managed to find a place where there was also a stable where we could park Bela, our horse.

There was no trace of Soviet troops, but also no trace of German troops!

Rumors kept flying about the German troops surrounding Timisoara, my hometown . . . The Soviet troops approaching, etc., etc. Finally, being all dead tired we went to sleep.

Next morning the town was full of Soviet troops, tanks, trucks, all kind of vehicles and lots of foot soldiers. It is extremely hard to describe our feelings. They were our liberators; they brought us the hope of a new life, a free life without persecution. 'Hope springs eternal.'

People always hope for the best, even in the face of adversity. This saying is from "An Essay on Man," by Alexander Pope.

In the evening there was a bombing attack by German planes. It was in the outskirts of the city and I don't know what the target was. By the next morning, the fields near the city were full of Sukoi and other Soviet planes that could operate from any flat surface, field or whatever, not necessitating a long runway and a proper airport. They were giving close support to the troops fighting on the front-line.

A couple of days later, Timisoara was also liberated and we heard what happened. Apparently, the German troops, chased by the Yugoslav partisans of Tito, were retreating and in the process surrounded our town on three sides. According to the story, the Soviet troops entered the city on the fourth side and then surrounded the German troops. They took a lot of prisoners.

After a couple more days, we decided to take the train back to Timisoara.

The train service restarted several days after Timisoara was liberated. After spending a few days home, I had to go back to Lugoj to get our Bela and the carriage back. Bela was well rested, well fed and full of energy.

I was dressed like a crossover between a Yugoslav partisan and a Soviet soldier. I had on boots, a military cap like a Soviet soldier and a khaki windbreaker. After about twenty kilometers a group of twenty Kozakhs (Cossacks) on horseback caught up with us. I spoke some Russian at the time.

One of them (I guess who was in charge of the group) came to me and said: "Davay Kuni" "Give me the horse." I told him I cannot because I have to get home to Timisoara. To which he answered, "I have to go to Berlin!" After a little chat they took off and let me go.

I don't know if you ever saw a group of Kozakhs on horses. They moved quite fast. My well-rested Bela must have noticed a glorious looking mare, because he took off after them at full speed, ignoring the fact he was pulling our carriage (me included) behind him.

Shortly after the beginning of this amoroso chase, I lost any control or even contact with Bela, and I just hung on for dear life while my carriage careened from one side of the road to the other, but my little, overfed, slow city horse was no match for the lean Kozakh horses, used to galloping at top speed. Finally, my Bela, foaming at the mouth and breathing heavily, came to a stop. Not only came to a stop, but was not willing to move even after a good rest. After he had cooled down properly I gave him some water, but he still wouldn't move.

For fifteen or so kilometres I walked in front of Bela holding some hay in my hand, knowing that the road to a man's heart leads through his stomach. This was our 'triumphant' return to my hometown!

Les Préludes

Chapter Eleven

THE END OF WAR

On August 23, 1944, Romania changed sides and entered the war on the side of the Allies. Shortly after, the German Army was expelled from Yugoslavia by Tito's Partisans. After nearly six years of giving up any hope to survive the war, the anti-Semitism, and the Fascists, it still took me several months to adjust to the feeling of relative safety. It was amazing to my psyche that I had managed to survive the war and Fascism and that I, like any other normal person, would have . . . a future!

This is 1944. Romania has switched sides, and my new friends are the Russian soldiers guarding the German POW's working in the bakery.

Safety truly is a relative term. The first few months after the war were still shrouded in uncertainty. The rule of law was an unknown quantity. Break-ins, murders, even kidnappings were reported daily. There was mail censorship. There was no regular train or bus connection from Timisoara to Budapest; and the borders were, for the most part, closed. So the war was ended for us, though it did not end around us.

By the fall of 1944, there was no more fighting in Romania; though fighting was intense in Germany, Hungary, and other countries, my country was comparatively secure from major military action. We started to see the arrival of many of the Hungarian Jews who had been doing forced labour for the Germans in the copper mines of Bor in Yugoslavia. As Hungary and Budapest were not yet liberated, these former slave labourers were exiles, stuck in Timisoara. At one point we had thirty-six Jews sleeping in our apartment and all over the large bakery, which had the advantage of always being warm from the ovens. The local Jewish community did what it could to feed, clothe and house them until early 1945, when they were finally able to return to Budapest after the liberation of the Hungarian capital by Soviet troops.

My parents and I at the end of the War, 1945. I was never slimmer in my adult life!

Two members of this group, who stayed in our apartment for several months, became lifelong friends of mine. One was the son of a baker in Budapest, Doli Gross, who worked very hard in our bakery. I never had cause to criticize his work habits, but his appetite left something to be desired. I will never forget the eight — eight! — scrambled eggs he wolfed down every morning.

The other was Istvan Kecskemeti, an accomplished pianist, who later earned a Doctorate in Musicology. The two of us played chamber music together and since then we have maintained contact for more than fifty years. Whenever I visit Budapest, we have lunch at the Feszek Club (in English, "The Nest"). The Nest is Budapest's official home for its artists, writers, actors, and musicians.

When groups of Jews started to return to Budapest, they

spread the word about the hospitality, food and clothing available in Timisoara. At the time, after the siege and partial destruction of the city, there was famine in Budapest. The starving population was carving up the frozen, dead horses lying around in the streets in order to eat something.

Liberation from death meant the rebirth of my activities in musical performance. It was by a roundabout course. A friend of mine had a sister in whom I was interested. I took to visiting her family's house, and I found the Naschitz family to be a bunch of music-loving doctors and lawyers.

Before long, we started to have chamber music concerts in the home. Gradually, a number of young musicians from Budapest joined us in these concerts. They included the great cellist, Janos Starker, pianist Georg Sebok, violinist Gabor Radnai, who later became the Concertmaster of the Rotterdam Philharmonic Orchestra, and others. On one occasion, I even performed with members of the well-known Lehner Quartet.

Through these exceptional musical experiences and through the pleasure of making music with these wonderful musicians, it gradually dawned on me that I could return to my original love and to pursue a serious musical career. The Naschitz family and these visiting musicians strongly encouraged me to do just this. They unanimously recommended that I should leave Timisoara and go to Budapest to continue my studies. They gave me valuable advice on whom to study under when I arrived in Budapest.

My new friends suggested that I should study the violin with professor Dezso Rados. Rados was an expert in how the human anatomy can work in harmony with the postures and movements required to play string instruments in general, and the violin in particular. Even Janos Starker, a cellist, studied with him. I decided that I should try to go to Budapest, meet Professor Rados, and in general get acquainted with the local situation, including the Franz Liszt Music Academy, and the National Conservatory of Music where Rados taught.

It was 1945, and the war had finally ended, but the movement of people from one country to another was very

problematic. Then, a miracle happened!
Or so it seemed.

Chapter Twelve

GETTING TO BUDAPEST

Late in 1945, I saw a large ad in the newspaper from a travel agency, stating that there would shortly be a trip to Budapest with a 'collective passport' for the passengers, which allowed entry to Hungary. My father and I went to the travel agency's office where he paid a large sum of money for my trip. I was to leave for Hungary to meet Professor Rados and explore the situation in Budapest. It is hard to describe my emotional state at this turn of events.

There was no regular mail to and from Budapest, and what mail did get through was heavily censored. Many people in Timisoara's Hungarian community gave me letters to family members to smuggle into Budapest. Many of these families had been split apart and incommunicado for years due to the war, and their needs were urgent. Despite the possible penalties, I did my part. I chose some extra-baggy golf trousers and stuffed more than forty letters in the legs of my pants.

On the day of departure we reported to the designated point. It turned out that we would be traveling on a Soviet military truck outfitted with benches for about forty-five people, covered with a tarpaulin and open at the back. The passengers included three babies, a doctor and a nurse accompanying one of the babies who needed surgery done in Budapest. Everything looked quite legitimate. We climbed on board and the Russian soldier closed the tailgate. After about two hours of travel, the driver stopped at the side of the road, came to the back of the car, and put his index finger to his lips, signaling that we should keep silent. He then lowered the tarpaulin over the back. So this was the 'collective passport!'

The soldier started driving the truck again and about half an hour later we stopped. The engine turned off. We thought that we were at the border itself, but in fact we were only in the village of Nadlac, several kilometres from the border with Hungary. We sat under our dusty 'collective passport', holding our 'collective breath' for several minutes. One of the babies started to cry, then our driver started the engine and we took off.

Sitting there under the tarpaulin, we all sighed with relief because we believed that the pause had been the wait to let the border gates open. We thought we were in Hungary and safe. This was not the case. After about twenty minutes the truck and the engine stopped again. We heard the Romanian border guard ask our driver in Russian if he had any civilians on board. THIS WAS THE BORDER! Our driver said "Nyet". The Romanian border guard walked to the back of the truck, lifted the tarpaulin and looked in the truck. We must have been quite a sight. Forty-five men, women, children and babies huddled together in silence.

The border guard said nothing, but walked back to his post and phoned up his headquarters to report his find. Realizing that this is most likely the end of our trip to Budapest, we clambered down from our 'collective passport' and walked around or lay on the grass waiting for the developments. The Russian truck driver also lay on the grass smoking.

Finally, an officer and some additional border guards arrived and our whole group was shepherded to the headquarters. They interrogated our driver first. My trousers were full of letters, a tricky thing to explain to suspicious military men. While waiting in the field outside the office I ripped the letters into small pieces and threw them in a well. The locals must have been fishing wet paper fragments out of there for months afterward.

It turned out the Soviet soldier did have official papers ordering him to go to Budapest. He declared that we were 'hitchhiking' — all 45 of us, including the infants. They let him go and began to interrogate us. Luckily, some of the group had copies of the newspaper ad about the "Trip to Budapest with Collective Passport." It took us hours, but we managed to convince them that we were victims of a confidence trick and not criminals attempting to cross the border illegally. After we were released by the border guards, I managed to phone my father from the border post and told him what had happened. My father was an extremely strong person with a powerful voice and a dominating personality. I knew that if anybody would be able to get back the large sum of money we spent on the trip, it was my father.

It was late afternoon when we were set free, but we were in the middle of nowhere, with no transport, many kilometres from Timisoara. I had no desire to sleep in a field, and I wanted to get back to the security of my family as quickly as possible. I found out through conversation that there was a train station at Nadlac, about sixteen kilometres from where we were. I decided I had to get there.

Getting to the train station meant a 16 kilometre hike in the dark along the Maros River, the physical boundary between Romania and Hungary. A fellow with a backpack decided to join me. I only learned later that he had been carrying several million rubles in his backpack! He was some kind of smuggler or criminal who had been conned along with the rest of us. This forced march along the border was one of the most exciting and exhausting nights of my life. We could have been stopped at any time by the roaming patrols of border guards, questioned, imprisoned, or even shot, especially if they discovered what my companion was carrying in his backpack.

After several physically exhausting and terribly tense hours, the two of us arrived at the train station in Nadlac. There were some empty passenger wagons on the tracks. I literally collapsed on one of the wooden benches. I had huge blisters on my feet from the forced march and I had perspired so profusely that the sweat had smudged the ink on the documents in my jacket pockets. I was back in Timisoara before noon the next day.

By the time the rest of the group returned to Timisoara the 'Travel Agency' had disappeared and all of them had lost their money — except for my father. True to form, he rushed off immediately after my call and had gotten his money back into his hands.

Naturally, I got quite depressed because of this fiasco, but I was not disheartened. My determination remained firm and I kept my eyes open for possible ways into Hungary. I had a very good friend and relative George Kurtag, who also wanted to go to Budapest to study music. Later, he became a very well known avant-garde composer. He was not as adventurous as I was, but he told me if I went he would take the risk with me. After several months, we found out that there was a train being organized by 'J.O.I.N.T.', a Jewish organization, to repatriate displaced Hungarian Jews to Budapest.

We reported in the evening to the train station along with all of the legitimately displaced persons. The train consisted of freight cars, disturbingly reminiscent of the wartime transports which took Jews to the camps, each holding around forty people. During the trip to Curtici, the Romanian border town, we told several of our new acquaintances that we had no official papers and were trying to sneak through the border.

They were very nice to us and covered Kurtag and me under several layers of winter coats, blankets, and sweaters. Kurtag was scared to death and started to tell me in a trembling voice: "You deserve to go through, but I will not make it, my legs are not covered." "Shut up!" I whispered to him. "Pretend that you are the 'Mute of Curtici,' a reference to an opera called 'The Mute of Portici'.

Luckily, the border guards did not come in the boxcars to check our papers.

The 'passengers' themselves collected the papers and handed them to the border guards. At that moment I knew that we were OK, but I quickly drew up a scenario anyway. In case a guard inspected the boxcar, and discovered the two of us, I was ready to claim that I had given my papers over to the rest of the people in the car. I was confident that this ruse would have worked, but I was not called upon to act. The papers were handed back, the door closed, and the train chugged its way out of the station and into Hungary without event.

Finally, we arrived in Budapest. George and I went our separate ways to meet with our future professors, make arrangements for our living accommodations and get to know as many people and places as possible during our few days in Budapest.

I mentioned earlier that my pianist friend, Istan Kecskemeti, stayed in our home for several months in 1944 before returning to Budapest. I now stayed with his family. His mother was very kind with me. Not only was I able to stay with them a few days, but she agreed that I could stay with them indefinitely when I came back "officially" to Budapest to study.

Les Préludes

Chapter Thirteen

THERE AND BACK AGAIN

After all the drama of our incursion across the Hungarian border, George Kurtag and I spent a peaceful, but busy, week in Budapest making all the arrangements necessary to start our new lives in Budapest. We had to visit the schools, find out the entrance requirements, search out teachers, and arrange accommodations for the future. I would be staying in the apartment of my good friend, Dr. Istvan Kecskemeti. Of course, he was a young man not much older than me at this time; he received his Doctorate in musicology years later.

I managed to make an appointment with my future violin teacher, Professor Dezso Rados from the National Conservatory of Music. Professor Rados was a very interesting human being. He had unkempt, uncombed hair, a hooked, "Indian" nose and he seemed, most of the time, to be in some kind of half-trance "seeing" or concentrating on some distant problem. A classic absent-minded professor type, focusing his entire attention on some abstruse problem which others ignored – valuable certainly, but often to the detriment of his relations with the "real" world. Dr. Rados' chosen problem was the interaction between the human anatomy and the demands of playing stringed instruments, the violin in particular.

You can literally count on one hand the violin teachers who know human anatomy sufficiently well as it applies to holding the violin, maintaining the independence of both arms, hands and fingers, the use of automatic reflexes, and how to apply all this to the individual student's anatomy. And Rados knew more than all of these other teachers put together. Rados used himself, his own body, to try to solve the physical problems of his students, each one considered as a unique set of problems. Sadly, through his experimentation he ruined his own violin technique.

Professor Rados had developed a technique of working in harmony with human anatomy instead of fighting it. His 'mechanism' of playing the violin was based on using the natural reflex motions of the body, instead of using force and effort. This approach made it easy to play the violin for literally hours without fatigue. Another aspect of his approach was his insistence on not applying the same rules or methods to every student. For him, there was no such thing as "one method fits them all".

In my own case, I have extremely long arms; in spite of this, my bow kept going backward and my childhood violin professor had kept hitting my elbow to get the bow to move parallel to the bridge of the violin. As I mentioned earlier, the strains of contorting my body to the "proper" position had resulted in pain and scoliosis. Worse, it was clear to me, that if I did not find a way to eliminate these problems my career in music would be very short. I would probably have to give up playing before I reached my thirties.

I played a few pieces for him and explained the problems and pains connected with my violin playing. Later on, when Professor Rados made me hold the violin and use my arms according to the dictates of my anatomy, I could see that I would also have to buy an extra-long bow because my bow now went in the opposite direction. Rados would also make me get a Huberman chin-rest, which enabled me to hold the violin way out to the left side, thereby taking advantage of my long arms and giving me plenty of space to use both of my arms and hands.

At the time, Professor Rados suggested that I not touch the violin for several months and when I return to Budapest we would start from scratch. I would learn how to hold the violin again, how to place it under my chin, where to put my bow arm in position, how to move my fingers from position to position on the neck of the violin...in short, everything.

This did not upset me at all. I looked forward to working

with this clearly brilliant man and developing the tools which would allow me to play the violin effortlessly.

My meeting with Professor Rados threw an interesting light on an experience I had had in Timisoara. I mentioned that a number of Hungarian Jewish musicians had come to our city, and I had played a lot of chamber music with them. One of these musicians was a former student of Professor Rados and I decided to take some lessons from him. Unfortunately, he believed "one method fits all". This man was quite a short fellow with short arms and Professor Rados had him acquire a Flesch chin-rest, which made it possible for him to bring the violin into the centre of his body so he could reach the violin comfortably with both hands. Compared to him, I was a tall fellow with gorilla-like arms.

He tried to make me follow the same route that Professor Rados had devised for him. Obviously, this couldn't work for me. The unfortunate fellow had been taught, but he had not learned. When I went to consult with Professor Rados he immediately had me doing the exact opposite, which was proper for my body type.

The comparison of these two experiences emphasized the great lesson and great wisdom of Professor Rados: there is no one technique which is "right" for your instrument; there is the technique which is "right" for your body. Know your body, know your strengths and weaknesses and how your proportions and movements may differ from the ideal. Find a teacher who will let you develop and learn the way which results in the least physical trauma and you will find more pleasure in your playing — and so will your audiences.

All too soon, the time to go back to Timisoara had arrived. There was still no public transportation available between Hungary and Romania, no trains, no buses, no planes, nothing. Soviet military trucks were the only viable means of transportation. I found out that the parents of an actress friend of mine, who were visiting her at the Studio in Budapest, (where she was filming) were to leave the next morning for Timisoara. They agreed that George and I could hitch a ride with them, which turned out to be a very interesting experience. When we showed up at the departure point, we found the Soviet truck almost fully loaded with a jumble of furniture, a rat's nest of upturned chairs, carpets, cupboards, chests of drawers, and other household valuables.

Our traveling companions were almost as much of a jumble. There were the parents of my actress friend, a Russian soldier, George and myself and the strange duo of a Romanian detective with his Jewish prisoner. The Jew, it turned out, had masqueraded during the war as a member of the anti-Semitic Fascist Arrow Party of Hungary. He had lived his part to the extent that he helped the Fascists in executing (with machine guns) a group of his fellow Jews, on the ice of the Danube. After the war, he had been caught and denounced; the authorities had taken him to Budapest to confront survivors of the massacre and now they were returning him to Romania for his trial. The fellow aroused curiously mixed feelings in me. On the one hand, I could understand the extremities of desperation which would lead someone to do uncharacteristic things to survive; on the other hand, I thought of how I could have been one of those Jews, victims of him and his chosen companions.

The truck was covered with a tarpaulin and I ended up sitting on an upside down chair, holding the tarpaulin up with my head. It was raining most of the day and as the truck jerked and rolled for six hours over roads not yet recovered from the war, the coarse, wet canvas nearly rubbed my head raw. The only thing that saved me was my youthful thatch of thick hair. Even so, my scalp would ache for a week after we got back to Timisoara.

When we got to the border, everybody got off the truck and went inside the border post with their documents, except George and me. We did not have any documents, as we had sneaked over the border with a boxcar load of displaced persons. The two of us were hoping that the border guards would be busy with the others and not look in the truck. Unfortunately, one of them turned up and started to question us, who we were, and what are we doing there. George, in his inimitable manner, asked in a shaky voice, "Could you tell me where the washroom is?", and he got off the truck. I was left to explain the situation.

Lying like a bandit, I told him that the driver of a Soviet truck had been kind enough to take us to the Romanian countryside to buy some chickens. It turned out that he took us over the border into Hungary and these people in their truck had been kind enough to offer us a ride home. I think even Baron von Munchausen would have been proud of this lie. The guard was not completely convinced of the veracity of my story, and he went into the office to make a report. In the meantime, George and the others returned to the truck. After a couple of tense moments we pulled out; as the truck accelerated, I saw my interrogator walk up in the company of two armed guards; obviously, with the intention of arresting us. I resisted the urge to wave goodbye, one of the few episodes of good judgment that I managed to demonstrate in the entire adventure.

I spent the next several months in Timisoara in a frenzied state of activity. I applied for my Romanian passport in order to go to Budapest to continue my studies, but it was not clear at all how long it would take to get it, or even if the powers-to-be would be willing to issue a passport and permit me to go. I spent a great deal of time helping my father in the bakery; but this was a mixed blessing, since I could not conceal my dislike of some of my father's business arrangements. A lot of energy was spent in getting my passport and visa in order to go to Hungary. This was just after the war, and bureaucrats and policemen were still hunting for collaborators and Fascists and their sympathizers and every request to leave the country was a cause for much suspicion and cold-eyed scrutiny. I was still only twenty years old, and so I put whatever energy I had left into my social life with my friends and girlfriends. I even went skiing for a week with a group of friends. In general, the winter and spring of 1946 was a sunlit and pleasant time after the darkness of the war years.

Word spread through the community that George and I were planning to go to Budapest to continue our musical studies. I even gave a farewell recital with my piano teacher. The program included Beethoven's Kreutzer Sonata, among others. I also participated in an "emergency" recital.

My composition teacher, Professor Eisikovitch, had been planning an "author's" night where he would perform his own compositions accompanied by a locally well-known female violinist. However, she got sick the day before the concert and I had to jump in at the last moment. I was an excellent sight reader and I knew I could perform the program with Professor Eisikovitch without any problem. Throughout my conducting career I have never had stage fright. To the contrary, I literally cannot wait to get on the stage, where I feel totally at home.

For my "farewell" concert. I was only twenty years old, and I was far less confident than I looked.

Many prominent people of our community were present at the concert, including our Rabbi Drexler. When my turn came, I simply lost control of my bow arm and the bow glided over the strings, producing little more than a series of whispers. I still don't know for sure if it was stage fright or an actual physical problem. I felt uncomfortable on stage for the very first time. Our Rabbi, God bless him, came backstage to see us afterward. He came up with a most diplomatic musical criticism. He said, a serious tone, "This was the most discreet violin playing I ever heard." This particular problem never recurred, but I found out many years later, that I was not the only violinist to have suffered this fate of silence. I was at a concert in Budapest where Yehudi Menuhin, a far more accomplished and famous violin soloist, had similar problems with his bow arm.

At this time, crossing borders was still a very major matter, even between two neighboring countries not at war, and I wasn't sure when and what kind of difficulties might arise in the future. Any particular border could be closed for a shorter or longer period of time without notice or logical explanation.

At the beginning of April 1946, I got the news that my passport and visa were ready and that I had to go to Bucharest in person to pick it up. My trip to Bucharest provided me with an unexpected and unforgettable musical experience. George Enescu, the great Romanian violinist and composer, gave a concert at the Atheneul Roman, Bucharest's famed Concert Hall. He, too, was leaving Romania for good, moving to Paris. Enescu was one of the most important musicians of the Twentieth Century. Yehudi Menuhin studied with him, and many other great musicians did too. He was also an accomplished cellist. In this farewell performance he played the Bach E Major, the Beethoven, and the Brahms Violin Concertos with the Bucharest Philharmonic Orchestra, now called the George Enescu Philharmonic Orchestra.

Obviously, this was the musical event of the season, perhaps of the decade, and everybody with any standing in society, including King Mihail, intended to be there. I don't remember how I managed to get a ticket, but I did. I remember the Royal Guard, looking incongruously like the Swiss Guard at the Vatican, lined up in two rows between the Royal Palace and the concert hall, while the King and his entourage walked over from the Palace, which was on the other side of the square from the Atheneul Roman.

The concert was unforgettable. Not just because of the occasion and emotional reasons, but also for musical reasons. Enescu's physical posture was very poor; he bent over almost like the Hunchback of Notre Dame, but in spite of this, he played like a deity. With my musician's eye, I noticed that he was having a problem with the little finger on his left hand during the last movement of the Beethoven Violin Concerto. When he had a chance, he glared down, almost as if to scold it. In spite of this microscopic problem, the overall performance was heavenly.

The emotional atmosphere of this concert simply cannot

Vera and the determined young musician, 1946, just before I left for Budapest.

be described in words. Perhaps it could be only described through music. But alas, music is not only the most enduring art form, but it is also the most ephemeral. You would have had to be present at the concert to savour the moment. There could have been no better incentive to keep firm my resolve to leave for Budapest to study music!

In some fit of bureaucratic pique, perhaps at the loss of an existing cultural treasure, the authorities told me, upon picking up my documents, that I had to leave the country within two weeks. Saying goodbye to my parents, friends, girlfriends, my hometown, my home; in fact, my whole twenty years of life-experience was, indeed, traumatic. Throughout the war, even though I had often been faced with death, I had always had my family and friends, and now I was facing an unknown future alone.

This time, I left for Budapest in style. Not only did I have a legal passport and visa, but I was going by train and I must have gone first (or at least second) class, because I still remember the green, plush seats in my compartment. I knew it wasn't third class, because third class had hard, uncomfortable, wooden benches and I would have remembered that. My parents came to the station to see me off, and I waved goodbye with many conflicting feelings.

I approached Budapest filled with ambition, hope and trepidation.

Chapter Fourteen

FIRST MONTHS IN BUDAPEST

When I left my hometown in late April of 1946, Timisoara had a population of one hundred thousand. Obviously, in my childhood it had had fewer inhabitants.

Today, it has a population of more than three hundred thousand. I remember that one of my concerns as a child was that I might have to live all my life in the same small city. At the time, I had no idea that I would be a citizen of three countries in my lifetime, and that I would have permanent residences in six cities, some of them with populations in excess of two million people — not even speaking of my worldwide travels as a conductor.

When I arrived in the spring of 1946, Budapest had a population of close to one million, even after all the death and destruction of the war. I felt like Alice in Wonderland, enjoying the sights and sounds, even smells, which were not always pleasant, of this great city. Budapest still showed the fresh scars of war. All the bridges over the Danube had been destroyed and there was only one crossing from Buda to Pest, the Kossuth Bridge, a temporary structure which was to stay up for more than ten years.

Many buildings were piles of rubble and the buildings that remained were pockmarked by bullet holes. Although there was no more famine in the city, and horses were once again safe on the streets, there were great shortages in staple foods, a high rate of inflation and the Hungarian currency literally had no value. One US $1 was the equivalent of one gram of gold or one kilogram of bacon or bread. Most people were forced to barter for their food.

Knowing the situation in advance, I arrived with a large,

huge, oblong wicker basket full of food. A whole smoked pork leg, sugar, oil, flour, and so on. On my arrival, I handed over all the food I brought with me to my landlady, Mrs. Kecskemet,i in addition to the room and board I was paying while I attended school. This led to some amusing situations between my landlady and her sister 'Nelly Neni,' who always ended up taking home some pastries made from the extras I had brought over.

Summer went by quickly, and I was having regular violin lessons with professor Rados.

Now, my first violin teacher had no idea of anatomy, and he taught me a posture for playing which was completely wrong for my body. Although I have longer arms than most people, for eleven years he kept hitting my right elbow so the violin bow would go forward and straight, parallel to the bridge of the violin and not backward. So I played, despite the discomfort it caused me, and I developed scoliosis; a curvature of the spine. Professor Rados corrected my posture. Not only did he allow my bow to move forward, which was a natural movement for my length of arm, he suggested that I buy an extra-long bow. Suddenly, I was able to use my bow correctly, without any effort.

Rados also suggested that I use a Huberman chin-rest, named after the great Russian violinist Bronislav Huberman. It was a flat chin-rest enabling the player to find the most comfortable position, while the 'normal' chin-rest forces every player into the same, sometimes unpleasant, sometimes even painful, position. As the music stores in Budapest didn't have it in stock, I had to have it custom made. The violin-maker who made it for me asked for five dollars. I ended up paying him with five kilograms of bacon — a princely sum, because bacon was far more rare than dollars in those days shortly after the war.

Fifty-six years later, I am still using the same chin-rest.

Though Professor Rados' changes were good for me in the long run, in the short run they caused me great trouble. It was almost like learning the violin all over again. Every exercise, every finger position, every scale, was now strange to me, and it took me months to regain my facility with my instrument. But it was all to the good. If I had not had the tutelage of Professor Rados, I would have ended my playing career after only a few years, suffering from chronic pain.

After a couple of months of lessons, the time was approaching for me to enter the National Conservatory of Music where Professor Rados was teaching. Together, Professor Rados and I agreed that I would enroll in the Fourth Preparatory grade, one class below the First Academy Class. Once I had put my technique in order, I knew I would catch up fast. And it turned out to be so; in the next school year I skipped three classes.

As I planned to continue my violin studies at the National Conservatory, and not as a private student, I had to pass an exam to be accepted. I had finished my academic studies already in Romania, so my exam was strictly practical. I had to audition to get in. At my exam, I played the first movement of the First Violin Concerto by Paganini and also the Caprice Number 24 by Paganini, an etude from the Ecole Moderne of Wieniawsky and a Bach prelude. Since each piece alone was longer than the time allowed for the exam, I only played excerpts from each one, until the admission committee stopped me. In view of the fact that I had performed material corresponding to the Fourth Academy level, four classes higher than the entry level, I was accepted in the Fourth Preparatory Class of the National Conservatory.

This led to a very embarrassing situation for me. The Director of the Conservatory was also a violin professor. He called me to his office and told me that if I would study with him, he would put me in the Fourth Academy Class, and end my studies with my present teacher, Professor Rados. I explained to him that I already finished my academic studies in Romania, playing Paganini, Wienyawsky Ecole Moderne, most of the standard violin concertos, and so on, so my academic grade had no importance for me. I explained to him that I didn't come to Budapest to get a degree as fast as possible, but to work with Professor Rados to get my violin technique in order. I am sure that he could not understand my refusal of his generous offer. The Professor was most irritated and took my rejection as a personal slight.

This incident gave me my first insight of what was going on behind the scenes in the professional world of music. Here I was, a kid coming from the musical 'boondocks' in Romania, ending up in a tug of war between the Director of the Conservatory and my own professor. I realized later, that most professors for reasons of ego, tenure, and professional recognition, try to stack their classes with the most talented students. For me, an outstanding teacher is the one who takes his whole class and makes them all outstanding, rather than a teacher who has one or two shining talents in his class — because quite often these talents succeed despite, rather than because, of their professors.

Both my friend, George Kurtag, and I had to pass an exam at the Franz Liszt Academy of Music, in order to study with the wonderful composer and professor, Sandor Veress. After a little more than a year, Veres left suddenly for Switzerland and his class was taken over by another very gifted composer, Pal Jardanyi. I continued to have luck in learning from a selection of outstanding teachers.

And I had to pass an exam in order to study conducting with Maestro Janos Ferencsik at the Academy. I think, this was the first year when conducting studies became a regular four year course. Prior to that, conducting was just a second subject, like piano, during the fourth year of composition studies. Ferencsik was a wonderful musician and was quite widely known in Europe and later in the USA. For many years, he was the Music Director of the Hungarian State Opera House. Later, he also conducted quite regularly at the Vienna State Opera.

Just before the 1946 school year started, the Orchestra of the Capital, now the State Philharmonic Orchestra, had auditions for violinists. I talked over whether or not I should take the chance with Professor Rados, and he agreed I should go ahead. Maestro Ferenc Fricsay was, at the time, the assistant conductor of the orchestra, and overseeing the audition. While I waited, I heard some superb violinists playing various concertos, sonatas, and orchestral excerpts, all brilliantly. I felt like leaving right there and then. My violin playing at the time did not come close to these seasoned soloists. After their solo pieces, Maestro Fricsay asked them to sit beside the concertmaster, Vilmos Tatray, and sight-read Weber's Euryanthe overture.

None of them were able to do it. None! These soloists were used to studying and learning a piece, one page at a time, over a period of weeks or even months. In an orchestra there is no time for this. You play pieces on short notice, often several different pieces a night and orchestral musicians have to be able to sight-read at a glance whatever music is on the stand in front of them.

Finally, my turn came. I must confess that my solo playing did not come close to the standard of those who preceded me. I was still in a transition period, changing my technique with Professor Rados, and responding to the intensely rich musical environment in which I found myself. I survived the solo audition somehow and my turn came to sit beside the concertmaster. I was ordered to play the Euryanthe Overture. From early childhood I played a lot of chamber music, string quartets, and other pieces, and I played in our amateur orchestra, so I was used to sight-reading, which is the most important thing for an orchestral musician. I played through the whole overture without pause or problem. Fricsay caressed my hair; almost like he was saying 'Good Boy' to a dog, which had just performed a trick...and I got the job.

There I was, not even four months in Budapest, accepted into the fourth level of the preparatory class, the school year not even begun, and I already had my first professional job. I cannot claim enormous talent, but I had an excellent work ethic, a variegated musical education, regular performances of many different pieces of music in everything from orchestras to chamber music groups, and a firm grasp of musical "literacy" — the ability to sight-read.

For the seventeen years I performed as a violinist in the Hungarian State Philharmonic Orchestra, and as a violist in the Montreal Symphony Orchestra, I don't think I studied or practiced my orchestral parts at home for more than a grand total of four or five hours. In contrast, I know that some of my colleagues spent ten to twenty hours a week practicing their orchestral parts. So I suggest, to all prospective orchestral musicians, that you learn to sight-read; you'll probably get a job more easily, and the job itself will be easier once you have it.

Chapter Fifteen

CONDUCTORS - 1

My wish to become a conductor begs the question: what is a conductor? It is actually a very good question, and worthy of a detailed answer. Asking "What is a conductor?" is like asking, "What is a stage or a film director?" They don't create the work performed, neither do they perform it themselves, yet they are necessary to the successful production, and can even become stars in their own right.

The current exalted status of conductors is a recent development in the long history of music, and the star conductor is an invention of only the last one hundred and fifty years. For centuries, conductors really were human metronomes. In the Medieval, the Renaissance, and the Baroque periods, conductors stood in front of a group of musicians and pounded out the beat on the floor with a large, heavy staff. Even then the life of a conductor was not easy; one such conductor, having pounded the end of his staff through his toe and later dying of the resulting infection. If you want to see this very early style of conducting, get a copy of the 1991 French film, *Tous les matins de monde*, and you will see a heavily made-up Gerard Depardieu pounding out the beat for the viol, the bass viol, and other instruments in the Seventeenth Century French court.

There are physical reasons for the need for a conductor. The conductor provides a single visual focus for all of the musicians so that they can stay in time, no matter how complex the music or size of the performing group. The conductor keeps not only a united time for the piece of music, but provides cues for different sections during rest periods when they are not playing, so that they may come in at the right time. The conductor gives cues to the different sections to make sure that they are playing at the correct relative volume for the piece to be heard properly by the audience.

But today's conductors are not merely metronomes and volume knobs. If they were, they would have been replaced, a long, long, time ago, by meticulously-engineered German devices with several arms. These devices would be programmed, like a player piano, for the best pace for every musical piece, and would deliver absolutely consistent performances. And these performances, though they would be music, would lack the "spontaneity of the instant" of the human-conducted performance.

What are the musical reasons for a conductor then?

Think about it: the word conduct means to guide. The conductor is ideally a conduit, a channel. The modern conductor reads the score of a piece of music, hears that music in his inner ear, and then finds a way to bring the music he hears to the audience. The composer writes the music; the orchestra performs the music; the audience hears the music...and the conductor brings it to life.

The conductor must, by turns, be domineering, humble, diplomatic, honest, and a good listener — to the musicians, to the audience and to the music. Professional musicians are all individualists, all proud of their ability with their instruments. They all have their own background of musical experiences and musical training which has given them particular tastes, preferences, and biases in music and musical performance. A large group of such people could not give an integrated, synchronous, balanced performance of any piece of music without some form of outside direction. The conductor, by hook or by crook, convinces, persuades or directs the players and the sections to perform in a manner consistent with the directions of the composer, with the physical performance space, with the audience and their particular expectations, and with his own reading of the intentions of the composer.

This was my ambition.

Chapter Sixteen

BUDAPEST IN RECONSTRUCTION

When I arrived in Budapest, in April 1946, the city was just starting to make the transition from the war years to Reconstruction. Travel in the city was difficult as a result of the damage from the street fighting between the Soviets and the Germans and their allies, the Hungarian Fascists and the retreating German Army having blown up all the bridges over the Danube. Buda and Pest were separated, and the trek to the nearest standing bridge was quite a few kilometres. On January 18, 1946, the first anniversary of the blowing up of the last bridge over the Danube, the temporary Kossuth Bridge was inaugurated. This "temporary" bridge lasted for sixteen years, somewhat longer than my career in Hungary.

The stores and store windows were totally empty. High inflation progressed to hyperinflation in a few months' time. One couldn't buy an ice-cream cone in the afternoon from the salary received in the morning. As cash depreciated in value too fast for anyone to spend it, employers started to pay their workers with staple foods: so many kilograms of flour for a week's work, so many litres of oil, so much of butter, etc. Inflation rose to such a degree that after they printed the One Billion Pengo banknote, they ran out of room on the bills for zeros and just started over. The new Ado Pengo (Tax Pengo) was the equivalent of the former One Billion Pengo. In a few weeks' time, we were back again to the Billion mark. If you had a good memory, you knew it was actually a Billion, Billion Pengo note!

Then one day a miracle happened. The new Forint was introduced and inflation ended overnight. The store windows and stores were full of merchandise. Hyperinflation was over.

Young Jewish kids and Jews in general, whose lives were saved and liberated by the Soviet Army, were open to Socialist ideas and ready to build a New World. Capitalism and the West had failed them, after all, and failed them catastrophically. With the rebuilding of bridges and reconstruction in full swing, there was an air of optimism and even enthusiasm.

At that time, I didn't know the backroom intrigues; how the Communist Party took over, who did what to whom, or the roles of our Big Brother Comrade Stalin and his local representatives in the establishment of Hungary's postwar Socialist/Communist state. Gradually, two names emerged: Gero "A Hidvero" (Gero the Bridge Builder) and Comrade Rakosi the "Father" of Hungarian Socialism. Unfortunately, both of them were Hungarian Jews, although at this early stage of the game it was not an important factor one way or the other.

In general, I was not familiar with the political situation, who was who and what was going on. I was busy with my own career.

Chapter Seventeen

PEAK EXPERIENCES

In my first month with the Orchestra of the Capital, we had an interesting experience. The orchestra, staffed with a full contingent of dedicated and professional musicians, still lacked many of the extras an orchestra needed to put on a fully esthetically pleasing concert. For instance, there weren't enough tuxedos to dress all of the sections of the orchestra. Many of us had to rely on older, dark suits to maintain the illusion of full dress. An American Jewish organization (JOINT) came through with some assistance and provided the men in the orchestra with some used full-dress uniforms. I imagine that the ladies also got some long black skirts and white or black blouses. Though a bit worn, the formal cloth looked just fine from the viewpoint of the audience many metres away. Finally, we started to look like a symphony orchestra!

YEHUDI MENUHIN & ANTON DORATI

During my first season with the orchestra, we had three extraordinary artistic experiences. First, we hosted two prominent guest artists. Yehudi Menuhin, the great American violinist, came with Anton Dorati, who was at the time the Music Director of the Cincinnati Symphony Orchestra. The two of them came to perform Bartok's First Violin Concerto and the Hungarian premiere of his Concerto for Orchestra, which Fritz Reiner had commissioned for the Chicago Symphony Orchestra. Bela Bartok, a Hungarian, and one of the greatest composers of the century, had died in New York the previous year from leukemia.

Bela Bartok had lived in self-imposed exile in New York after leaving Hungary under very poor conditions. He was too proud to accept donations, but he accepted money for commissions. This is how Fritz Reiner commissioned the Concerto for orchestra for the Chicago Symphony. I believe that Bartok received $1,000 for that piece of music. I had guilt pangs many years later when I occasionally received $5,000 for just conducting it, one of the greatest masterworks of the Twentieth Century! Yehudi Menuhin commissioned Bartok to compose the Solo Sonata for Violin.

Both Menuhin and Dorati were extremely elegant in their brand-new full-dress clothing. They oozed American wealth, comfort, and confidence. Artistically, both Menuhin and Dorati's performances were in a class by themselves. Dorati conducted everything by memory and Menuhin gave a wonderful performance on the violin.

It was my first experience to be part of music-making with artists of the highest standing in the international music world. Although these rehearsals and concerts took place almost fifty-eight years ago, they are still as vivid in my memory as if they had happened yesterday. The other great experience was with Leonard Bernstein.

LEONARD BERNSTEIN
August 25, 1918 - October 14, 1990

Leonard Bernstein was the first internationally-successful American-born and trained conductor. After his success in replacing Bruno Walter with the New York Philharmonic Orchestra, Bernstein embarked on a European Guest Conducting tour, which included concerts in Prague and Budapest. On his way from Prague, he missed his plane to Budapest and arrived one day late, missing two rehearsals. This upset and offended the orchestra, and we were not at all in the best of moods when Bernstein breezed in.

Bernstein was a good-looking, young American, typically sporty, youthful, athletic, and chain smoking. A young conductor, just starting out, Bernstein oozed talent and musicality from every pore. He sat down to the piano and asked us what he should play, Beethoven or Ravel? Then he played a few bars brilliantly, with great panache and charm. We were so impressed that we made an unheard-of decision in the orchestra-conductor relationship.

Bernstein had missed two rehearsals because of his late arrival. And this particular day the orchestra was very busy doing recordings until 11 PM. Most orchestras would not have agreed to extend their work day even further for a conductor who had flown in late. But such was Bernstein's staggering charisma and obvious talent that we agreed to come back at midnight and do an extra rehearsal with him.

Bernstein decided to play the Ravel Concerto and conduct the orchestra from the piano. Most of the musicians were not familiar with the Ravel piece. I don't think they had ever performed a concerto without a conductor, or at the least with minimal conducting from the piano. As he used a smaller orchestra for the Ravel, I didn't have to play, and therefore stayed behind the door at the stage entrance, where I could see through the little window and also hear the performance. When he came backstage after the Ravel, he went into a mock crying fit on my shoulder sobbing, "What happened with the trumpets?" There were minor problems, but nothing outstandingly bad.

What I was most impressed with was not his piano playing or conducting, but his ability to multi-task. During the rehearsal, our first clarinetist asked him if he could help him with the interpretation of his clarinet sonata. He agreed. In the rest period of the rehearsal Bernstein sat down to the piano with his jacket on his shoulder and a cigarette dangling from his mouth. While playing the piano part, he smoked and sang the clarinet part, his left leg beating out different rhythms. He was a one-man orchestra, playing all the parts, and playing them all magnificently, and off the cuff.

Bernstein was a brilliant composer, a brilliant pianist, a brilliant conductor, a human being of ineffable talent...the kind they call genius. Yet, when he was asked in his last year of life where he thought he had made his greatest contribution to Twentieth Century music, he said, "Teaching." And when you look over his staggering career, you see over and over again his dedication as an educator. The young people's concerts of The New York Philharmonic Orchestra, his regular instructing at Tanglewood over several decades, and many other examples. Whatever Bernstein touched, it was of a superior quality.

Chapter Eighteen

CONDUCTORS - 2

The conductor's job looks very simple. He waves his hands around in time to the music, sometimes glaring at the musicians and sometimes making funny faces. Of course, it's not that simple. If it were, there would be numerous good conductors and the standard of conducting would be much higher than it is right now. What skills and what background does a conductor need?

A conductor must, first and foremost, be a gifted musician. In fact, he must be a musician's musician. Now, an orchestral musician's basic skill is the ability to sight-read music. But, conductors must be able to read a musical score. A musical score contains on each page the musical notation and instructions for all of the separate instruments playing in the piece. A score is arranged vertically by pitch and section. The line of music at the top of the page would be the notes played by the highest woodwind, followed, in descending order, by lines for the other woodwinds, down to a line for the bassoon. Then there would be the lines for the various brass instruments: trumpet, French horn, trombone and tuba. Below that line there would be the lines for the percussion instruments, the drums, cymbals, and miscellaneous instruments such as the harp and celesta. Last, would be all the strings, from the violins, down to the double-bass.

These lines have radically different notes, melodies, sequences, and musical instructions for the musicians — faster, slower, louder, softer, lightly and other directions. Forthwith, the conductor must be able to scan the page, listen to the individual players and the sections and to hear and correct any mistakes by the players. The pages of a musical score can be very long in order to accommodate the array of different instruments being used. With a large number of instruments, there can only be one line of music for each instrument on each page, so the scores of some long orchestral pieces are very thick.

The conductor does not read the score. Rather, he experiences it. As his eye scans the page, he hears the music in his inner ear, hears the instruments, whether it is a chamber group or a 120-piece orchestra, hears it as he believes it should sound. So the conductor studies the score, studies it the way he would study a great novel. He identifies themes, notices patterns, and slowly and steadily works his way to the heart of what he believes is the true intention and essence of the composer. This formidable undertaking may take as many as twenty years or more to master; or, it may never be fully completed in the conductor's lifetime because every performance is unique, never completely matching the music in his inner ear.

The conductor's ultimate challenge is to take his concept of the composer's work to the audience. And whereas a conductor may spend years with a piece of music, the audience will hear it performed in that way only once.

And to do that well, the conductor should know with reasonable intimacy, the sound, the key, and the playing requirements of every instrument in the orchestra. I once studied the bassoon intensively for several months so I could know the problems of the double-reed instruments. How could I, as a conductor, direct a bassoon to play in a certain way, if I did not know the capabilities and limitations of the instrument, and if I was not able to imagine the particular sound that would come from a note or notes in the score.

These days, there are quite a few conductors who conduct everything by memory. Some have photographic or eidetic memory. Some memorize the score using mathematical formulas or other tricks. If I am really familiar with a composition, I prefer to conduct it from memory. In most concerts, I make a point of conducting certain pieces from memory and some others using a score. The essential is what you do with the music and not the score. "Look Ma no hands," said the kid on the bicycle!

Later on in his life, a conductor becomes so familiar with pieces that he can conduct from memory and still do a good job. But every new piece of music he wishes to conduct comes with its own "textbook"... the score...which he must study. In the end, the conductor uses his memory and some cues from the score, to direct, with command, a performance. A common joke amongst musicians is that "some conductors have the scores in their heads . . . and other conductors have their heads in the score." However well the conductor may know the score, he must also know the musicians who actually perform the music.

A conductor should be a practicing musician. He must know at a very deep level how musicians play as part of a unit. He should know the tremendous strain of playing a difficult solo part. He should be closely familiar with all the arguments and personal strains within an orchestra.

A conductor must be a musical scholar. He should know as much as possible about the background and the personality of the composer whose music he is conducting. What was going on in the composer's life when he wrote the piece? Was the composer trying to make a musical or political point through his music? Was the music commissioned, and if so, for whom, and for what purpose? The conductor should not impose his own "interpretation" on the music — the conductor should strive to get as close to the composer's original intent as possible, and communicate that to the audience through the instruments of the orchestra. Of course, there is no such thing as mental telepathy, nor is there conversation with the dead — in the conventional sense. I will never know what actually went on in Beethoven's head while he wrote his Fourth Symphony, or what Tchaikovsky was thinking about while he wrote a particular passage in The Pathetique. I can only make my best guess and communicate that sincerely to the audience.

A conductor must be a leader. After all, there may be anywhere from sixty to one hundred twenty musicians and vocalists (if you are conducting the later Mahler) on the stage with you, and they must follow your directions in order for the performance to be good. Being a leader doesn't mean yelling and shouting, though the old 'dictator-conductors', Toscanni among them, did just that. Now, with the growth of musician unions and better labour standards, amongst other improvements, leadership is manifested in different ways. Being a leader, to me, means establishing mutual respect between the conductor and the players and mutual knowledge of the conductor's intentions.

A conductor, for instance, cannot get too close to individual musicians. The orchestra is a hotbed of jealousy, gossip and intrigue, and the perception (accurate or not) that some of the members of the orchestra are getting individual attention from the conductor (whether a promotion to first chair, or occasionally to play a solo part), destroys the cohesiveness of the group. Sometimes, musicians have to be demoted or let go because their skills are not adequate. This is crushing enough for the individual involved; that pain is also sometimes difficult for the conductor, and would be worse if there were intimate relationships involved. Leadership is lonely, and the conductor must be prepared to be lonely and to go without some of the camaraderie that unites the musicians under him.

Have I mentioned that a conductor must be, first and foremost, a psychologist and even a social worker? Romantic relationships of all kinds, up to and including wife-swapping, develop when musicians play at the same desk. How do you handle such situations? You'd better figure out a way because you will be faced with situations like this over and over again, and many other small petty conflicts that take place among the often highly-strung people you will be working with during your career as a conductor. Despite their education and attainment of high culture, a group of musicians acts exactly like any other group of human beings under the direction of a single person, most often as a well-functioning team — and sometimes like four-year olds. I have often felt like a kindergarten teacher riding hard on seventy-five fractious children with the vocabulary of adults. In fact, despite everything I have said here about the necessary musicianship of the conductor and the orchestra is true, I have to say that ninety percent of the art of conducting is psychological.

I will recount one story. While I was a violist for the

Montreal Symphony, Charles Munch was invited to guest-conduct. Munch was one of the most famous conductors at the time. He brought a great reputation and a great talent to Montreal, and the auditorium was full for the performance. Unfortunately, we were playing on the night of an important ice hockey match for the hometown team, the Montreal Canadiens.

While Charles Munch stood at the podium and conducted the dozens of professional musicians performing some of the greatest music ever composed, calling on them to pour their talent, energies, and refined sensibilities into a dynamic interpretation of these great works of art, one of the players had a small transistor radio plugged into one ear. He was listening to the hockey game and signaling the goals to the other musicians as they were scored.

Les Préludes

Chapter Nineteen

TRIUMPH AND DESPAIR IN 1948

At the age of twenty-three, I got my first professional conducting assignment. I was engaged to conduct the State Philharmonic Orchestra in three "educational" concerts. The first performance of the identical programs was slated to take place in the Great Hall of the Franz Liszt Academy of Music, in Budapest, the second in a school and the third at the Communist Party Academy. The very fact that I would be conducting at the Franz Liszt Music Academy on the same podium— where some of the greatest conductors, from Gustav Mahler, through Erich Kleiber, to Otto Klemperer, and others had all conducted— filled me with both pride and anxiety. Would I measure up to my own expectations and to the expectations of my colleagues and audience?

I knew the program by heart which included one of my favorite pieces, Tchaikovsky's Romeo and Juliet concert overture, and I was determined that I would set the world on fire with my brilliant conducting. The first concert was so-so. No major mishaps, but no sparks either. The second concert went more or less the same. I did not set the world on fire . . . but the third concert...!

The Party Academy was located in an elegant old building with marble floors; the heating ducts were concealed in the floor and the heat came out through some copper grates at our feet. When I came out to take my bow on the podium, this heat suddenly engulfed me. It became the most exciting concert of my life. I was in ecstasy from beginning to end!

To illustrate the intensity of the concert I experienced, while conducting the last chords of Romeo and Juliet, my baton was feeling so very heavy that I had to hold it with both hands. When the piece ended, my hands were grasping the baton with such a force that I could separate my hands only with great difficulty. Yet, not one musician or any member of the audience criticized me for any kind of 'show business', or hamming it up because they realized then, that I had had to do it that way to handle the enormous musical energy which was flowing through me.

From early childhood I had had tremendous musical experiences, listening, for example, to a great artist, or later playing with some fantastically talented conductors and soloists. But this was the first time I had actually experienced what it means to be at the centre of music-making, to be the focal point between the music of the composer, the orchestra and the audience. The question is not really 'controlling' everybody and everything but acting as a channel, creating a harmony between all the disparate elements so that the audience and the musicians all experience the same thing.

Since the memorable Bronislaw Hubernan recital in my early childhood, I had become totally convinced that a great performer or conductor has to control the breathing of the audience, in order, to have a uniform breathing pattern; otherwise, he has to fight hundreds of different breathing patterns. As difficult as it seemed, I had achieved that level of control and early in my career. Would I ever be able to achieve this again?

Throughout my professional career I kept looking for those heaters in the floor — but in vain. At one point, I even considered bringing my own heaters on the podium. This was the only concert in my life where I could have done whatever I wanted, perhaps even stood on my head, and the musicians and audience would have accepted it... because the intensity of the musical performance was so electric and the shared experience so powerful.

Parallel to my musical advances, I started to hear noises in my ears. At first, they were only intermittent buzzing sounds. After some months the noise became less intermittent and became more and more regular more and more a continuous and unwelcome accompaniment to normal life. Finally, I went to see a hearing specialist. The examination took place in a strange-looking room in a hospital, having separate enclosures that looked like shower stalls. I sat in one stall, soundproofed, of course, and the doctor sat in the other stall, he playing sounds of various frequencies and volumes through the headphones I wore. The verdict was Ottoschlerosis, an ossification of the delicate bones of the inner ear, a degenerative condition which would progressively worsen and could render me deaf. My whole musical career was in jeopardy.

My father was a baker, a businessman, a millionaire in Romania. He had three sons. He also had a substantial hearing loss due to this ossification. The two non-musical sons had excellent hearing. I was the only musician in the family and it was I who inherited this degenerative hearing condition. I also inherited two beautiful red crystal ashtrays.

The emotional shock was severe. In the 1940's, there were only two known solutions, both of which were presented to me by the specialist. One was to have an operation called "fenestration", which meant making a hole in the skull behind the ear and having some kind of an implant. This procedure was very crude, and usually left the patient with a constant vertigo (dizziness), while only slightly improving the hearing threshold. I decided that I could not risk the operation. After all, a violinist or violist can sit down during his performance, but a conductor has to stand for hours at a time.

The second solution would have been to wear a bulky hearing aid on my waist with thick black cables leading to my ears.

I decided against both proposals. I opted for the third possibility, which was to "grin and bear it" and carry on as if I had no hearing problems. I felt that I had to wait and see how bad the problem became, hoping that sooner or later the medical establishment would come up with an effective cure or treatment. Imagine in what kind of mood I was when I left the hospital!

It is strange to recount, but my hearing problems never affected my playing of the violin or piano, my conducting, or my hearing music. The growing ossification never bothered me as far as the performance part of my career was concerned; I had difficulty only with spoken words. This was especially pronounced in meetings, where people might be scattered around a room and would talk over and interrupt one another. As a conductor, it was a great strain on me when I tried to hear voices at a rehearsal. When somebody in the back of the orchestra asked a question and I could not hear it, I had the choice of guessing what the question was and perhaps giving a wrong answer, or asking the musician to repeat the question. In retrospect, once hearing aids had become less bulky, I should have started to use them.

Vanity! Vanity! A conductor suffers no loss of reputation or respect if he wears glasses, so why not hearing aids? We take it for granted that other accomplished professionals, doctors, artists, even athletes wear aids of various kinds, and Itzhak Perlman uses crutches, but wearing a hearing aid is a no-no! This, in spite of historical facts: that Beethoven had to use a very bulky hearing aid and that Smetana became totally deaf overnight, and that many other musicians (both ancient and modern) have had hearing problems. Surveys have proven that after twenty years of playing, musicians in the brass section of the orchestra are almost as deaf as rock guitarists. Modern hearing aids are tiny, powerful, computer-controlled devices which nestle behind your ear or even in your ear canal. I wish I could have rerun my life and started to use hearing aids at an early age, and save myself all the strain of trying to hear or pretending to hear.

I will skip ahead and go over my history of aural surgical intervention. In 1966, when I was forty-one years old, I had a stapedectomy operation in Montreal. This greatly improved the hearing in my left ear. In 1967, I became Music Director of the Victoria Symphony Orchestra and moved to British Columbia. One year later, I had made all the arrangements to return to Montreal to have my right ear fixed too, when my surgeon suddenly died. I looked for a local expert and, in 1969, I learned about an ear specialist in Victoria who had just returned from the United States where he had taken special training in ear surgery. As the operation on my left ear had been so successful, I decided to let him operate on my right ear. The doctor performed the operation, but the hearing in my right ear did not improve at all, much to my disappointment.

I refused to give up. In 1970 I had my ENT specialist try again. Once again, however, there was no improvement whatsoever. The situation became so frustrating that I made arrangements with BC Medical Insurance (the government medical plan) to pay for the expenses to have an operation done in Los Angeles, at the Otological Institute.

When the Institute's Dr. Sheehy opened the eardrum he exclaimed "My God! Today I will earn every penny!" I was under local anesthetic and still able to hear through my left ear. I replied, "I hope so." It turned out that a facial nerve had herniated and covered up completely the 'window', which was itself totally ossified. Dr. Sheehy had to pull the nerve aside with a pair of forceps while drilling a hole in the 'window'. This was an extremely delicate operation, as the slightest damage to the facial nerve could have caused a paralysis of the right side of my face.

The operation was a success in that my face was not paralyzed and I regained some hearing; but I still ended up with a sixty percent hearing loss in my right ear. What I found criminal was that both surgeons in Victoria had opened up the eardrum and, seeing the complicated nature of the situation, they had simply closed the eardrum. Both of them had pretended that they had actually performed an operation!

No wonder some doctors need malpractice insurance.

Les Préludes

Chapter Twenty

MORE PEAK MUSICAL EXPERIENCES OTTO KLEMPERER 14 May 1885 - 6 July 1973

Starting my second season as violinist with the Hungarian State Orchestra, (1947 - 48) I was blessed to work regularly with the great German conductor Otto Klemperer. If the name seems familiar to you, it is. His son, Werner Klemperer, played the fatuous and ineffectual Colonel Klink in the popular 60's sitcom, Hogan's Heroes.

In my opinion, no other conductor got as close to the soul of Beethoven and Mozart as Klemperer. Why do I say Beethoven and Mozart? It is because Klemperer's interpretations of their music were consistently outstanding. Most of the great conductors have an affinity with particular composers or with a certain musical epoch, for example, Charles Munch and French music. And as great as they are when conducting their favourites, some of these genuinely great conductors can be completely out of their depth when it comes to the work of other composers.

Every year, Klemperer conducted a Beethoven Festival which included the nine symphonies, a few concertos and some overtures. Budapest was the site for this festival in the late '40's, and I played violin in the orchestra he conducted. One morning, he came to the rehearsal, placed the full score of Beethoven's Symphony #7 on the music stand and went through the entire score. He looked at each page as though he had never seen it in his life. It must have taken him a good ten minutes before he went through the score. While he turned the pages interminably, the musicians made silent signals to each other, asking, "What is going on here? Surely, he cannot be this unprepared! How bad is this rehearsal going to be?" These were some of the thoughts which musicians shared when subjected to the whims of musical "greats."

Finally, he closed the score. Klemperer looked out over the seventy musicians gathered behind their music stands and asked, "You know this symphony?" We answered in a variety of voices, "Sure", "Yes", "Of course." He said: "You know it, I know it, why rehearse?" and left.

The performance that night was the most exciting 7th Symphony that I have ever played. All of us were on the edge of our seats for the entire performance, giving him all our attention, watching intently for every move of his hand, every gesture of his body so we could respond properly. Klemperer could not have done a better job of leading the musicians to a great performance. Instead of rehearsing and over-rehearsing this wonderful, but familiar piece of music, he challenged us to use all of our skills as musicians to play in the moment, rather than from memory or habit. We came through with flying colours.

Klemperer was the best example of a conductor who could make the musicians feel that they were playing the way THEY wanted to play, whereas in fact they were playing the way HE wanted them to play. This only seems like common sense, but in the world of classical music, the majority of conductors adopt an authoritarian attitude and try to coerce the musicians to do their bidding.

Klemperer was already in his sixties and in poor health when he came to Budapest to conduct. Several years earlier, he had had a brain tumor operation which had left him partially paralyzed. He could not even hold a baton, though his charm and skill were such that the orchestra followed him as well as if the baton had been there.

Klemperer loathed any stripe or colour of dictatorship. Erich Kleiber, a contemporary of his, a conductor, a German, and a Jew to boot had been photographed in an S.A. (Nazi) uniform in the early 30's in Germany. After the war this photograph was circulated. When Klemperer found that Kleiber had also been invited to conduct in Hungary, he created an unholy scandal when he threatened to leave Hungary and abandon his performances if such a Fascist were allowed in the country. In the end, Kleiber did come and Klemperer stayed. But Klemperer had other interesting ways to show his displeasure.

The great conductor held Comrade Rakosi and the other Hungarian Communist cohorts in total disdain. Once, he had to conduct the Hungarian National Anthem at a Communist Party function with all of the Party functionaries in attendance. Klemperer came onstage with a cigarette holder and a lit cigarette dangling from his mouth. On another occasion, he came on stage in full formal dress, but wearing rubber boots! He had a wonderful sense of humor.

Kleiber and Klemperer were different in other ways too. Klemperer didn't like to rehearse. Kleiber did. Klemperer's rehearsals were slapdash, sometimes even cancelled, but his performances were great. Kleiber's rehearsals were fabulous, but his concerts never reached the same level. We musicians used to say that the ideal concert would have had Kleiber doing the rehearsals and Klemperer conducting the public performances.

I think I found out why Kleiber's concerts were never up to par with his rehearsals. At one concert of his I was not required to play in the first number of the program, so I was standing near the stage door before he went on stage. Here was this poor man, this great conductor with decades of experience, famous, successful, lauded internationally, breathing hard and perspiring profusely before going on. It was obvious to me that he had severe stage fright.

It is hard for the general public to understand the tremendous pressure classical performers are operating under, even if they are great artists and have been performing for several decades. The same pressure is placed on orchestra musicians playing solos during symphonies or concertos. The Max Planck Institute of Germany once biometrically wired all the musicians in an orchestra and recorded their physiological reactions during a performance. Just before his solo, the clarinetist's blood pressure hit two hundred.

Though I have been blessed with having no stage fright at all during my career, I have had very funny experiences with this phenomenon. During one concert that I was conducting, my soloist was a world-renowned lady pianist who had been performing in public for forty years, since the age of twelve. The last thing I expected from a soloist with such a background was stage fright. But there we were, sitting backstage, waiting for the orchestra to tune up. My wonderful, talented, famous soloist was sitting in a chair embracing herself with both arms, shaking violently and repeating "I cannot go on! I cannot go on!" She was a beautiful woman so it was easy for me to caress her, kiss her and to try to comfort her.

"We will just make chamber music," I whispered. "Ignore the audience; they're all cabbage-heads. This went on for some time. The orchestra finished tuning up. There was a hushed silence in the hall as the audience and the orchestra waited for us. The silence dragged on. We simply could not stay backstage any longer, so I literally pushed her out of the chair.

As she started to walk in front of me, I stepped on her large, beautiful, crinoline skirt, pinning it to the floor. She stepped right out of it. She didn't even have stockings on, only little sexy panties! Luckily, we were still backstage. We both laughed, she refastened her skirt around her waist, forgot completely about her stage fright and played magnificently.

Unfortunately, this remedy is not always applicable, particularly to the men.

Chapter Twenty One

AGNES & MARRIAGE

The summer of 1950 was very hot in Budapest. As usual, the State Philharmonic Orchestra had its Summer Concert Series in the Karoly Gardens.

During the intermission of one of our concerts in July, a gorgeous blond girl came backstage and told me that she was looking for the secretary of the Academy of Music. While she was waiting in the doorway, I looked through several rooms backstage and finally returned to her to report that he was definitely not here. After the concerts, the musicians, as was our custom, went over to the Carpathia Garden restaurant for some snacks and socializing. I still remember the menu that fit my meager finances: soda water, an order of French fries and a cucumber salad.

To my great surprise, that gorgeous girl was seated at a table nearby. Though I carried out my usual animated conversations with my colleagues, I could not take my eyes off her. Agnes was a real beauty. Great blue eyes, beautiful, cascading, blond hair. I even remember what she was wearing: a grey skirt, a beige blouse and a fire-red jacket. She was an apparition of beauty in the still-threadbare surroundings of Budapest during Reconstruction.

At the time, I was living on the Szabadsag Hegy (Freedom Mountain, formerly Svabhegy, or Schwab Mountain). This is one of the most scenic parts of Buda and I had to take a cog railway up a steep hillside to go home. As I had a long bus ride and the last car left at midnight, I said my goodbyes after not too long and headed home. The cog railway consists of two cars. One contains the engine and pushes the other car uphill or brakes coming downhill. The front car has an open platform. It was a beautiful starry night and I decided to go outside onto the platform.

Who was standing beside me? The same girl whom I had met for the first time in my life a couple of hours ago, for the second time in the restaurant an hour before, and now a third time! If this was not the hand of destiny, then I could find no other explanation. We had a nice chat and I walked her to the apartment building where she was staying, located one station past my stop. When we parted company, she said to me that she hoped to see me again. I flew home down the mountainside on wings of happiness.

When I met Agnes she had so many suitors, that I told her jokingly that she needed me as a traffic cop to direct the streams of jostling rivals.

But after only a few weeks, I managed to climb on the top of the heap. We spent some very happy times together. We went together to Siofok on Lake Balaton and had several other excursions. We had met in August 1950 and married by November.

With her gorgeous blond hair and blue eyes she looked the prototype of a pure member of the Aryan Nation, but she was, in fact, Jewish. At one point, during the war, she ended up hiding in the very building where the headquarters of the Fascist Arrow Party was located. The Hungarian officer who helped her there even managed to get her parents off of a train leaving for Auschwitz.

When I first met Agnes, she was still a member of the Choir of the National Folklore Ensemble. She had a lovely voice and not-so-secretly aimed at becoming an opera singer. Agnes wanted to study at the Franz Liszt Academy of Music, but she failed the admission tests. She did not forgive the Secretary of the Academy, one of her suitors, for not helping her with the admission. She ended up taking singing lessons at the Music School of the Post Office. This is not so strange as it sounds. In Budapest it was common for a number of government institutions to have their own music schools.

One of the vocal exercises her teacher gave her was "Yepipi, Yepipi, Yepipipiye." So the teacher's nickname became Yepipi. I also tried to coach her for a while, but I was not very successful. She was more interested in the beauty of her own voice than in counting the beats in a bar. Finally, I just gave up.

The government provided so called re-training courses mainly for members of the aristocracy and other displaced elements under the new social order. It was not a bad deal. People who took part in the program were actually paid for studying. I don't remember how Agnes got into a program studying fine mechanics, but she had a good time. Usually, I would go with her in the early morning. Sometimes, I would wait for her until she finished work.

She was working with a baroness who kept giving her food recipes. Once, she ended up cooking a soup which hardened so much that we had great difficulty extricating the serving spoon from it. So much for the aristocracy knowing better, I thought! For

Agnes and I before our marriage in Siofok on Lake Balaton, the largest lake in Europe, 50 kilmeteres outside of Budapest. We would be married by November.

years, I teased my wife that we had to use an ax to get it out.

After a couple of years, she had found a job as a wardrobe mistress with one of the film companies. Agnes had excellent taste and fashion sense and could design her own dresses, which later on proved useful in landing her an important position in a dress factory in Montreal. Her beauty also caught the eyes of one film producer, who wanted to cast her as a harem girl. Unfortunately, fate intervened with this career move because Agnes got pregnant. Some harem girl she would have been with her belly sticking out between the veils! Due to her intervention, I had my first assignment as an actor, being one of a crowd of several hundred people at an air show in the film Two Times Two is sometimes Five.

The first five years of our marriage was perhaps one of the happiest times of my life. I adored Agnes and we enjoyed each other's sense of humour, being able to see the funny side of even some impossible situations. Our laughter saved us many times since our living conditions bordered on hopeless.

Even though I had a well-respected professional position in the Hungarian State Philharmonic Orchestra, life still fell under the shadow of the war. Much of the housing in Budapest had been destroyed by bombing and fighting, and what with the baby boom and the industrialization which brought rural residents to the city to find work, there were many more people in the city than living spaces. Housing was in very short supply for years and years after the end of the conflict.

For the first few years, our kitchen consisted of a two-plate electric burner on top of a shelf that I built in the bathroom. We used to say, with a smile, that we could cook sitting on the toilet. And it wasn't a joke. We could. When I moved our kitchen to the foyer, the owner of the apartment took me to court for "disturbing the property". I won my case, but, as a consequence, our friendship suffered.

Upon the arrival of our baby, we bought a crib and the situation became even more desperate. We literally had to step over the bed to get to the other side of the room. But, shortly afterward a miracle happened.

My career had taken a good turn and I began working for Hungarian Radio (HR). I was very productive, and, wonder of wonders, they gave me a "service" apartment; an apartment I could use as long as I worked for HR. It was a one-bedroom apartment with a living room, a kitchen, and separate rooms for the bath and toilet. Such luxury! And just what my family needed.

Chapter Twenty Two

RADIO CALLS

Musicians are, in general, quite a jealous breed and they resent it when somebody from the ranks of the orchestra gets up on the podium and tells them what to do. I had come to the conclusion that being a member of the orchestra made it more difficult to develop a career as a conductor. Agnes and I talked over the situation and she came to the same conclusion, so, in 1953, I left the Hungarian State Philharmonic Orchestra. However, the only job I was able to find was a position teaching violin to adolescents in the Budapest Music School system. This position paid much less than what I had earned in the orchestra, which was not, incidentally, a great deal to begin with. I was assigned to teach at a school on Tomori Street in Angyalfold, a working class district.

This turned out to be a very rewarding experience. The music school provided violins and tuition free of charge for the children, and I suppose it was my role to provide the passion and direction. What can I say about the privilege of introducing children to musical performance, of watching them grow in mind and body, of seeing them perform and interpret music with their own natural and unforced joy? Early music training has been proven over and over again to enrich the lives of children. By stimulating their minds to grow and process information in different ways, early music training encourages creativity and allows individuals to express themselves in ways both subtle and profound.

By the end of the school year, I had thirteen children

performing as a small orchestra. At our end-of-term recital, the parents (mainly mothers) sat around proudly enjoying their children's performance. In thanks, they gave me a little Czech crystal ashtray which I managed to take with me when we escaped from Hungary. This ashtray is still my prized possession, virtually the only memento of my ten years in Hungary.

The school year was eventful for me, too. During that time, a former colleague of mine, Istvan Vermes, from the State Philharmonic Orchestra, became the Head of the State Philharmonic Association which organized concerts all over the country. Though I had not managed to conduct often, I was on their roster of conductors. Knowing of my organizational abilities, which he had witnessed on several occasions during our tours in different countries, he asked me to join him in running this organization. To put pressure on me, he cancelled one of the conducting engagements for which I already had a contract. And it was at this time that I found out about my hearing problems.

I refused his offer. Though I could doubtless do the job, I was not interested in administration. I only wanted to conduct. Months later, Istvan was appointed Head of the Music Department of Hungarian Radio. Then he offered me the job of Head of the Symphonic and Chamber Music Department of Hungarian Radio. I accepted this offer for a variety of reasons; first, my hearing problems were causing me to doubt my long-term future as a musician and conductor, secondly, conducting opportunities themselves were diminishing, so combining my musical background and my organizational abilities would keep me in the field. And finally, the job offered better pay. With a wife and baby to support, I thought that taking the offer was the best decision at the time.

Radio was one of the three mass-media in existence (print, movies, and radio) and had a powerful and influential position in the cultural and political life of Hungary. Hungarian Radio was highly sensitive to politics in general and to the dictates of the Hungarian Communist Party in particular. No wonder that Hungarian Radio was the first target of the revolutionaries on October 23, 1956.

But in 1954, I had only one condition for my friend. I wanted to have my background check completed by the Personnel Department before any confirmation of the job. In Communist Hungary after the war, one's background and family history had a lot to do with one's employability. I had relatives in Canada and Israel, which could make me an object of suspicion, and I came from an unregenerate capitalist family, my father being a successful businessman. I didn't want some busybody to find out about my background once I was already working at the Radio, then to denounce me, harass me, and cause problems for me and my family.

After I was cleared, I accepted the position of Head of the Symphonic and Chamber Music Department of Hungarian Radio. The Department had been operating without an executive for six months; although, it was perhaps the most important section of the Musical 'Establishment' at Hungarian Radio.

We at Hungarian Radio, were responsible for programming 80 (!) hours of classical music a week, live as well as recorded music. We had to program the eighty-piece Radio Symphony Orchestra and the forty-voice Radio Choir; we also recorded and broadcast other symphony orchestras, such as the opera orchestra, the Hungarian State Philharmonic Orchestra, the Magyar Allam Vasutak Szimfonikus Zenekara (Hungarian State Railways Orchestra) and others and we recorded hundreds of hours of chamber music.

As the members of my department had operated without a boss for the past six months, I was initially greeted with hostility. Janos Decsenyi, a gifted composer and senior member of the department, told me bluntly, "If you came just to play the boss, we don't need you!" I comforted him by saying that if I saw there was no need for my services, I would quit. And later we became lifelong friends.

When I started, I had neither an office, nor even a desk. I began my career in Hungarian Radio out of a drawer in Janos' desk. The first thing to do was to get to know my co-workers and the tasks at hand. I had several editors who programmed the recorded music, several producers who did the actual recordings, a financial department, and all the ancillary supports a sophisticated organization normally requires, regardless of the political system in power. The situation was even more complex, since I had to liaise with the Technical Department and some other departments of Hungarian Radio and each of these departments had their own agendas and competed for resources to get their projects done.

In my department I had eight people under me, programmers, recording engineers, and administrators. And I had my own finance department of four people. They had all been working on their own for six months. So the first thing I did was to have a 10-minute meeting with my staff every morning before work, setting duties, goals, and project schedules. Gradually, I began to get the department under control; I established a disciplined and productive atmosphere where people knew what their responsibilities were and when they had to have things done.

I also worked with an in-house 80-piece orchestra and a 40-voice choir and their music directors. They performed not only in the studio, but also had public performances around the city, many of which I was involved in. Hungarian Radio broadcast all of their performances and recordings.

As if all of this was not complicated enough, I had to learn about sound recording to work productively with the technicians in the recording studio. Actually, this worked out very well; they knew things I didn't, but I also had knowledge they lacked. The learning curve was steep, but it helped us build a real team.

After about six months, I had us programming weeks ahead and the orchestra and choir were recording and performing regularly. I felt we were finally well-organized. We were, in the main, a happy and productive group. That was when I came across a real problem, which I turned into an opportunity.

I realized that we had a crazy situation. Hungarian Radio had its own Department of External Affairs, just like an independent country. And, just like an independent country, once a year, one or more delegates of this department went to Beijing, Moscow, Warsaw or some other Communist country for international conventions and conferences. They had a great time wining and dining each other, buying leather coats, sightseeing and being out of their countries, none of which was a problem for me. My problem was their official activities. They agreed to a plan stating how many hours of music each state radio operation would send the others. Again, a laudable goal. The trouble was that we, the professionals in the Music Department, were responsible for programming that music, and finding an appropriate place for it in our broadcast day.

This was the problem.

Some statistics to

In 1954, I saw my brother Dodi for the first time since 1940. He visited us while he was living in Belgrade, Yugoslavia. The meeting was joyful indeed. We picked up as though we had been apart only a few days. Our spirits remained simpatico in many ways.

There was only one small tension. As Dodi was an Israeli embassy attache, he felt he had to make sure that Agnes and I were not targetted politically.

consider: Soviet State Radio sent us twenty hours of music per month, Chinese State Radio ten hours per month, and so on down the line. We even got five hours of Egyptian music per month! Egypt's President, Gamal Nasser, was adroitly playing his game of getting favourable world opinion by playing with both the West and the Warsaw Pact. We had this kind of musical exchanges only with members of the Soviet bloc and Egypt.

In order to fulfill their quota of twenty hours per month, our friends in Moscow would sometimes send us the same music four and five times over, and we, the Music Department, were supposed to broadcast that music and report the use of the tapes to the directors of Hungarian Radio.

One day, I saw in a Russian magazine a scathing critique of Takaishvili's Fourth Symphony. Hungarian Radio already had four or five copies of that piece of junk. I went to the Collegium of Hungarian Radio with a scathing critique of the Takaishvili work from a Russian paper and asked them if this is how we were supposed to show the superior quality of Soviet artists and culture.

I told them we should have a direct transmission from the Bolshoi Opera, or a recital by David Oistrakh or another great Soviet artist. I was told that the only high quality connection between Budapest and Moscow was the 'hot line' between Comrade Rakosi and Comrade Khrushchev. I told them I would find another 'line'. After several weeks, I finally succeeded. I went to the headquarters of the Hungarian Post Office, which at the time was in charge of radio communications, and after some research, the technicians, who always loved a good challenge, found a slightly convoluted but good quality cable that snaked from Moscow to Budapest via Stockholm and Berlin.

Luckily, our first tryout was not broadcast live, but recorded. We heard a wonderful violinist, Henryk Shering, but we also heard international phone conversations, feedback, interference, beeps, whistles, and all other kinds of electronic noise. But it was possible!

After proving I could find a solution to one problem, I approached the Collegium with my take on the other difficulties plaguing my department at Hungarian Radio. I explained how the Department of External Affairs was making arrangements for musical exchanges while leaving the Department of Music (of Hungarian Radio) responsible to execute their silly agreements, and how, in the end, it made for an impossible situation. I asked them if they thought we could broadcast, for example, ten hours of Chinese or five hours of Egyptian music each month on Hungarian Radio or four copies of the Fourth Symphony of Takaishvili.

I got the Collegium to agree that we, the Music Department, would establish an independent department in charge of musical exchanges. I became the head of this new Musical Program Exchange Department, but I didn't get two salaries or even a raise because then I would have earned more than the Director of the Music Department.

I hired the former wife of an old composition teacher of mine, Professor Pal Jardanyi, to be the secretary of this new department. She was a wonderful lady and a tremendous help. Her nickname was 'Cica' (little cat); although, she was physically fairly big. I simply had to tell her my problem and I knew that she would find a solution. Organize a banquet for visiting delegation? I just had to tell her how many people were attending and she took care of the rest. She really was my right hand. On my last visit to Budapest I went to see her. Sadly, she was living in a single small room, chain-smoking herself to death. I wish I could have kept the memory of the young 'Cica', instead of this self-destructive old person.

Although we kept receiving offers from the BBC and other radio stations for program exchanges, we were only allowed musical exchanges with Soviet bloc countries and Egypt. One day, I took a program offer from the BBC literally out of the wastebasket, and asked my secretary to order from them the Verdi Requiem with Sir Thomas Beecham conducting. After only one year at Hungarian Radio, the political situation had improved enough for me to do that without being arrested and jailed.

By the fall, of 1954 the political climate in Hungary became much freer than during the worst Stalinist era just after the war, or under Zhdanov's cultural dictates. The Hungarian press had not just published critical writings and sarcastic parodies on the existing Communist regime, but even complete three-act theater pieces lampooning the whole political shebang. I remember a joke at the time: A student says that Attila Jozsef, a well known "proletarian poet", has already shown by his birth the importance of the worker-peasant alliance, his father being a worker and his mother a peasant. The professor yells at him "Already by his birth?" The trembling student answers, "Already before his birth!" The Communist system was upside-down according to many standards of logic and common sense, and Hungarians were beginning to want a clearer view of the world.

Though I was an excellent administrator, my life's real meaning came from music, and the greatest fun I had was when taping or broadcasting live operas or concerts. I remember three great events: the opening of the rebuilt Berlin Opera with Wagner's "Die Meistersinger aus Nurnberg", the farewell concert of Benjamino Gigli from Vienna, and the re-opening of the rebuilt Vienna State Opera with Beethoven's Fidelio. Short of actually being there, we were part of musical history.

By the mid-fifties, I spoke five languages fluently: Hungarian, German, English, French and Romanian. I perfected my Spanish later during my frequent visits to Mexico and Latin America. This skill turned out to be very useful, if not indispensable. When a concert of ours was being broadcast live and direct to the West, I would be moving from one phone to another speaking to Paris or Brussels in French, to Vienna in German, to Bucharest in Romanian, to London in English. How can the human mind do such things? The answer is that we can do it as well as we can make music. (The Pope speaks twenty-five languages.)

The live broadcast of Beethoven's Opera Fidelio, performed in honour of the opening of the rebuilt State Opera House in Vienna, became memorable to me for several reasons. As was the routine, the host radio broadcaster was in charge of the proceedings, directing you, the receiver/transmitter of their program, how long the different acts would be when and how long the intermission would be, etc. In view of the fact that this opening was a major international event, many celebrities, politicians, including John Foster Dulles, U.S.

Secretary of State, were present and so were the most important international news organizations. We at HR wanted to send somebody from the Music Department to the opening, but the only person who had a passport valid for Western countries was our sports reporter, George Szepesi.

Although he knew much less about music than I knew about soccer, we had no choice. It would be our sports guy going to the grand opening of the Opera. We agreed that during the intermission, which was supposed to last twenty minutes, he would give us a live report, an interview, of whatever he thought would interest our music-loving audience. As the opera was Beethoven's Fidelio, we had prepared on tape some other music by Beethoven to fill the gaps before and after George's report. The intermission started on time, but our reporter was nowhere to be found. Five, ten, and then fifteen interminable minutes passed, with no Mr. Szepesi. Normally, we would have a five-minute warning before the next act but we received no such sign from Vienna.

To cut a long story short, the intermission lasted a whole hour instead of twenty minutes. We, in Hungary, had no idea what was going on. We kept running to the music library to get some more music, all this going on live! Our 'reporter' whose trip was paid by the Music Department had simply vanished. We were really left in the dark. It turned out that our 'reporter' had also taken assignments from other departments, in this case, from the Agitation & Propaganda Department, so he was busy pursuing interviews with John Foster Dulles and other important personalities for a subsequent broadcast, while leaving us in the dark and in the silence.

The official reason given for the one hour long intermission was that the soprano got a sore throat and she took a long time to recuperate. My personal opinion was that it had taken this length of time to have all the luminaries interviewed, posed, photographed, and filmed. The political theatre of the occasion was as important as Beethoven's Fidelio.

BERLIN-BUDAPEST-LIVE

Today, it is totally common to see somebody on the screen,

talking live on the TV in New York, and to see on the same screen somebody else answering from London. In 1955 we did not yet have television in Hungary, but we were very interested in the proposal of East Berlin Radio to do a live musical program between Berlin and Budapest. This proposal created great interest because this would have been a first for Eastern Europe.

I was assigned to work out the details. I went to our first meeting in the Czech border town of Komarno. The head of the radio station let me have his Tatra car, so I drove in great style to the border. The Czech Tatras were wonderful cars with an avant-garde aerodynamic shape. The engines were in the rear of the car and I enjoyed a very smooth ride. Unfortunately, they stopped making them many years ago.

We had a very good meeting with the representatives of the Berlin Radio. We had our orchestra from the light music department with soloists and Berlin did likewise. The bilingual program was a lot of fun and it gave us a good experience in this type of programs.

Hungarian Radio had a huge stumbling block in its plans for program exchanges with the West. We had a law which forbade us to export anything that we imported. Our audio tapes were imported from Agfa, the well known East German company, but we were not allowed to export them. That is, we were not allowed to record music on the tapes, then send the tapes outside Hungary.

I found a solution. At first it was a secret — a year earlier I could have gone to jail for it — but gradually, it became official. It was rather simple, and saved us money, time, and organizational pain. We didn't order new tapes from Agfa. Instead of broadcasting the four copies we had received from the Russians of Takaishvili's lousy 4th Symphony, we erased the tapes, recorded on them the music we were sending to the various Western radio organizations. This was a practical way of getting rid of all the unwanted music and having the needed tapes to record and send our music all over the world.

This small, worn pamphlet, still spattered with mud and blood from the plane crash outside Munich, is all that is left of the culmination of my career at Hungarian Radio. This contained all of HR's major programs, including live as well as recorded concerts for the entire year. We were only the second radio broadcaster to plan and publish our programs a whole year ahead of time. The program was not for the general public, but was for all of the other radio programmers throughout the world who might want to exchange music with us. The program was printed in five languages, and was significant because it represented a break from the political and cultural isolation of the Communist regime in Hungary.

When I came to Hungarian Radio, we didn't have any musical program exchange with the West. When I left two years later, we had regular musical program exchanges with 44 stations all over the world. During my last stay in Budapest in the late '90's, I visited the Musical Program Exchange Department at Hungarian Radio. It is still going great after 45 years.

Les Préludes

Once a week I had to take part with my program editors in the 'Eight-Weeker' programming session. HR planned the programs eight weeks ahead of time; in the first week of January we would actually program the first week of March and so on. Gradually, I realized that this system was not satisfactory as far as planning the musical programs is concerned. By programming only week by week, we did not have an overall view and plan for the programs. For example, we just realized in hindsight that from time to time we programmed the same symphony, string quartet, sonata or other piece two or three times during one month.

So I changed the programming to three months in advance. The program editors and I color-coded the programs, using various colored paper strips, on a large sheet of white cardboard pinned up on the wall.

As my program editors were all young women, my colleagues from the other departments would tease me saying 'Here comes Gati with his harem girls", or "Here comes Gati with his washerwomen." Despite the snickers over our unconventional artwork, within two years, HR became only the second broadcast organization in the world, after RAI, Italian Radio, to advance-publish a one year musical program.

This program was printed in five languages. English, French, German, Russian and Hungarian and was a great accomplishment. Due to the revolution in 1956 and the upheaval that followed all this work was in vain.

I took a French copy of the program with me when we left Hungary. This program was in the inside pocket of my jacket during the plane crash outside of Munich, on December 22, 1956. The mud and blood on that program will always remind me of the happy and sad moments, of victories and defeats, of the good and bad times I had at Hungarian Radio.

I left many good friends and colleagues behind when I left Hungary. Since 1964, when I went back the first time to Budapest to see Professor Zoltan Kodaly, I have had several occasions to return and renew old friendships with my colleagues.

Chapter Twenty-Three

OCTOBER 23-NOVEMBER 26, 1956 THE HUNGARIAN UPRISING

Many people in the West have the wrong idea about the Hungarian Uprising of 1956. In anti-Communist mythology, brave Hungarians threw off the yoke of their Stalinist oppressors, and stood up for freedom and Western democratic and capitalist values. The truth is something else again. In 1919, in the aftermath of the First World War, Hungary became Europe's second avowed Communist state after Russia. Hungary was Communist only for a few months, then the international reactionary forces, headed by the British and the Americans, installed Admiral Miklos Horty as the fascist dictator of Hungary. His regime lasted until the Second World War. Fascist Hungary allied with Hitler during the War. When Stalin made Hungary one of his satellite states, many of the Fascist leopards changed their spots and became loyal Communist apparatchiks.

What did happen after the war was that Stalin's style of monolithic, personality-cult Communism was imposed on Hungary; Hungary's "Stalin" was "Comrade" Rakosi, who kept tight social and political control until 1953, the year Stalin died. Then, the U.S.S.R. was more concerned with its own political upheaval than controlling affairs in Hungary. In that atmosphere, Hungary began to liberalize itself. I have mentioned that some of my activities at HR in 1955 and 1956 could have put me in jail in 1953. As silly as it sounds, I could have been jailed for erasing the tapes we received from Moscow and recording our own music and shipping the tapes to the West. Such was the state of Communist paranoia and bureaucracy at the time.

The liberal reforms were very much like the 1968 reforms of Czechoslovakia's Dubcek, who had wanted "Socialism with a human face."

Hungary's 1956 Revolution was aimed at getting rid of Stalin's supporters and their influence, but in no way was this a Capitalist revolution. All that happened was that Stalin's Communists were replaced with naive, idealistic, Hungarian Communists who wanted to 'do socialism right." The revolutionists miscalculated and the U.S.S.R.'s response was bloody indeed.

During the week preceding the "October Revolution", or "Counter-revolution" as it was referred to from time to time, I was in Warsaw, Poland, attending the conference of the O.I.R. (Organization International de Radiodifusion- the International Radio Organization) as a representative of Hungarian Radio.

My trip to Warsaw had started out in a strange way. In Hungary in the 1950's, if you were sent out on an official trip to another country, you received neither hard Western currency, nor the local currency of the country you were visiting. Instead, you got a book of coupons. Once you arrived at your destination, you were able to exchange the coupons for services such as hotel, meals, a taxi, and even exchange them for cash. Naturally, the coupons were seen as worthless and in reality the black market provided the goods and services the coupons could not. My own experience with the coupons was rather arresting.

I was to go to Warsaw by train from Budapest, through Hungary and Czechoslovakia before arriving in Poland. The train was four hours late arriving from Bucharest and four hours late in Czechoslovakia, so we missed our connection for Warsaw. We had to sit in our railway car through the whole cold night at a small station on the Czechoslovak-Polish border. So, instead of arriving in the early morning in Warsaw, we ended up arriving nearly eighteen hours late.

The train started up in the morning and trundled through the Polish countryside. I had no Hungarian money, as I was not allowed to take any out of the country. I had the coupons, but they could be exchanged only in Warsaw. I had no Polish money, not a single zloty, and I had neither eaten, nor drank for nearly twenty-four hours. All around me Poles were eating savoury lunches and drinking fresh, cold beer.

I had never thought that I would be hungry enough to eat raw meat, but when servers began to pass by me with plates of tartar steak, my stomach growled and my eyes grew large. I still remember those dishes, the colours and the smells sharpened by my hunger. In the middle of the round plate sat a fat, luscious, pile of ground beef, pink and fatty; in the centre of the mound was a depression in which rested a bright yellow egg yolk, shiny and appealing. Framing the meat around the edge of the plate were sliced, sweet onions (their smell pungent in the small, shaking confines of the railway carriage), a slippery, greasy, salty sardine, tangy capers, a dollop of mustard, and other spices.

By noontime my stomach was making louder and louder noises. I realized that I had to find a solution, and I found it — in my socks.

In postwar Eastern Europe, men's nylon socks were not available in Hungary or Poland. On a previous trip to Czechoslovakia, I had bought two pairs of nylon socks for myself. I carried them both around with me on all of my subsequent trips. My usual routine was to wash one pair by hand and wear the other pair. I had washed yesterday's socks that morning.

I called over the waitress in the dining lounge and negotiated a deal; whereby, I exchanged my still-wet socks for a tartar steak and a beer. What a relief! The rawness, which, otherwise, would have revolted me, did not put me off at all. I consumed every bit of the meat, spicing each bite with mustard and onion and an occasional nibble on the greasy sardine, washing it all down with excellent Polish beer. For those twenty minutes everything was perfectly right with the world. That meal stands out in my memory as one of the most satisfying I had ever eaten, although, naturally, I had many more "elaborate" meals in my lifetime. Appetite is indeed the best spice!

Les Préludes

The Warsaw Music Festival was in full swing when I arrived and we attended many concerts in the evenings. We stayed at the Bristol Hotel, where most of the visiting artists, such as David Oistrakh, Yampolsky, Lev Oborin, and others were staying. Some idea of how non-monolithic the Soviet Bloc was came to me when I arrived at the Bristol. When I addressed the hotel clerk, I called him "Tsovarich", or Comrade, a proper revolutionary greeting. He corrected me saying: "Here we call each other Pan (Mr.) and not Tsovarich!" I found this quite strange, as in Hungary, Czechoslovakia, Romania, and other countries in the Eastern Bloc, "Tsovarich" was the proper and only way to address each other.

As the delegates were in various meetings all day long, we did not closely follow events in Warsaw. I learned that something unusual was taking place, when talking to my colleagues in Budapest on the phone. They were very anxious to find out what was causing the excitement in Poland. Being in Poland, but not aware of any excitement, we started to follow things by watching Polish Television whenever we had a chance.

We learned that parallel with our O.I.R. meeting, the Polish Communist Party was having its own convention. Gomulka, the former General Secretary of the Polish Communist Party, whom the Russians had replaced a few years earlier, was to be re-elected, prompting the Russians to try to intervene. Molotov, the Russian Foreign Minister and Khrushchev, another high functionary, were, apparently, in Warsaw and we heard rumors that Warsaw itself was surrounded by Russian tanks. When we went outside, we saw many men running around, and others standing guard, with armbands of the Polish flag.

Obviously, the Russian intervention was not successful, because Gomulka was re-elected as Party Chief. Why the Russians decided not to intervene militarily remains a mystery. Perhaps they knew that the Hungarian situation was about to explode, and did not want to intervene in two of their satellite countries at the same time. The situation was so tense in Warsaw that up until the very moment our plane took off, we were not sure exactly where we were going. And after the plane attained altitude, we were still unsure if the plane would land in a Western country, or if it would be shot down or if we would ever get to Budapest!

I returned to Budapest on October 22, 1956, on the eve of the Hungarian Uprising. That evening I was in charge of a live broadcast of a concert of the Annual Bartok Festival, which was fed to several foreign radio stations. Suddenly, during the broadcast, we lost contact with Romanian Radio in Bucharest. We learned, only later, that some forces involved in the Revolution had been sabotaging communication cables in order to cut off Hungary from the outside world.

Not many people are aware of the fact that the Hungarian Revolution started off with a sympathy demonstration for the Poles. The demonstrators marched to the statue of Behm Apo (Father Behm), the Polish General, who helped the Hungarian revolutionaries in 1848. From there, one armed group headed straight for the HR Building, where they intended to broadcast their revolutionary declaration. The HR was defended by a detachment of the AVH (Allam Vedelmi Hatosag), the State Security Service.

Shortly after their arrival, a gunfight broke out between the revolutionaries and the AVH. After several hours of fighting, the HR Building was partially destroyed, with the remaining portion held by the revolutionaries.

I was still in the building when the fight broke out, because the Radio Symphony Orchestra had a late rehearsal with the well-known Italian conductor, Mario Rossi. The HR complex occupied a whole city block. To this day, it is still bewildering to me that the demonstration and the actual attack were limited to the main entrance on Brody Sandor Street. I do not consider myself a military strategist, but I would have surrounded the whole complex and attacked from all sides. But the revolutionaries didn't, and this made it possible for me to get the members of the Orchestra, Maestro Rossi, and myself out of the Radio complex via the car entrance, which was on the opposite side from the main doors.

Upon arriving home, I phoned up HR to see what was going

on. A member of the AVH answered the phone while I heard machine gun fire in the background. He said, "I cannot talk now. There's a big fight going on!" and slammed down the phone. Apparently, forty-six members of the AVH lost their lives in the attack and likely he was one of them.

The first few days following the events of October 23 were chaotic. The tearing down and destruction of the huge statue of Stalin and other Soviet era "memorabilia" were some of the major activities of the first heady days of the revolution, but the main preoccupation of the revolutionary crowds was to chase down the members of the hated AVH, the Hungarian equivalent of the KGB. Although some of the agents managed to get rid of their uniforms and change into civilian clothes, they were often recognized by their brown boots, and sometimes they were lynched on the spot in the street.

Some elements of the army took part in the revolt, but most of the army stayed in their barracks. The takeover and establishment of the Imre Nagy government went smoother than one could have anticipated under the circumstances. Amazingly, the large Soviet military forces stationed in Hungary stayed in their barracks. It looked for a while that the forces of the victorious revolution would not be challenged by the Russians. This led to various developments.

Some of the Fascists who had escaped from Hungary in the final days of the Second World War, and who had lived mainly in Austria and West Germany, started to trickle back to Hungary. Naturally, there were all kinds of rumours floating about. There even were rumours of pogroms against Jews being committed or at least threatened to take place in various communities.

A few days after the Uprising, "Revolutionary Worker's and Peasant's Committees" were formed in the various factories and workplaces, including Hungarian Radio. Their role was to identify members of the Communist Party and management, prior to the Revolution, and, if justified, to eliminate them from the workplace. As is depressingly the case in this kind of situation, the extremists carried the day.

This led to some tragicomic situations. I will never forget

the scene when one of the "Comrades" was called to task for the sin of bragging about having received a Soviet Decoration. I will never forget the deprecating inflection of his voice in the way he said, ". . . *Soviet Decoration* . . ." before setting out to prove that the whole thing wasn't even worth mentioning. It also turned out that some high ranking Comrades (members of the Communist Party) were actually former Fascists, and that even some former members of Szalasy's Fascist Arrow Party had been posing as Communists for over ten years! But in the topsy-turvy world of the revolutionaries, it was better to have been a loyal, nationalistic Hungarian Fascist in the past than to be a Soviet today. After the Russian intervention less than two weeks later, it turned out that these claims of former Fascist membership were all untrue! Apparently, the officials just used it in self-defense so they wouldn't lose their jobs, or worse. Extremism drives out truth.

I was present at a couple of meetings of this Revolutionary Committee. Here, I became totally disgusted with what was going on, and I think this precipitated my departure from Hungary. I simply could not see myself working any longer with these kinds of turncoats, in an atmosphere of total distrust and loathing. Totally disparate elements with various motivations took part in the revolution, from disgruntled and progressive members of the Communist Party, to Fascists, who wanted to re-establish a Fascist regime. They were all fighting side by side, especially after the Soviet intervention.

The progressive wing of the Communist Party, headed by Imre Nagy and his new regime, aimed at getting rid of the excesses of the Stalinist, dictatorial "personality cult" of the Rakosi era, and sought to establish a Socialist State with a "human face." The Fascists and many right-wing elements who took part in the revolution, wanted to re-establish a Capitalist or even a fascist state.

Imre Nagy, the new Prime Minister of the Interim Revolutionary government, was a high-ranking member of the Communist Party who had been sidelined by Rakosi, the former Stalinist First Secretary of the Communist Party.

Naturally, in these revolutionary times, there were perhaps as many stories as there were people, everybody having his or her own tale to tell of what happened to whom, how and where. Doubtless hundreds of books could be written just about that eleven-day period between the Hungarian Uprising and the Soviet Invasion (October 23- November 4, 1956).

In view of the fact that the Radio building and some of the studios were destroyed during the attack on October 23, we were forced to broadcast from a temporary studio in the Parliament buildings. Walking to work in this totally different atmosphere amongst the memorabilia and slogans of the Revolution was quite an experience. While the "cleansing" work of the Revolutionary Worker's Committees continued, life started to return to "normal." The World watched the scene in awe — the first revolution against the State Capitalism of the Stalinist era and Soviet domination seemed to have succeeded!

In retrospect, if we had been able to be objective during these heady days, it should have been obvious that Khrushchev and Co. would not let this revolution succeed. The Soviet Union would have faced the danger that their other satellite countries would follow Hungary's example. The tension in the air grew day by day. Frightening rumors were flying: "The Russian troops were re-deployed" and "Budapest was surrounded by Soviet tanks."

November 4, 1956, dawned with the roar of Soviet airplanes dropping thousands of leaflets ordering the revolutionaries to surrender, and with the rumbling of Russian tanks on the streets taking up positions around strategic objects, including the Parliament buildings.

Imre Nagy, the Prime Minister, issued a call for help to the Western World, which, naturally, went unheeded. He then quickly sought refuge and asylum at the Embassy of Yugoslavia.

Fighting broke out almost instantly. Soldiers, civilians, even children, took up the fight with whatever they could get their hands on. It was not unusual for children to have destroyed or immobilized Soviet tanks with Molotov cocktails. Soviet troops were met with sniper fire from various apartment buildings along the Korut, the main circular avenue in Budapest. The Soviets did not bother to find and flush out these snipers. The Soviet tanks simply started firing on the buildings themselves, partially or fully destroying them, and killing large numbers of civilians.

Despite some Hungarian tanks and military units taking up the fight, they were no match to the superior forces of the Soviet Army. After a few days and tens of thousand of casualties later, the fighting was over. If we count the one hundred and fifty thousand dissidents who left Hungary, and the number of those who were killed, it is a safe say that Hungary lost more than a quarter of a million people, a devastating loss for such a small country.

Even before the Soviet intervention my wife and I decided to move to her parents' place downtown, so she would not be home alone with the baby. It was also closer to my work, since our own apartment was quite far from downtown and public transportation was erratic. Agnes, Suzanne and I spent several days in the cellar after the Soviets attacked. It was quite a scene with crying babies, old people, and all the habitants of the apartment building huddling together, listening to the guns, and the drone of the planes and the frightening rumors.

After several days, when the fighting finally subsided, somebody came back with the news that they were distributing bread at the market on Klauzal ter. (ter means "square" in Hungarian). As we were running short on food, I decided to take a chance and go. There was already a fairly long and noisy lineup in front of the steel door of the market. As we were waiting in line, a Soviet tank came around the corner, stopped, and aimed its gun towards us.

Suddenly, the din of the crowd stopped and there was dead silence. We had to make a Shakespearean decision: "To be or not to be?" Should we give up on getting bread and run for our lives? Or should we take a chance and stay? I still don't know if it was a subconscious, collective decision, or simply, if we were afraid to move, but we stayed there in silence waiting and waiting for something to happen. I really don't know how long this situation lasted, but at the time it seemed like an eternity. Finally, the tank turned around and left.

At the time of the revolution and the Soviet intervention, Agnes and I came to the conclusion that the situation would have either of two most likely outcomes. One, the Russians would stay and then we could probably expect a worse dictatorship than the one we experienced under the Stalinist personality cult of Rakosi. Or, the Soviets would pull out of the country, in which case we would have a return to Fascism and institutionalized anti-Semitism looked quite plausible. At the time, we could not foresee that in order to prove that the Hungarian Uprising was not necessary at all, the Soviets would allow Hungary to steer a much more liberal course under Prime Minister Kadar. This led eventually to Kadar's becoming quite popular in Hungary. Though he was partially blamed for the Russian intervention and the execution of Imre Nagy by the Russians, under his rule, Hungary became the envy of the other satellite states with its "pseudo-freedoms" and relative prosperity.

Based on our assumptions, my wife and I came to the conclusion, that if we could leave legally, we would flee the country. Having a fifteen-month-old baby, we did not want to take a chance of an illegal flight, which would mean crossing minefields at night, evading border guards who had orders to shoot, and other manifest dangers. But legal flight was not a picnic either.

To have a passport was some kind of extraordinary privilege. The only person in all of Hungarian State Radio who had a valid passport for Western countries was Georg Szepesi, our soccer reporter. For the purposes of my prior trip to Warsaw, I had been issued a so-called "Service Passport." This passport was only valid for countries of the Soviet bloc. I was supposed to have given it back to the authorities at HR after my return.

In view of the tumultuous events of the revolution, I had not yet returned this "Service Passport". At our Radio convention in Warsaw, I met Mr. Kalcic, the head of the Music Department of Radio in Belgrade, Yugoslavia, who gave me his business card. I put the date of 26 of November on his business card, and went to the authorities in HR. I told them that I had to be in Belgrade on that date to conduct the Symphony Orchestra of Yugoslav Radio.

After the end of the fighting, a general strike was declared in Hungary which was supposed to last until the withdrawal of the Soviet troops. If the citizens had stuck to their guns, this strike would have lasted thirty-three years. The general strike affected every public service. As there was no telephone or any kind of communication with the outside world, I knew that the HR authorities could not check on my story about conducting for Belgrade Radio. I used the lack of phone, mail, and telegram service as an argument, asking how can I leave my wife and baby behind under these circumstances, when I would not be able to communicate with them in case of an emergency?

In the end, by mid- November, I was issued a passport for my wife and child, valid only for the Soviet bloc and Yugoslavia. However, our tribulations had just started.

First of all, I needed a Yugoslav visa. The Yugoslavian Embassy was still surrounded by Soviet tanks, because Prime Minister Imre Nagy was still inside. I made an appointment with the officer in charge of issuing visas to meet in a different building away from the Embassy. After I told him the same story and answered various questions, he was getting ready to stamp the visas in our passports. Before doing so he told me the following: "I have to warn you, that if you wish to stay in Yugoslavia, there is a mixed Hungarian-Yugoslavian committee which decides who should get asylum and who will be shipped back to Hungary." He was acting suspiciously, and rightly so.

I told him that we had no intention of staying in Yugoslavia... which was not a lie. My parents were already living in Montreal, Canada. My brother was a commercial attaché at the Israeli Embassy in Belgrade. Our plan was made up: we were going to Canada! Naturally, I did not tell the officer in charge all of this.

After obtaining the Yugoslav visa, it turned out that we also needed a Soviet military visa to leave Budapest, as the capital and all of Hungary were under Soviet military occupation. I went to the Soviet Embassy. While waiting to speak to somebody, I witnessed something incredible.

The scene closely resembled one in Charlie Chaplin's satire, The Great Dictator. The film itself is hilarious, but the scene played out in front of me was not at all funny. Every time I see the movie I am reminded of this moment. In the film, Hitler (Chaplin) tears off Goering's many medals, including the buttons off his coat, flinging off handfuls until Goering ends up in his striped undershirt, looking like a clown. Chaplin made it funny. The real scene at the Soviet embassy, (which happened on Saturday morning, the 24th of November) was frightening. A man in civilian clothes was yelling at the top of his voice at an extremely well-decorated Russian general; this civilian began tearing the medals and decorations off the chest of the general and flinging the decorations on the floor. This was obviously one of the Soviet political agents, KGB or NKVD, disciplining the general; and the general was taking it because the agent clearly had the arbitrary power of life and death. I huddled, frightened, in the corner. I wonder if the general was demoted, sent to a labour camp or just shot.

After going through my story, and my trip, and why I had to go to Belgrade several more times, I finally obtained a Soviet military visa.

We quietly made preparations for leaving Hungary, leaving our previous life, leaving my wife's parents and sister, our friends, our careers, our "new" apartment which we had waited five years for, our whole life in Hungary. It was painful watching the grandparents come to grips with the idea that they might never again see their grandchild. Since our "official" story was that we were leaving just for a short time, we could take only a limited amount of baggage with us, in order not to raise suspicion.

I had the complete edition of the works of Tchaikovsky, the volume that contained the three different versions of his Romeo and Juliet, (one of my favorite pieces); it also had a dedication to me by the great Romanian conductor, George Georgescu. I ripped this portion out to take with me, along with a few other favourite scores. Eight years later, when I returned to Hungary for the first time, I retrieved the rest of the scores and took them with me back to Canada, so the book is complete again.

Finally, all the documents were ready, we were more or less packed, and it seemed that everything was ready to go, except for a small detail — the GENERAL STRIKE! No train, no plane, no bus, nothing was moving, in or out of the country. I knew that we had to get to the Yugoslav border somehow because my brother could come from Belgrade to get us once we reached a Yugoslav border post.

Sunday morning, November 25. Still no end in sight of the General Strike. We were getting desperate. Early in the afternoon, we heard the news that a taxi service between Budapest and the provinces was to start operating on a limited basis on Monday, the 26th of November. I phoned up the company, and ordered a taxi for the next morning to take us to a little village near the City of Szeged, named Roszke. According to the map, it was a little border post on the highway to Belgrade. This seemed to be the shortest and most inconspicuous route.

I don't remember exactly how much this taxi ride cost us. All I remember is that it was a very substantial sum in relation to our finances.

Leaving everybody and everything behind us proved to be a terribly difficult emotional experience. I will never forget the scene: our baby daughter, Suzy, was sitting in the middle of the double bed playing with some toys. Her grandfather was lying on the bed fully dressed, propping up his head with his arm and watching her play. I will never forget the look on his face, the pain, the Jewish "I've seen it all" expression, the expression of hopelessness. He almost looked like somebody who was in a daze after a sudden shock.

This was the second time I was leaving a country for good, but this departure was totally different from leaving my birthplace and country of origin, Romania, to go to Budapest to continue my musical studies. Then, I was a twenty year old youngster, full of hope, excitement and expectation, anticipating my new life in a vibrant metropolis. In 1956, when I closed the door of our cherished Budapest apartment for the last time, I felt that I was closing the door on perhaps the most important period of my life and heading into an unknown future.

We decided to spend the last night downtown, with my wife's parents and her sister and leave from there. We slept very little that night, talking and talking with my wife's family, for perhaps the last time in our lives.

The taxi arrived at 9 A.M. sharp, and we had to say our final good-byes. We were all crying, waving, as we drove away, until we could not see them any longer.

Shortly after our car turned into the Korut, we drove by one burned-out and destroyed apartment building after another. Four or five blocks down, we were stopped at the first Russian army checkpoint. We had to stop several times before we left the city itself, and again a couple of times in the countryside, before we reached the border. After a stop in Szeged for lunch, we reached the border at Röszke in the early afternoon.

It turned out that between the Hungarian and the Yugoslavian border posts there was a kind of no-man's-land. I believe it was flanked on both sides by minefields, due to the former unfriendly relations between Marshal Tito and Comrade Rakosi.

Chapter Twenty Four
November 26 to December 22, 1956

BELGRADE TO MUNICH

Agnes, Suzanne, and I reached the Yugoslavian border in the middle of the afternoon. There was an empty area of about one hundred metres between the Hungarian border post and the Yugoslavian border post. I had to walk back and forth several times with our baby, luggage, bags, and everything else we had managed to snatch in our flight. It was almost an hour before we settled down at the Yugoslavian border post.

I tried to phone my brother in Belgrade several times. By this time Dodi was a commercial attaché at the Israeli Embassy in Belgrade, the capital of Yugoslavia. When Dodi answered the phone, he thought my call from the border post was some kind of ruse or trap; he had not heard from us in months, and his position as an Israeli diplomat made him justifiably cautious. He hung up, then called us back at the border to assure himself of our genuine location. He then told me it would take several hours for him to get there and pick us up.

The family settled in at the border post. The guards cleared a room for us with Suzanne, my fifteen-month-old daughter, sitting on her potty in the middle of the room, supervising the situation.

Dodi and the First Secretary of the Israeli Embassy arrived around 10 P.M. in a small Vauxhall, a popular British car. Somehow, we managed to squeeze our belongings and ourselves into the compact car. Fortunately, we drove only a couple of hours until we reached Zagreb, where we spent the night in a hotel. The next morning, we loaded the car again and headed for Belgrade. Hours later, still many kilometres from Belgrade, the poor little car's axle broke under the heavy load and we were stranded on the side of the road.

The embassy's First Secretary volunteered to hitchhike to Belgrade and send another car for us. Shortly after, he got a lift from a truck driver and we settled in for a long wait. In order not to raise suspicion when we left Budapest, we did not take very many belongings with us. I remember the pain I suffered, ripping out of my complete edition of Tchaikovsky's works, including the version of his Romeo and Juliet overture I usually conducted.

Still, we had a huge, oblong basket, heavy with many additional orchestral scores packed between our meager personal possessions. I also had my violin with me and we had some smaller suitcases. No wonder that the poor Vauxhall expired under the weight of the five of us, plus the luggage!

After a couple of hours, the driver of the Embassy arrived in a brand-new 1956 Chrysler Plymouth. This was my first experience of seeing and actually travelling in a big American car. Compared to the miniature, underpowered, and insecure confines of the Vauxhall, it was sheer heaven.

We arrived to Belgrade and unloaded our stuff at Dodi's apartment, where his wife and their two baby daughters were waiting for us. Next morning, my brother told me: "Here are the keys to my apartment in Jerusalem; you will leave shortly for Israel."

I replied: "Not me!"

Which may require some explanation.

We had arrived in Belgrade during the Suez crisis, when the Israelis, the British and the French occupied the Suez Canal after Nasser had nationalized it. The tension in the Middle East was reaching the boiling point and the whole region was a hairsbreadth away from outright war. I told Dodi that we had just come from a revolution, filled with street fighting, invading tanks, and civil insurrection, and I had no intention of getting into another fight right away. I also told him, half-jokingly, that there were already too many Jews in Israel and especially too many Jewish musicians. How would I be able to establish myself and support my family?

This put Dodi and his family in a very difficult position at the Israeli Embassy. His wife, Margalith, also worked there. He had to explain why his brother would not go to Israel. I did not envy him, but we had definitely no intention of going to Israel. Looking back over all the upheaval in our lives from 1939 on, Agnes and I wanted to get as far from Europe and the Middle East as possible.

What options were open to us? After the war, my parents had moved to Israel to be with their two older sons. But life in Israel just after the creation of the Jewish state was hard; living conditions were poor and the country itself was threatened on all sides. Finding life too difficult there, my parents decided to join my father's brother, Ferdinand, in Paris. No sooner had they arrived in Paris than Ferdinand received his emigration papers for Canada and left for Montreal; so my parents applied for Canada as well. The process was difficult and protracted and my parents gave up and prepared to move back to Israel. Their possessions were already in Marseilles ready to be shipped when the Canadian embassy delivered their papers. In the end, they joined my father's brother in Montreal.

Canada seemed to be our best option, so we went to the Canadian Embassy to check out the possibilities of emigrating. We met Mr. Albert Hart, the First Secretary of the Embassy, who became our guardian angel. Later, he and his family became our life-long friends. They even named their adopted daughter after my younger daughter, Kathleen. If it weren't for Mr. Hart, we would have not come to Canada,

Mr. Hart explained to us that there was no agreement between Canada and Yugoslavia regarding refugees, and the only way we could go to Canada would be if my parents were to sponsor us. Hungarians escaping from the revolution who went to Austria were accepted as refugees into Canada and the Canadian government even paid for their transportation. We, on the other hand, would have to pay our fare ourselves.

While staying in Belgrade, we lived in limbo, neither in immediate danger, yet not truly safe, having neither a destination, nor a home. We had left our life in Budapest, our family, friends, jobs, our apartment, belongings, and all the things, all the status, all the experience and all the potential we had, without knowing what the future might hold for us.

Compared to Budapest at the time, Belgrade seemed to be a Western European city, with a lot of car traffic and coloured advertising everywhere. You could find newspapers and periodicals from all over Europe. Sometimes, I just walked around the city by myself, looking at various historical sites or I just walked around aimlessly, wondering at the turn my life had taken and where my family and career were headed.

Our Yugoslav visa was good for only thirty days, so it was touch and go as to whether we would get our papers in time. Mr. Hart promised that he would expedite the proceedings. So we settled in for our 'holiday' in Belgrade. The two wives went to the park with the girls and sometimes I joined them. To familiarize ourselves with Canada, we started to visit the Canadian Embassy, where they had a reading room, maps and other information about Canada. On Wednesday afternoons they used to have film showings that we visited regularly.

We shared the preconceived notions of most Europeans about Canada. Canada was a cold country, with snow year-round, with Eskimos, igloos, polar bears, and the Northern Lights. Slowly, we came to realize how much more there was to this country. At the second Wednesday film showing, the film was about a plane crash in the Canadian wilderness. We felt no disquiet at the time, but in retrospect it was a harbinger of things to come.

One day, Albert Hart and his wife invited us for something called, "afternoon tea." I will never forget my feelings of being in the garden of a gorgeous home of a Canadian diplomat, and being served tea by a male attendant in a white jacket on their patio. I will never forget the sight of the cream dissipating in the gold colored tea. Coming from the conditions we were living through in Budapest, the contrast was almost surreal.

My brother and his wife went to a diplomatic reception almost every night. In view of the fact that basically they met the same people, the same diplomats and their wives every night, whether the reception was held at the U.S., British, etc., Embassies, we felt that these receptions must have been pretty boring.

In the meantime, our immigration proceedings were making some progress. Mr. Hart had arranged our medical pre-clearance without having to wait for an OK from Ottawa.

The easy, peacetime travel people experience nowadays was not available to us then. Yugoslavia was a Communist country, and on the wrong side in the eyes of the Americans and Canadians. In view of the Suez crisis, British and French planes were not allowed to fly between Cairo and Paris. Only the YAT (Yugoslovensky Aero Transport), the Yugoslav national airline, was flying twice a week, Wednesdays and Saturdays, between Cairo and Paris, with stopovers in Belgrade, Vienna, and Munich. No non-stops for us, no waving through Customs. Because of the stopovers, all three of us had to acquire Austrian, German and French transit visas. Although my service passport was not officially valid for the western countries, we managed to obtain the necessary visas. Since we had no money, my parents had to send the money to purchase the tickets.

Our excitement grew daily. By the middle of December, our Yugoslav visa had only a week left, so we made airline reservations for that Saturday, the 22nd of December 1956. We were supposed to fly with YAT from Belgrade to Paris and then on Trans Canada Airlines from Paris to Montreal. Finally, on Tuesday the December 18th, with only four days to spare, we received our immigration papers for Canada! Wednesday afternoon we went again to the film showing at the Embassy. They showed the same film about the plane crash, and again I felt not a shiver of doom. Thursday, I received a telegram from Trans Canada Airlines informing us that they had canceled our reservations from Paris to Montreal.

Trans Canada Airlines gave a discount of 20% to immigrants, but this fare was available only if they were unable to sell the seats at the full price. Naturally, passengers paying full fares had priority and could "bump" discounted immigrants. Such was our situation. As we already had reservations for the YAT flight leaving Saturday (the expiration date of our Yugoslav visas), and the next flight would have been only the following Wednesday, I decided to leave on Saturday as scheduled, and wait in Paris for a flight to Montreal. I didn't even tell Agnes about the telegram.

Dodi and his wife took us to the airport. My family had been jostling about in his apartment for a whole month.

Our plane was a new Convair 44 turbo jet. This was one of the first passenger planes to have a nose-wheel. We were used to flying with DC 3's or Ilyushin planes, which had their third wheel hanging off the tail of the plane.

After saying our good-byes, we boarded. The forty-four seats on the plane were filled to capacity. We took off at 5 P.M. In about an hour we were approaching Vienna. Our approach to the airport was quite bumpy. It was a little bit like a ship riding the waves, once going up, once going down, but we landed safely in the Austrian capital. Later, we learned that the pilot had had problems with the automatic pilot and had switched to manual controls for the approach and landing. Most of the passengers disembarked in Vienna and only sixteen, including my family, continued to Munich.

Before leaving Budapest, my wife had made a nice sleeping bag filled with down for our baby, and now Suzanne was sleeping peacefully in the seat in front of us. As we were approaching the Munich Airport, the "Fasten Seat Belt" sign came on. Suzanne started to cry, perhaps feeling the sudden change in air pressure.

I told my wife to take her in her lap for the landing.

I looked out through the window and saw some lights.

When I regained consciousness (which I found out was about fifteen minutes later), I was sitting on the snowy ground. I was not even aware that I had been hurt. When my eyes adjusted to the dim light inside the plane, I noticed that the seats were on the 'ceiling', the real ceiling had been ripped off, and I was freezing on the snow. Gradually, I realized that we must have crashed.

It turned out that the plane hit the ground about one and a half kilometres from the München Grub train station, in a plowed field near a little forest, about fifteen kilometres from the Munich airport. As the crash happened without any warning, there had been no panic in the plane, and I did not remember the pain of being knocked out. The plane struck the ground with the left wing, which broke off with the engine. Then the fuselage tipped over completely and the right wing broke off too, leaving the trunk of the plane to skid several hundred metres upside-down on the snow. The pilot and the navigator were killed, likely because the cockpit was the first part of the plane to hit the ground when it flipped over. The second pilot survived unscathed. One passenger was mysteriously ejected and found dead several hundred metres from the plane. The Convair itself broke into hundreds of pieces leaving a long trail of debris in the fields. In 1997, forty-one years after the crash, they found a propeller blade from the plane embedded deep in the soil.

The flip and the skid had left me sitting in this hole in the ceiling, in snow, mud and blood. Suzanne and Agnes were alive, but I didn't know it at the time.

This was the beginning of our three month stopover in Germany.

The remains of our airplane sitting on the snowy field. The fuselage has been turned right-side up.

The left wing of the aircraft.

Investigators search the ground for pieces of aircraft and clues as to the causes of the crash.

This is the inside of the plane, right-side up, with the winter light coming through the hole in the roof. The hole in the roof of the plane was where I was sitting, on the ground, when I regained consciousness.

Workers stand beside the righted cockpit. This was a smaller aircraft, not the huge people-movers we are used to seeing nowadays.

Here one can see the name of the airline, Yugoslav Air Transport. These photos are from the official government report on the accident.

TRANSCRIPT OF COMMUNICATIONS BETWEEN MUNICH AIR TRAFFIC CONTROL TOWER (ACC) AND YUGOSLAV AIR TRANSPORT (YAT)

ACC : Yankee Delta Alfa, Munich Control - Continue to descend to four thousand - Report passing six. Over.

YAT : Go Ahead

ACC: Delta Alfa is cleared for a straight-in ILS runway two five. Over.

YAT: Roger. Cleared for a straight-in IIS approach. Delta Alfa

ACC: What is your present altitude. Over

YAT: Present Altitude six thousand three hundred

ACC: Roger Contact Munich GCA on this frequency

YAT: What frequency is GCA please

ACC: On this frequency. On this frequency.

YAT: Munich GCA for radio check. How do you hear?

GCA: GCA

YAT: Read you five

GCA: Roger. If you lose communications for five seconds on final - turn right to a heading of three four zero - climb to three thousand five hundred feet and contact Munich control for further instructions.

GCA: What's your present altitude please.

YAT: Three thousand five hundred.

GCA: Descend to and maintain three thousand feet. Position now seven miles each of Munich

YAT: Descending to three thousand.

GCA: Perform your final cockpit check - gear down and locked.

YAT: Roger

GCA: What's your present heading right now?

YAT: Present heading two.

GCA: Pick up heading of two four zero - two four zero - you are right up on course four and a half miles from touchdown - maintain three thousand feet - you are going dangerously low - level your aircraft off - bring it up - bring your aircraft up - dangerously low - you're very low - bring your aircraft up to three thousand feet.

GCA: Are you reading, GCA over.

ACC: How me --

GCA: Roger Control. He went very low out there and I don't see him on my scopes yet.

ACC: Do you read. Over

ACC: Do you read. Over

ACC: Do you read. Over.

Les Préludes

Chapter Twenty Five

ESCAPE FROM DEATH

The YAT Convair 340 departed Vienna at 18.37h for a flight to Munich. The captain was acting as an instructor on this flight in the right-hand seat; the co-pilot acted as pilot-in-command. At 20:33 the flight passed the Munich NDB at FL 120. The aircraft then started the descent. After reaching 3500 ft. at 20.58 the flight was cleared to 3000 feet msi (which is 1268 ft. agl), which altitude was to be maintained. One minute later the crew reported leaving 3000 ft. GCA then told the crew to pull up and maintain 3000 ft. GCA did not receive an answer. The Convair 340 descended fast and struck the ground left wing and left undercarriage first, at a point 6.85 km from the runway threshold and 200m right of the glide path. The aircraft came to rest with both wings detached after a ground slide of 400 m. Weather at the time of the crash was: wind 210 - 240 deg/3-5 kts; visibility 1 - 2.5nm, possibly only 0.7 - 1.0 nm; moderate snowfall; cloud base 60 - 800 fet; ground temperature -1 C.

At approximately 9 P.M. on December 22nd, 1956, our YAT plane fell out of the sky.

The impact was violent, and the plane broke into hundreds of pieces.

The friction from the 1,200 foot skid made a hole in the ceiling, which had become the bottom of the overturned craft. I found myself sitting in this hole in the snow, mud, and blood.

I was unconscious and unaware I was hurt for about 15 minutes. The first things I saw were the seats upside-down on the ceiling, and Agnes sitting on the floor near me. Her skull seemed to be open from ear to ear and she was bleeding profusely. For a moment, I thought that I could actually see her brain. It turned out later, that it was just her scalp peeled back from the skull. She also had a couple of broken vertebrae in her neck.

She saw me bleeding from my own head wound, and because the blood had covered the right side of my face completely, she thought I had lost an eye.

My first question was, "Where is our baby?" Suzy was already outside in the snow. Fortunately, one of the passengers who had regained consciousness earlier had used a cigarette lighter to look around and had seen Suzy on the floor, picked her up and took her outside. This saved Suzy from being trampled to death in the dark by the other passengers escaping from the plane; in fact she was one of the first to leave the plane.

Because of the nature of the crash and the serious structural damage to the plane's body, the passengers were unable to open any of the doors or emergency exits. Finally, a male steward kicked out one of the windows. We were very lucky that the gas tanks broke off with the wings, so there was no fuel around to ignite.

Agnes was helped out of the plane. I managed to get out on my own. It was snowing, pitch black, and quite cold. Naturally, our overcoats were still inside. The flight attendant was holding Suzy, who was bleeding from a little wound beside her ear. As I stood in the middle of the ploughed field, I saw a train stopping at a small station about a mile from where we were. Agnes was bleeding so badly that I was afraid she might bleed to death. I had to get her to that station for first aid to stop the bleeding.

No authorities had arrived. No police. No doctors. And no ambulance could have driven over that ploughed field, even if a road had been nearby. And there was no road. So it became of paramount importance to get Agnes to that station.

One passenger was a veterinary doctor from Yugoslavia. He and the stewardess helped Agnes out of the plane. I took Suzy in my arms and put a handkerchief over her head, sheltering her a little from the cold and covering her head wound.

The walk through the snow-covered field, with its deep furrows was quite difficult. Making our way in a fog of shock, oblivious to the cold, the snow and the pain. We finally reached the station. I left Agnes in the care of the vet and Suzy with the stewardess and went out onto the highway to flag down a car. I managed to stop the first ambulance on the scene. When it halted, I collapsed. Until that moment I was not aware that I had been hurt. My right leg ended up in a splint for five weeks. I have no idea to this day how I was able to walk that mile to the train station.

The ambulance took us to a hospital in Munich called the Krankenhaud Rects der Isaar. They took me into one operating room and Agnes to another. My head needed a few stitches and my right leg was put into a splint. Once finished in the operating room, I had them push my wheelchair to a telephone and called my brother in Belgrade. By that time, it was close to midnight and I woke him up. He didn't know our plane had crashed.

About an hour later, Agnes was wheeled out of the operating room. Her head was completely swathed in a heavy bandage. They had had to shave her head completely to close her wounds. We were taken to a room where our baby was already asleep in her crib. The room was our home for the next two months.

The staff at the hospital nicknamed us "Die Heilige Familie" (The Holy Family) because we came from "heaven" two days before Christmas Eve. One day, our nurse came in the room and said, "Holy Family, you have a call from Jerusalem." Under any other circumstances this would have been quite funny. It turned out to be Nandi, my eldest brother.

During the first day in our room, the head of YAT visited us with a dozen long-stemmed roses for Agnes. He started to tell us how much safer air travel is compared to a car or any other method of transportation. I told him to tell that to someone else, not the 0.0000003% who had just come out of a plane crash.

As a Jew, Agnes had had terrible experiences during the Second World War. Now stuck in Germany, home of her erstwhile persecutors, she was upset and fearful. When the nurses asked her religion for one of their forms, she answered Catholic. I claimed Atheist. (I don't like sectarian Gods.) So the Catholic priest came every day to visit my wife, and when he was leaving the room, he blessed Agnes with the sign of the cross. He was very careful to aim his blessing only at Agnes, avoiding me entirely. We always had a good laugh after he left.

Suzy's scratch healed in a couple of weeks and she had to find other ways to amuse herself, while her battered parents recovered.

Our daughter played outside our room for a couple of hours every day with our nurse, Brigitte. At the time of the crash Suzy was not yet walking. So imagine our surprise, when one day the door to our room opened, and our baby walked in, holding out a hairbrush in one hand to balance herself. Her knuckles were white from the effort. She was such a beautiful baby. I think the whole nursing staff must have spoiled her. Agnes had some family in Munich who visited us, and would take Suzy out of the hospital on outings.

While the days seemed to pass very slowly, especially as we were immobilized and largely bedridden, the weeks trotted by. Around the 7th week, we started to have discussions with our doctors and YAT to decide where we would continue our convalescence when we no longer needed full-time hospital care. At the end of February we moved to the Ebenhausen Sanatorium about 30 kilometres south of Munich in a pastoral sub-alpine setting.

At the Sanatorium, we started walking around, first the premises, then venturing out to the village. Suzy played in a sandbox in the garden. Agnes became more and more restless, hating every minute in Germany and wishing to continue to Canada as soon as possible. She hated the food. Everything German irritated her. And my parents urged us to come, saying we could go to a sanatorium in Canada. This last was crucial, as we needed another couple of months for complete rehabilitation. The Sanatorium gave us massage, physiotherapy treatments, the best of everything.

Another complication reared its head.

In January, Agnes missed her period. The doctors said it was just the shock of the crash. It happened again in February, with the same diagnosis. In March, the doctor said, "Congratulations!"

Can you imagine someone in our situation, in fragile health, heading to a new country with no job or prospects, faced with having a new baby in only a few months! (Don't feel sorry for us. Kathy, our second daughter, brought us only happiness and good luck, in spite of the bad timing of her arrival.)

Someone had a Mercedes Sports Coupe and offered me a lift to the Canadian Consulate in Munich to make arrangements to continue our voyage to Canada. There are no speed limits on the Autobahn and the fellow drove at 120 miles an hour. What with my concussion and recent catastrophic experience with speed, I was weak, dizzy, and sick by the time we got to the office. I talked to the Consul and asserted that we would not consider flying after our crash. The consulate agreed to make arrangements for us to get to Canada by train and boat.

Once these arrangements were made, we had to sign documents saying that we were leaving the Sanatorium on our own responsibility, as we were not fully recovered. Both of us were still weak, but we had been assured by my parents that we could continue our recuperation in Canada, and Agnes desperately wanted to leave Germany.

The die was cast and we were on our way. YAT, which had been paying our hospital expenses, was delighted to see us go.

Agnes' relatives took us to the train station. We boarded the train for Bremerhaven to meet our ship, the Arosa Star.

Recovering at the Sanatorium

After the accident, we were taken to the Rechts der Isaar Hospital for treatment. We were there two months, then moved to the Ebenhausen Sanatorium for one month.

Chapter Twenty Six

THE AROSA STAR TO HALIFAX,

While we were in the Sanatorium Ebenhuasen, outside Munich, we received letters from my parents exhorting us to hurry up and come to Canada. They assured us that we would continue our medical treatment in Canada, that we would have access to a sanatorium or hospital. Our injuries were hardly minor. I had a foot injury which required a brace, having also sustained various bruises and cuts, and most dangerous, a concussion, (brain-bruise) which led to fainting spells. The injury to my foot also put blood clots into the blood vessels in my leg, and I had to take blood thinners to reduce the chances of sudden, catastrophic stroke. Agnes had a deep scalp wound, a minor concussion, and two broken vertebrae in her neck, as well as all the regular bruises, strains, and bodily insults that come from an airplane crash; and she had maintained her pregnancy. Suzanne had been blessed by the miracles that accompany childhood, having sustained only a small bump on her head. We stayed two months in the hospital and one month in the sanatorium, which I guess would be called an extended-care facility now. The treatment was excellent, the very best the German government and the insurance company could give us.

I was aware all the time how lucky we were. The headlines about the crash blared "MIRACLE!", and other such words; the pictures showing the airplane opened up and twisted like a very large tin can were disquieting to me. At the time, YAT (Yugoslav Air Transport) was not giving us any trouble, but

Here is the whole family on the Arosa Star, B.W. (Before the Waves).

they warned us that if we signed out "AMA" (Against Medical Advice]") they would consider their obligations regarding our treatment finished. Against this I had to balance the demands my parents were making, my own desire to leave Europe, and Agnes' intense desire to be out of Germany.

My wife hated every minute she had to spend in Germany, even the food we were eating. Agnes' experience as a Jew hiding from death for five years during the war had created a revulsion of everything to do with Germans or Germany. Although both of us were in very poor health requiring several more months of treatment, we decided to sign ourselves out of the Sanatorium and head for Canada, having received assurances from my parents that we would be able to continue our treatment at our new destination.

After an overnight train ride we reached Bremerhaven on the North Sea, and boarded our ship, the Arosa Star, which flew the Swiss flag. No more plane trips for us! It turned out that this ship had been converted from transporting bananas to transporting immigrants to Canada. It was quite a small ship, about 8,000 tons which, though well-maintained and safe, was very, ahem, responsive to bad weather. This gave us passengers quite an adventure as we crossed the North Atlantic during an enormous spring storm.

I realized later, that for the amount of money we had paid for our tickets, we could have crossed the North Atlantic in a ship five times larger and more luxurious— such as the United States, the Ile de France, or the Bremen. I was convinced that there was some collusion, if not outright corruption, between some of the employees of the Canadian Consulate in Munich and the shipping company. But I found all this out later, and so started our trip in good spirits.

Naturally, we were quite excited about boarding the ship, and looked forward to the trip and our new life in Canada. Our

Agnes in her privileged seat in the exact centre of the ship, getting the minimum of movement

trip from Bremenhaven, through Le Havre in France and finally Southampton in England was more or less uneventful. Once we hit the open waters of the North Atlantic the situation changed dramatically. It turned out that we were heading into one of the biggest North Atlantic storms of the year. Much larger ships than the Arosa Star had had to turn back, returning to their ports with some passengers suffering bruises and even broken bones from the violent motion. The captain of the Arosa Star was made of sterner stuff, as were his passengers, and we steamed resolutely through the storm for eleven days.

During this time, I, a land-locked lad, learned what writers mean by "mountainous seas". Our little ship would literally climb up to the crest of a huge wave, a wave several times higher than our ship, and then descend into a trough just as deep. We would tip upward for several seconds, climbing the wave, pause level at the crest for only a moment, then tip forward into the trough and run "downhill" with what seemed like suicidal speed. Then we would repeat this motion, several times a minute, hundreds of times an hour, day after day.

By that time we knew that Agnes was pregnant, so I took her out from our cabin, which was in the forward section of the ship where the motion was particularly strong, and made her lie in the middle of the ship on a lounge. This minimized the up and down motions of the ship. I was afraid the extreme, continuous motion might cause a miscarriage, so I also set her at right angles to our forward direction so her body moved sideways instead of back and forth

For eight days we were unable to eat anything. I remember that on the first day they served a steak for dinner. On the second day, the meat reappeared as hamburgers and from the third day on we couldn't care less what they served in the dining room. On top of everything they kept painting the ship and the smell of the heavy oil paint was all we needed to be totally seasick. The crossing took eleven days instead of the customary seven to eight days. Suzanne was the only person on the ship who was not seasick. Everything she ate stayed down until the very last day of the crossing, when somebody gave her a bunch of salty, greasy, roasted peanuts and even her iron stomach finally rebelled.

The ship dropped anchor in Halifax harbor eleven days after we set out. When we landed the next day, we were greeted with some free promotional foods from Kellogg's and other brand names. It was our first experience with Western commercial indoctrination; Canadian and U.S. companies obviously had intended that newcomers would also be new customers. After our eight days of starvation, I will never forget the taste of Kellogg's Corn Flakes cereal with pear conserve. I don't remember anything else tasting so good as this bland North American, heavily-processed food, except perhaps my tartar steak on the train to Warsaw. As for the severe, austere look of our surroundings where we were processed, we ignored it. I remember only that some ugly green colour seemed to dominate everything.

We took an overnight train to Montreal. I woke up after midnight and looked out the window when we stopped in Moncton, New Brunswick. Here I saw huge piles of snow like it was still midwinter, even though it was mid-April. Not only was it odd to see deep winter so late in the year, the architecture also surprised us. Coming from Europe where houses in general were built of brick and mortar, we were surprised to see all these wooden frame houses in different colors. We wondered when we would see real houses.

On the next day we arrived in Montreal, and were greeted by my parents. Unfortunately, the very first night turned into an enormous fight. The real reason my father wanted

Our first night in Montreal. My father and I had already had a tremendous fight.

us to come to Canada as soon as possible was not out of paternal love, but because he had plans to open a bakery and he intended that I, who spoke English and French, would be in the store serving the customers. He had completely ignored the fact that I was a musician and had been a musician for over ten years. My two brothers, at one time or another, had been trained and involved in the bakery, but not me. I had absolutely no plans to get involved in a bakery.

Within hours, Agnes and I realized how irresponsible it had been for them to mislead us, for it turned out that we would have no opportunity to continue our treatment in Canada unless we paid for it ourselves, which was out of the question. Canada had not yet established a government-funded medical system, and all medical care was either private or private charity for the worst cases. YAT (Yugoslovenski Aero Transport) had happily washed its hands of any further involvement in our medical treatment and expenses after we left the German sanatorium. So we were in a real pickle. I had no money, no job, a small child and another on the way, still sick, and unable to practice my profession.

When we realized the situation we were in, my wife burst out, "I can not take this, I will die!" My father answered back, "There will be one corpse more!" This little exchange set the tone for the future: a relationship filled with fights and arguments between my parents and my wife. I was the punching-bag between them. My parents had been living in a very small apartment behind a store. The apartment consisted of a bathroom, a small kitchen and one very small bedroom, so it had been out of the question to stay with them. Before we arrived, my parents had arranged to rent a room for us from a French-Canadian couple. When we met them, I found that because I spoke Parisian French and they spoke in Joual, the Quebecois dialect originating in the Bretagne of France, I didn't understand one word of what they were saying. The room we were in was very small, painted in dark green. The window opened up on a flat roof and there was a heavy April rain. All in all, our first day in Montreal was not very auspicious.

Chapter Twenty Seven

FIRST YEAR IN MONTREAL

We arrived in Montreal in a fragile state of health. Then we took another big hit when we found out that, contrary to my parent's assurances, there was no way that we could continue our treatment. Once we signed out on our own responsibility from the Sanatorium Ebenhausen in Germany, the obligations of the YAT ended, and from then on we were on our own. For the first couple of days after our arrival the skies were dark and raining, a reflection of our own poor state of mind.

My parents paid for our trip and I realized that for a short time we would continue to need their financial help. Seeing the dismal conditions they themselves were living in, scarcely better than our own, I promised to pay back every penny (with

Suzanne in Montreal, 1957. She is wearing the skullcap I wore when I was employed singing in a choir in a synagogue. $25 each Sabbath

interest) at the first occasion. In fact, I did repay the debt, with interest, four years later when we received our settlement from the YAT.

In order to get to know Montreal, to find another place and be mobile, I needed a car. Not having any money, naturally, we could not consider buying or even renting a car. The solution was to become a taxi driver, thereby, not only having a car but possibly also some income. Within two weeks of our arrival, I had passed my Conductor's test and became licensed to drive a taxi. To be a taxi driver, you had to pass a conductor's test— an operator's test was not sufficient. It became a standing joke that I was the only licensed 'Conductor' in Canada.

As I spoke six languages, including English and French, the bilinguality requirement of the test was not a problem. I also needed to get to know the city, so I studied the map of Montreal the way I would study a score and soon I knew the names of most of the forty-five streets that crossed Saint-Laurent Boulevard, without ever having driven on any of them or even seen them in real life.

I soon had a job driving for a company named Lasalle Taxis. The car that I rented belonged to a fleet of two hundred taxis owned by a Romanian. The arrangement was as follows: I paid ten dollars a day for the car, plus gas, and whatever remained from my fares and tips was my (very modest) profit. At the time, an average fare was anywhere from fifty cents to a dollar fifty. It became very obvious that this was not the way to great riches. I remember one day, I netted the princely sum of four dollars after driving for sixteen hours. And in Montreal traffic, too!

For my purposes, driving a taxi was a kind of shortcut, not just for getting to know the city, but also getting to know the people, how they talked, how they acted, what made them laugh, what they were passionate about. As I didn't know the city very well, I would tell my customers, "I know the city like the palm of my hand, but if you know a shorter way to your destination just tell me!" However, being multilingual has its perils. One day a French- Canadian told me, "Tout droit." I understood "tout" in English (to), and "droit" (right) in French, and made a right turn. He started yelling at me: "J'ai dit tout droit" ("I said, tout droit!" which in French means "straight ahead." Thank God I wasn't at the waterfront!

Another time, after getting some directions from my passenger, we ended up in a dead-end street at a golf course. I turned around and found my passenger having a good snooze. I didn't wake him, but put the car quietly back in gear, went back to Decarie Boulevard, and then woke him up to ask for his directions.

I had an unforgettable experience with Chinese food. It was my first or second evening on the job, when the phone rang at my taxi stand. I was instructed to go to a Chinese restaurant nearby, pay for and pick up twenty dollars worth of Chinese food and deliver it to an address on Desroches street. I was in seventh heaven because I just came back, I thought, from that street in the East End of Montreal, so, finally, I had an address which location I knew. When I arrived twenty minutes later, it turned out that I mixed up the name of the street with a similar sounding name. I arrived at my destination forty minutes later, only two blocks away from my taxi stand, with twenty dollars worth of ice-cold Chinese food. My reception was as cold as the food.

We quickly moved out of the tiny place my parents had arranged for us and rented a room with a family who also had children. As I mentioned earlier, my wife was an excellent dress designer who always made her own and the children's dresses. She started to do alterations for some ladies to bring in some income. As she gradually became more and more pregnant, her ability to kneel in front of those ladies while fixing their hemlines became more and more difficult for her, but she managed. She turned this little alterations business into a career; and several years later she became the designer for Auckie Senft, a major Montreal clothing factory. She designed their complete line of dresses.

After several weeks of driving a taxi and getting the feel of the city and the exact quality and methods of its police corruption, I switched jobs and became a driving school instructor. At least here my dollar fifty an hour was guaranteed. I practiced my violin evenings and weekends, and whenever I had a chance, preparing for the forthcoming auditions for the Montreal Symphony Orchestra.

In the meantime, I looked for other ways to turn my musical skills to money. I auditioned for several local conductors for work in different music groups. I formed a little trio consisting of violin, cello and piano. We played at weddings and other social functions. When I was still driving my taxi I would use the taxi for transport to these paying gigs. Sometimes that didn't work out. I remember leaving Victoria Hall in Westmount from having played a wedding, only to find a ten dollar parking ticket on my taxi. The fine ate up the entire ten dollars that I had just made for playing two hours.

There were other amusing experiences too. The trio played for a Diamond (sixtieth) Wedding Anniversary. The happy couple were to enter the hall at the back and walk through the crowd up to the front to Mendelssohn's familiar Wedding March. The couple were in their nineties, and we could play the Wedding March only as fast as they could walk. The joyous wedding tune became a dirge, the slowest Wedding March doubtless ever performed. We musicians almost fell off the stage laughing.

Both my wife and I continued to suffer from the effects of the crash and from our early withdrawal from treatment. I experienced dramatic proof of that at the end of July 1957. I had just dropped my last driving student off in Verdun, and I was heading off to an audition. For many months after the plane crash I had short fainting spells, often lasting only a few seconds. There was never any warning of these attacks. I must have had such a fainting spell then, because I drove through a stop sign. I hit another car, and demolished both it and my own vehicle. Luckily, nobody was hurt. This was the end of my career as a driving instructor.

This was also the beginning of several months of treatment at the Neurological Institute of Montreal. I became so friendly with my doctor that he asked me to play my violin at his wedding. The treatment worked and the fainting spells stopped, praise be. Now I was able to concentrate fully on my musical career. In some ways, the accident was fortunate because I could no longer drive a cab or teach driving or even

Suzanne, Agnes, and Kathleen in one of our apartments in Montreal. Kathleen is less than a year old, so it is 1958.

drive a car. I was, as a consequence, able to devote my time to our coming child and my forthcoming audition at The Montreal Symphony Orchestra.

It is amazing how a newborn baby has her/his character already established at birth. Our first child, Suzy, was born with a full head of beautiful black hair and when she cried (which was frequently), she opened her mouth so wide that she literally disappeared behind it. I used to joke that she was a big mouth with a small baby behind it. She was delivered after twenty-four hours of labour. She was not willing to accept mother's milk straight from the source and we had to get a special gadget to extract Agnes' milk and feed it to Suzy with a teaspoon.

Mademoiselle Kathleen Gati arrived on August 13, 1957. She was already halfway out when the doctor asked my wife not to push, so he had a chance to put on his gloves. When Kathy was born, she was totally bald and looked like Winston Churchill. She was born with a big grin on her face and she hasn't stopped smiling and laughing since. As for her feeding habits, she literally attacked the maternal mammary glands. No teaspoon for her! She has always embraced every challenge, everything and everybody in the same way throughout her life.

Aside from being bald, Kathy was a well-developed and beautiful baby, eight pounds, seven ounces. She brought us

The family in a Montreal park, fall 1957. Me, Suzy, Agnes, Kathy

nothing but pleasure from the moment of her birth. Her beautiful blond hair appeared in few weeks time.

Whether through fate or coincidence, the three ladies in my life were all born in August: Kathleen on the 13th, Agnes on the 22nd, and Suzanne on the 24th of August.

In preparing for Kathy's arrival, I had rented a luxurious apartment in a new building. I was very confident of my ability to earn a living as a musician, whether playing, teaching, or conducting. Besides accommodation for what was soon to be a family of four, I intended the apartment to be a studio where I could teach violin. This led to another ironic problem faced by refugees and immigrants: getting credit to buy furniture. This turned out to be a real problem; because we didn't have any debts, we didn't have a credit rating, and without a credit rating, we couldn't borrow money.

But we got a lucky break. When the mainstream society won't meet immigrants' needs, the immigrant community itself will provide goods and services to their own. A former colleague of my wife's from Budapest had moved to Montreal years earlier. Her husband and his brother had started up a business which specialized in selling furniture to new immigrants. Through them, we were able to buy two Sealy Posturepedic beds, a small desk, a kitchen table with four chairs, a large curtain and some additional chairs for my studio. The furniture in the apartment's large living room consisted of a crib, a dresser which my parents had bought for Kathy, and the large box in which the new refrigerator had arrived. To cover up the paucity of our furnishings, we hung a curtain over the open entrance to the living room.

I rented a piano for the studio at ten dollars a month and I was ready to advertise "European violin teacher accepting students. Will teach in studio and at home." I could see the lineup of students in my head. I had three potential students: Mr. Furman, a gentleman in his fifties, Mademoiselle Desroche, a French-Canadian spinster also in her fifties, and a six year old boy whom I was supposed to teach in his home.

Teaching led to new experiences. Furman and I ended up becoming lifelong friends. After several months of lessons I still couldn't get Mademoiselle Desroches to play with any speed. Finally, I realized what her problem was: she was trying to vocalize every note she was playing. After I held her lips forcibly closed with my hand, she was able to play almost twice as fast! As for the child, when I arrived at his home, he appeared in a football outfit, complete with shoulder pads. I couldn't even put the violin under his chin! This student-teacher relationship lasted only a few weeks.

Not for the first time, my plans did not turn out according to my expectations. It was obvious that my large body of students could not support my own studio and such an expensive apartment ($180 a month, a huge amount for 1957). Therefore, I started to look for a cheaper apartment. I found one on St. Kevin Street for ninety dollars a month. After living for two months in our luxury accommodations, we moved to an older, cheaper, two -bedroom apartment.

Les Préludes

Chapter Twenty Eight

MY MUSICAL CAREER IN CANADA BEGINS

The day of the auditions for the Montreal Symphony Orchestra arrived. I was aware of the fact that auditions take place behind a curtain. This is common practice in classical music circles in order for musicians to be judged on their talent alone, rather than their sex, colour of skin, or physical handicap. In general, this is a wonderful principle, but it has its drawbacks. What if, for instance, the audition is for second chair violin, and the best player is left-handed? A left-handed musician plays his instrument with different arms and sits facing the opposite way to the right-handers. Placing a left-handed violinist in the middle of a string section can cause a lot of problems. Fortunately, I am right-handed, so I knew there would be no problem for me on that score. Moreover, the curtain gave me another advantage.

I decided to audition for both violin and viola positions in order to double my chances for employment. I borrowed a viola from a violin maker friend of mine and practiced for a few days. I auditioned first, for the violin and later, under a different number, for the viola. When the auditions ended it turned out that I won both positions. I decided to take the viola position because there is always a shortage of good viola players. I was placed on the last desk of the viola section. The following year, when my good friend Steve Kondaks left the orchestra, I became the Assistant Solo Viola of the Orchestra and moved up to the first desk.

With the L'Orchestre Philharmonique de Montreal, conducting a benefit for the Societe de bon parler francais. My career is getting back on track -- I am freelancing and networking constantly.

Being a viola player also meant there was more chance to freelance and have additional income. This last point about income was very important. Though there was much prestige in playing with a symphony orchestra, there was not much money. In this lovely job I was to be paid one hundred dollars per week for a ten-week season— a grand total of one thousand dollars. Obviously, this was not enough to make a living and to support a wife and two children.

I started freelancing for radio, television, the National Film Board, studio recordings, public performances, weddings, etc. Working like this was dodgy, because to be a member of the orchestra, I had to belong to the Musicians Union. The union was good in that it mandated minimal payments for all kinds of work, but it also meant that a lot of non-union work went on "under the table", with musicians receiving far less than the union scale. The union frowned on this, threatening fines on any union musician playing non-union work, and thus, keeping a downward pressure on wages. Almost all of us did this non-union work occasionally, because we had to eat. One day, I got a call from a Monsieur Romeo asking me to do a three-hour recording session. The name of our personnel manager was Romeo Mastrocola, so I took it for granted that it was he who called, and so I expected a regular union job. When I got to the place where the recording session was taking place, not only did I find it was non-union work, but I found seven other musicians from the symphony waiting to play. It turned out that it was Monsieur Romeo Duhamel who organized this kind of non-union work.

I had a dilemma. I could leave the premises, denounce my colleagues to the Musicians Union, or do the job and get it over with, making forty dollars. So I did the job. I don't know who denounced me, but I was fined one thousand dollars by the union, which represented my total income for the year from the Montreal Symphony Orchestra. I had no choice but to pay. If I didn't pay, they would kick me out of the union and I could not play or conduct any union job. The union officials were 'nice' and set up a time payment plan. Up to this day, I don't know if any of the other seven musicians there were fined and if so, how much. Being a newcomer, perhaps they wanted to make an example of me. I put this experience in my bulging "injustices" file.

If I had had only my Montreal Symphony Orchestra income, the financial burden would have been intolerable. My freelancing helped, but our largest income that year came from another source. My wife was a singer and could read music. Together, we made five thousand dollars, five times my symphony income, copying and orchestrating music for the Chanson Canadienne TV program. All praise to the Canadian Broadcasting Corporation!

Now that I had an "establishment" job in the viola section of the Montreal Symphony Orchestra, extra income from freelancing, and my daughter safely born and living at home, I started to explore the musical scene in Montreal to see what I could do to restart my conducting career. I don't wish to brag, but even as a youngster I was a good organizer, and my successful experiences in Hungary and Hungarian Radio gave me added confidence. I set about to see what kind of conducting possibilities I could find, or better yet, make for myself in Montreal.

Les Préludes

At the time, there was an amateur orchestra in Montreal known as the Orchestre Philharmonique de Montreal (Montreal Philharmonic Orchestra). Through a musician friend who played in the orchestra, I was invited to conduct a special concert given for the benefit of the Societe de bon parler francais (Society for the Well-Speaking of French). The concert took place in front of a full house at the Theatre St. Denis, which had a capacity twenty-five hundred seats. It was a great success, and I enjoyed working with the members of the orchestra. I also got to practice my French in public.

Chapter Twenty Nine

VIGNETTES OF A MUSICIAN'S LIFE

There is no such thing as a typical musician. Age, culture, and language are all extras on top of the grand edifice of classical music education. Not long after I joined the Montreal Symphony Orchestra, I was playing alongside an elderly violinist of German-Jewish background who had sought refuge from Nazi persecution and spent the war years in Shanghai. After the war, he emigrated to Canada with his Chinese wife. Orchestra musicians have incredible intuition and insight into the foibles of most conductors and can spot a phony in an instant. If an instrumental soloist or singer is a dilettante, it is obvious to all of the musicians after a couple of bars, and the musicians will call them on their mistakes. Unfortunately, this is not the case with the conductor whose 'silent' instrument, the baton, apparently, cannot make any errors or play a wrong note. On one occasion we had a violinist and composer who had aspirations to be a conductor and who imitated the great British conductor, Sir Thomas Beecham.

When he rehearsed a piece he had composed at the Stratford Festival in Ontario, Canada, the musicians hated it, and almost walked out on him. In his best Sir Thomas Beecham style, he exhorted the musicians: "I don't understand you, I just conducted this piece in Israel and the musicians loved it and they did a magnificent job!" One musician answered: "It might be true, but I am sure they didn't do it to please the Jews, but to annoy the Arabs!"

This has become a standard saying in musical circles. After we were playing for a while, my colleague suddenly turned to me and said: "Tell me Gati, how far can you push bullshit?!" This great 'philosophical' question confronted me many times during my career.

Only once in my musical career did I encounter a musician who dared to tell the conductor his honest opinion. This was George Lapenson; a wonderful Latvian violinist recently arrived in Montreal. He was a real virtuoso, but also a total eccentric. Shortly after his arrival to Montreal, he bought a Cadillac which he drove at high-speed up and down the sidewalks until both the shock absorbers and the springs were gone. In mid-December he bought a ship which needed four crew members just to heat it. He wore a captain's uniform and everybody had to address him as Captain Lapenson. Naturally, since it was winter, the boat froze in Montreal Harbor and Lapenson went bankrupt and had to get rid of the ship before he was able to ever sail it.

Lapenson was the concertmaster of a little orchestra connected with Radio-Canada in Montreal and during the season we had rehearsed and recorded the program every Sunday. One day, George stood up in the middle of rehearsal and started to leave the stage. The conductor stopped the proceedings and asked George, "Where are you going, George?"

George replied, "I am sick."

"What's wrong, George?" the conductor asked.

"YOU MAKE ME SICK!!!" George exclaimed, and left, never to return.

A good colleague of mine, Steve Kondaks, and I were also always bitching about this and that during the rehearsals. Finally, one day, Steve turned to me and said, "Listen, Gati! If you were as smart as you think you are and if I was as smart as I think I am, we wouldn't be here!" Not long after this discussion we both left.

Meanwhile, I made no secret of my background and my ambition to resume a conducting career. Slowly, this became known in the orchestra and in Montreal music circles. One day, Jose Iturbi, who was our guest conductor, wanted to hear the orchestra from the hall and asked if somebody could conduct Beethoven's Third Leonore Overture. The musicians said, "Gati, Gati." I knew the piece by heart, but I hesitated. Iturbi was an excellent pianist and a film star, but not a good conductor, and I didn't want to upstage him. Finally, I assented. I got up and conducted the overture from beginning to end by memory. When I finished the orchestra gave me a big hand. Iturbi yelled from the hall, "I will never ask you to conduct for me again! You are too good!"

At the end of the rehearsal I went backstage to speak to him. I explained who I was, and that I was trying to restart my conducting career in North America. I asked if he could write me a short letter of recommendation now that he had seen me conduct. Iturbi dictated the most beautiful letter to his secretary, who promised to mail it to me the next day. This was my very first experience with one conductor helping another conductor. However, I never received the letter.

I had a similar experience when I asked Joseph Krips, the well-known Austrian conductor, for advice on restarting my conducting career in North America. Krips started to complain about Herbert von Karajan, how Karajan sabotaged him at every turn, how Karajan conspired to make sure his wife was unable to get shoes which fit. This pissing and moaning continued for some time. I ended up comforting him on the unfairness of his present life without getting any of the advice I had requested.

There had to be a way to get started.

Les Préludes

Chapter Thirty

CONDUCTORS - 3

CAREER ADVICE

Now you know what a conductor does and what skills a conductor must have. So how do you become a conductor? Becoming a conductor is a complex process; it encompasses the artistic and technical growth of a person and the difficult experiences of gaining and keeping employment in the world of classical music. I will switch back and forth between these two subjects.

If you want to conduct, conduct. Start by conducting your favourite orchestral music played on your home stereo system. Stand in front of the speakers and move your arms naturally to the music. If you feel like a child playing while conducting, that's fine. You can learn a lot from this exercise. You learn how to coordinate the movement of your hands and arms. You learn how to keep time. You learn how subtle conducting technique can be, how to speed up, slow down, and pause music, and what the effects are on the piece of music. Buy CDs of different conductors conducting the same pieces and you will not only hear the differences in conducting, you will feel them in your body. Listen to and experience the phrasing of different conductors. This is an excellent exercise for anybody of any age who wants to conduct. If you feel silly, close the curtains.

Acquire instrumental knowledge. Most conductors were string players. This is not a conspiracy. String players constitute, numerically, the largest part of an orchestra, so statistically it is more likely that conductors come from the strings section. There are other factors: brass, woodwinds and percussion are primarily solo instruments. Playing in the strings section is closer to conducting than playing in the other sections of the orchestra, so it is natural for more conductors to have been violinists, violists, cellists, and so on. Learning to play the piano can be very helpful. It is a complex instrument, nearly an orchestra in itself, and piano skills translate well to reading scores, adjusting orchestration, and so on. Step out of your instrumental specialty and learn other instruments, not so that you can play them in an orchestra, but so that you can appreciate the techniques, the potentials, and the limitations of the instruments.

Learn or be taught composition, orchestration, and arrangement. These skills help you read a score better and divine the intentions of the composer to a deeper level. They allow you to know the limitations of your conducting, how much variation in phrasing, volume, and speed you may impose on a piece before violating the underlying musical structure. Practice an analytical exercise, such as transcribing a piano or violin piece for an orchestra, or vice versa. Take a flute solo and transcribe it for the bassoon. See what changes this makes to the overall effect of the piece of music.

Be warned, however. Some conductors get stuck at the analytical stage and they never break through it to experience the lyrical and the spontaneous in music. And if they do not break through, neither will the players, nor the audience.

If you want to conduct, conduct! The addition of the exclamation mark means a lot. It means that if you want to conduct, forget about the money and orchestra. Go and conduct any group which needs conducting. Conduct a church chorus. Conduct a schoolchildren's choir. Conduct a student band, or a marching band. Conduct amateurs who gather in small groups to perform for their own musical pleasure. Form a group to play at weddings and dances and go conduct them. There is no such thing as a bad experience. The more conducting you get under your belt, the better.

Never stop studying; never stop listening. When you are not playing your instrument or conducting, listen to music, preferably live music. Listen to groups and to soloists; listen to styles of music outside your interest. Even if you think you will hate it, listen to music played in Schoenberg's 12-tone scale. Listen to music played on authentic period instruments, which is the latest fad in classical music. Attend New Music or avant-garde performances. Within the garbage there is always something you can learn. Go talk to other musicians and conductors before and after they play. Debate, argue, and learn.

Build a network of people who have seen you perform and conduct. Other musicians and conductors may help you — not everyone is threatened and not everyone views you as a direct competitor. Do not forget the members of the audience: wealthy patrons of the arts, people who sit on the boards of arts organizations, bureaucrats who sit on government grant committees, local politicians who approve grants for arts funding. All these people can help you in your career.

Take opportunities when they are offered and be prepared to move. Even a large city in a big, rich country can only have a couple of permanent conductors. When a job offer comes, you will have to be prepared to move yourself and your family, uproot yourself from your surroundings and your friends and start over. For years, your career may consist of regular guest-conductor engagements. Be sure you have a passport and a clean record. Conductors move promiscuously from country to country and continent to continent.

It is not necessary to speak two or three languages, as it is the case of all musicians who know Italian, which is used in musical notation and comments; also a conductor can make most of his desires known through his body, his baton, the tone of his voice, and the common musical expressions such as piano (softly), forte (loudly). Yet the ability to speak French or Spanish, German or Russian is extremely useful when communicating with musicians, musical bureaucrats, funders and audience members.

Maintain your focus and learn from every musician and soloist and conductor with whom you work. During the seventeen years I spent as an orchestral musician, playing the violin and the viola, I found I often pleased the conductors because they would catch me looking at them during performance and rehearsal. It is very gratifying to the conductor to have musicians (who spend most of their time reading the music on the stands in front of them) look directly at them to take their direction. In fact, I was studying these conductors, making note of particular bits of their technique or approach which I liked or which produced a big effect on the audience. I learned far more from observing the great, the near-great, and even the mediocre conductors than I ever learned from my formal studies in conducting. A greater part of that learning was learning what not to do.

Build your career as an instrumentalist while looking for that big break. If you are a violinist, your career might proceed in an orderly fashion from second chair, to first chair, then to soloist, then to concertmaster, then to assistant conductor, and finally, to Music Director. Without a "big break", your career might stall at any one of these stages.

Most careers do not proceed in an orderly fashion. Breaks may come in many ways. Become a well-known soloist and use your fame and large fees to arrange conducting work. Fill in, on short notice, when a conductor quits, becomes sick, or dies. Work on a recording career and come to the notice of an agent who arranges you to conduct for a CD. Enter international competitions as a soloist or a conductor. Take an internationally-recognized conducting course. Become a protégé of another conductor (usually by being an assistant or associate conductor). Find work in television, movie, and radio recording. Go out and aggressively promote yourself to cities, broadcasters, and national arts organizations. Master arts administration politics and procure grants to conduct and record. Apply for, and win, a conducting post against other applicants; and have that ineluctable variable— luck.

I received international exposure by going to a prominent conducting class, which led directly (with a wait of nine years) to my being offered a Music Director position to replace someone who had abruptly quit (in Victoria, BC). Later, I competed and won a Music Directorship over a field of over two hundred applicants (Windsor, Ontario). The competition for work never ceases, so you will have to use all these tactics more than once during your career.

You cannot be friends with the musicians you work with, but you can give and receive respect. Musicians "who respect you as a person and as a musician" (if I may be permitted to apply that description to a conductor) will play better for you and enhance your reputation. Therefore, when you rehearse and when you conduct, do not force the musicians to play your way; instead, lead them, persuade them, even follow them.

Respect the music and the composer of the piece of music you are conducting. Express your ego in the pleasure you give your audience, not the distinctiveness of your style. Refrain from distorting or changing the music in order to put some kind of personal stamp on it. Your own personality will make the music different without having to force it into a different shape. Do not expend great effort in trying to conduct a piece of music the same way each time; be sensitive to the conditions of the performance, whatever those conditions are. A concrete room sounds very different from a wooden room; an audience of 300 needs a different performance than an audience of 3000.

Finally, after all this acquisition of knowledge and all your accumulation of experience, you will have to learn to LET GO. I put this in capitals because it is so very important. The magic of music is that it does not last. It exists only for the moment. Once you, as a conductor, raise your baton, you must trust your instincts and trust the craft of your musicians to create a series of wonderful moments. You can plan for these wonderful moments; you can carefully build up to them; you can reproduce as closely as you can the exact conditions which led to them before; but you cannot guarantee them. Music is a helium-filled balloon, and it will not fly unless you LET GO.

Why should one endeavor to spend some twenty years in acquiring so much knowledge and experience? The conductor puts it to work when there is a catastrophe, such as when a prominent instrument is suddenly missing, or when a soloist or a section comes in a bar or a beat early or late; then the conductor consciously uses his skills to adjust the performance and continues. Do not worry. It will happen to you, and more than just once.

LETTING GO is wonderful. I use an anecdote from Jascha Heifitz, the great violinist, who was once asked what he thought about while he performed. He said, "I think about the wonderful ham sandwich I am going to have in my hotel room later. That's why I practice ten hours a day...so I don't have to think when I perform."

Chapter Thirty One

THE PAN-AMERICAN CONDUCTING COURSE

In 1958, I was Assistant Solo Viola in the Montreal Symphony Orchestra, but since this took up only ten weeks of the year, I made most of my income as a freelance musician. I played for radio and television, much of that work coming from the Canadian Broadcasting Corporation, the National Film Board of Canada (which was at that time a very active producer of Canadian non-fiction films), and working as a session musician in recording studios. I was supporting myself and family adequately, but I still yearned to become a conductor again.

That year, I became aware of a conducting course being given in Mexico and taught by the present conductor of the Montreal Symphony, Maestro Igor Markevich. The course cost $200, which was a substantial sum in those days, but the greatest part of the cost would be for travelling to Mexico, accommodations and food. Markevich supported me by procuring a $100 scholarship, and I managed to get a loan for another $600 to cover all the other expenses, which included, of course, lost income for the six weeks I would be away.

I saw the course as an opportunity to learn, but more than that, an opportunity to gain international exposure as a conductor. Not only would there be conductors from other countries, but many observers, sponsors, funders, politicians, and other musicians and music directors would be gathering there. I saw the course as an investment. As it turned out,

The INBA (Instituto Nacional de Bellas Artes) in Mexico City. A beautiful building about a century old, it has now sunk 17 feet into the ground. The sinking is a direct consequence of Mexico City's continued draining of the groundwater underneath the city.

this was one of the best decisions of my career. The exposure led not only to many guest-conducting jobs for me in Mexico and Latin America over the next forty years, but also helped earn my first appointment as Music Director of a major symphony orchestra.

I decided now that the powers that be would have to pay my wife and children a decent sum for any sudden plunge from the sky. This was the summer of 1958, before the introduction of jet planes for passenger service, so the trip from Montreal to Mexico City took fourteen hours. I went to the airport early to buy travel insurance. Nobody was selling insurance that early, much to my frustration. Fortunately, the plane had some engine problems and our departure was delayed by four hours. An agent arrived and I bought insurance to the tune of $150,000. During our stopover in Toronto, I popped out into the concourse and bought an additional $100,000 of insurance. I phoned my wife right after the transaction and asked Agnes if she thought that $250,000 would be sufficient for her and Kathy and Suzanne to live on if I didn't come back. She agreed, but added that she would prefer to have me back than receive the insurance money.

At the Toronto airport, about fifty Mexican school children (who were studying in Ontario) boarded the plane. Four hours after take-off, the plane ran out of any kind of drink, including water. We flew another ten hours without a drop of liquid. Upon arrival in Mexico City International airport, in spite of all the warnings "not to drink the water", I literally ran to the first water fountain. Luckily, the water was tepid, almost warm and quite revolting, so I just spit it out and headed off to buy a Coke, which was supposed to be safe.

I was alone in Mexico City, but I did not anticipate any problems. I spoke Hungarian, Romanian, English, French, German, and some Italian, so I expected to manage Spanish one way or another. As a precaution, I had purchased a dictaphone record and booklet on elementary Spanish, but I was so busy I had no time before leaving for Mexico to listen to the record or study the book. While on the plane, I had distracted myself from my thirst and pulled out the booklet for some quick study. I learned "Buenos Dias" (Good Day), "Como esta usted?" (How are you?), "Muy bien, gracias" (Very good, thank you), "Y usted?" (And you?), "Gracias, sin novedad" (Thank you, without any news.). I invested $12 in that dictaphone course and I tried to practice it on Señor Ariola (the Secretary of the Bellas Artes), who met me at the airport. It turned out that this greeting did not make any sense for a Spanish-speaking person — and it doesn't make much sense in English either.

Even so, I learned Spanish amazingly fast once I was in Mexico City. Many people are unaware that Romanian is not a Slavic language, but is one of the Romance languages, based on Latin, as is Spanish. I started by reading the local Spanish-language newspapers and very quickly puzzled out useful nouns, verbs, and adjectives. I had no problem at all communicating with my fellow musicians in the course, since virtually all musical vocabulary is Italian and all musicians know it. So when I started to conduct, all I had to say were things like, piu forte (louder), piu piano (softer), staccato, for

Some of the participants in the Pan-American Conductor's Course in 1958. Second from the left is Louis Auriacombe, the French assistant to Markevich. Third from the right is Volker Wangenheim, the German assistant. I am on the far right.

example, and the musicians understood me perfectly. I did pick up the Spanish phrases for "good morning" (Buenas Dias) and "once more please" (Otra vez, por favor).

The six-week course took place in the Sala Ponce, named after the prominent Mexican composer, Manuel Ponce (1882-1948). We had at our disposal the Orquesta Sinfónica de Bellas Artes. The Bellas Artes has several orchestras including, the Orquesta Sinfónica Nacional de Mexico, the Opera Orchestra, the Chamber Orchestra, and others. There were eighteen students in the Corso Panamericano de Dirección de Orquesta, (Panamerican Orchestra Conducting Course) headed by Maestro Igor Markevich. Markevich had two assistants, Louis Auriacombe from Toulouse, France, and Volker Wangenheim, the Music Director of the Symphony Orchestra of Bonn, West Germany.

I found a charming and reasonably-priced hotel called the Diligencias, not far from the imposing Palacio de Bellas Artes (Fine Arts Palace) where the course was given. At first, I was the only participant in the course who was staying there, but shortly after, some colleagues joined me.

In many respects, the course, the whole ambience in the Sala Ponce, the magnificent Bellas Artes, and Mexico City itself were all great experiences. There were eighteen conductors from many different countries, including Algeria, Canada, Cuba, Mexico and the US. There was great camaraderie among the participants. We often helped each other through constructive criticism. Although I was not, collegially speaking, the oldest in the group (at only 33), somehow I was treated as such.

Besides the theory classes led by Markevich, we worked mainly with the assistants. Markevich would show up once or twice a day at the orchestral sessions, make some critical remarks and leave. He expected all the students to emulate his conducting style. I used to tell to some of my colleagues, "Why have 500 copies of a questionable original?" At some sessions Markevich was not only critical of me, but told the other students, "Don't stay like Gati", or "Don't do this like Gati," and other remarks. I could not help but take this personally. One day, Volker Wangenheim, who was in charge at that session, asked me to put my left hand in my pocket and conduct with my right hand only. Just then Markevich came in the room and started to yell at me, asking me, "Why are you here at all if you always do the opposite of what I am teaching?!" I told him that Maestro Wangenheim had asked me to conduct that way.

After my turn ended, I went to sit in the last row of the hall and deliberated whether or not I should stay or go back to Montreal. If it had not been for the financial sacrifice, the bank loan and the foregone income, I would have gone home already. Just then, Markevich came and sat down beside me and started to explain to me that the reason for being so strict with me was because he thought I was the greatest talent among all the students, and he wanted me to win the competition. I told him that I was glad that he came to talk to me, because I was ready to quit. I told him that I thought I had developed my own conducting style and technique, and that I was not prepared to change unless it was justified.

Markevich invited me to visit him at his penthouse in the Ritz Carlton Hotel. By the time I arrived, he had sent his wife away so we were alone and could start our discussion in total privacy. I explained to him that if I were to follow his advice, just for instance, on how to hold the baton, my arm would get stiff before conducting even one note. Markevich slapped the table with his open hand and said, "This is how I hit the table." I banged the table with a clenched fist and told him, "This is how I hit the table!" This was not a highly technical discussion. I told him about the importance of the free swinging pendulum movement in my conducting and justified many other aspects of my conducting style.

Markevich never told me whether he accepted my arguments or rejected them. From the next day on, though, everything was the opposite. "Stay like Gati,"or "Do it like Gati." I had a hunch that I would never have any relationship with him. Now that I didn't have to fight an uphill battle with Markevich, I was free to conduct as I wanted to, and take whatever I wanted from the instructors and the other musicians.

Learning from the students was a multi-level task; not only did we learn musically, but we had to learn about each others' cultures. One example comes to mind. Our orchestra had a lady concertmaster. One day, after I finished conducting, she made a sign which musicians use when they hear an old and oft-repeated joke; they stroke their chins as though smoothing a very long beard. At first, I was insulted, but it turned out later that she wanted to convey a compliment, to let me know that my conducting was very good.

In the course we had to rehearse and perform all the Beethoven symphonies by heart, except for the Ninth Symphony, since we did not have a chorus or soloists at our disposal.

Markevich continued his instructions, promoting a number of, in my judgement, odd theories. For instance, he had a theory that the conductor should not perspire. One day, he came in when I had just finished conducting a fast movement which had required a lot of arm waving on my part. He said, "You see, Gati, how you perspire!" I said, "When should I perspire if not after this movement?" He believed that it was the musicians who should perspire, not the conductor. I told him that if the conductor did not perspire, the musicians would not perspire either. A few months later he conducted an excellent performance of Tchaikovsky's Pathetique Symphony in Montreal. He perspired profusely on the podium. Right after the concert I went to his room with a white handkerchief. While congratulating him, I wiped the perspiration from his forehead without any comment.

During our stay in Mexico, the Presidential elections took place. We didn't know what to expect, whether there would be street fights or just what. Just in case, we stocked up on food. By that time, five or six of my colleagues moved over to my hotel, which created a funny situation. I had bought a big pineapple and asked the cook to keep it in the fridge. My friends followed in my footsteps and also bought pineapples. For the rest of my stay I didn't have to buy any more pineapples. I just had to ask the cook for a slice of 'my' pineapple.

All the precautions were unnecessary; there were no great civil disturbances and no interruptions in the food supply. When Lopez Mateos was elected President the newspapers printed big headlines, "Elecciones sin pistolas," (Elections without guns).

We had Saturdays and Sundays off. One Friday evening, I decided to take an overnight bus to Acapulco and come back on an overnight bus on Sunday night, thereby getting two full days in Acapulco. I had hoped to sleep on the bus, but all through Friday night I was constantly tossed from side to side. The old highway between Mexico City and Acapulco was narrow and winding, with many "Curvas Peligrosas" ("Dangerous Curves"). The bus, however, was air-conditioned, so though I did not sleep I was generally comfortable.

When the door finally opened in Acapulco on Saturday morning, it was like stepping into a steam bath. Despite my climate shock, I found a room for $2 a night; it had no air-conditioning, but came with a mosquito net on the window. Not wanting to waste a moment, I went to the beach and ended up renting something which looked like a surfboard, but which came with paddles, like a kayak. By that time, it was midday and the Sun was literally burning up the sky.

All my life I had been a sun-worshipper, but this was too much even for me. I got burned so badly that I was worried that I would not be able to conduct at all on Monday. I decided to go back Sunday during the day and so at least I would take in the scenery.

As we started to climb up in the mountains, I saw a bus which had crashed on the way down into the valley; then I saw a second crumpled bus, and later on a third. I hung on to my seat for dear life. At least when I had traveled at night, I had missed these signposts of mortality. It was nearly as bad as my trip down the mountain in Romania on the back of that crazed pack-mule. After seeing eleven — eleven! — destroyed buses nestled way down in the crevasses; I swore that I would never again take a bus in Mexico. To this day, whenever I visit Mexico I always rent a car and I drive wherever I need to go.

The finale of the course was supposed to be a competition, the first prize being two concerts with the National Symphony Orchestra of Mexico. I don't wish to go into details because some of the protagonists are still alive, but I was 'disqualified' from the competition because I was a 'professional' conductor and it would have been 'unfair' to compete with the other students, one of whom was only fourteen years old. They felt justified to rob me of my right even to compete for the chance to show myself internationally. It was the cantor's son and the first prize for calligraphy all over again. I was beside myself with anger.

The last concert of the course was a performance with the OSN - Orquesta Sinfonica Nacional de Mexico (the National Symphony Orchestra of Mexico.). Ten of my colleagues from the class approached this second jury and demanded they let me participate in the competition. The jury took the position that they could not change the decision of the first jury. In the end, they didn't even hand out the first or second prizes and I ended up being a regular guest-conductor with the OSN. That was a prize of a kind.

The program of the final concert was Beethoven's Coriolan Overture, his Eighth Symphony and the Eroica. Each of the students conducted one movement of the pieces. Markevich gave me the most difficult piece, the second movement of the Eroica symphony, the Funeral March. I poured all the bitterness I felt from the injustice of my disqualification into the performance. Fortunately, my feelings were not inappropriate to the music.

While he was writing it, Beethoven had called his third symphony the Napoleon Symphony, from his great admiration for the then-new leader of France. Beethoven believed that Napoleon was a hero for the ages, and hoped that under his leadership Europe would experience a revolution in the quality of life. Napoleon quickly proved himself a megalomaniac dictator and plunged Europe into years of massive bloodletting. Beethoven's horrified response was to remove the dedication to Napoleon from the symphony, and replaced it with the phrase, "Composed to celebrate the memory of a great man."

My performance led to my appointment, nine years later, as Music Director of the Victoria Symphony Orchestra. Otto Werner Mueller observed me conducting this second movement while he was waiting to conduct the last movement. In January 1967, he invited me to conduct the Eroica with the Victoria Symphony Orchestra and this led to my being considered for the post of Music Director.

This insurance business led to a funny situation on my return flight from Mexico. They were repairing the runway in Mexico City and the plane could not take off with a full load of fuel, so we had to make a refueling stop in Atlanta, Georgia. When we arrived in Atlanta the visibility was zero. The airport was closed and totally fogged in. Unfortunately, we had no fuel, and so no choice, having to land come what may. At first, I started to panic, recalling the flight from Belgrade to Munich, but then I said to myself, 'If I stay alive I would never be able make this kind of money ($250,000) for my family.' So I relaxed. When we landed successfully, I felt cheated.

Fear, desire, tranquility — it's all in the mind.

Les Préludes

Chapter Thirty Two

ENTREPRENEURSHIP

In the centre of Montreal there is a mountain, or rather a hill, called Mount Royal.

On the west side, close to the top of Mount Royal, there is a large building with a spacious terrace overlooking the Saint Lawrence River. The terrace can accommodate two - three thousand people. I felt that it would be an ideal place to give some open air concerts in the summer. Before starting to look for sponsorships, I talked over my idea and the financial aspects of the project with my bank manager. He gave me excellent advice and I was to get his counsel on all my Montreal projects. In the process, we became very good personal friends.

I approached several companies, including the Steinberg Supermarket chain, with my idea. They liked it so much that they decided to sponsor a local Jewish conductor to give summer concerts at the Chalet on the top of Mount Royal. I was an immigrant Jewish conductor, and would have to get in line behind the natives for any opportunities. The Montreal Symphony Orchestra itself started giving concerts there in later years. Obviously, there was nothing wrong with my ideas. So much for that project. Another one into the file.

My next idea was to approach the Pepsi-Cola Company to sponsor eight summer concerts in Lafontaine Park. The school where The Montreal Symphony performed was also located in the park. The company agreed in writing to sponsor the concerts, provided that they would be broadcast by the Canadian Broadcasting Corporation. It took me only a few days to work out arrangements with the CBC. Then it turned out that another agent of the Commercial Department of the CBC had talked Pepsi Cola into sponsoring a series of hockey matches, instead of the concerts. I had not realized hockey's grip on Canada's psyche. Now I knew. So much for that project.

In the late 1950's, the Montreal Symphony Orchestra gave its concerts in Plateau Hall, which was the auditorium of the high school in Lafontaine Park. I had a brilliant idea. Plateau Hall had one thousand seats and the average price per seat was around ten dollars. The Forum hockey arena, on the other hand, had over ten thousand seats. My idea was very simple. Instead of one thousand people paying $10 dollars for a ticket, why not have ten thousand people pay $1 dollar per ticket? I discussed the budget and financial projections with my bank manager.

This project obviously needed a lot of promotion and publicity, so I approached The Montreal Star, the major English newspaper in town. The Star liked my idea so much that they started a "Dollar Concert" series of their own, consisting of four concerts with The Montreal Symphony Orchestra. These concerts were so successful that the series usually sold out in three-four days. The Star sponsored these concerts for years, until the newspaper went bankrupt and closed due to a lengthy strike — not the concerts. So much for that project.

When my bank manager friend saw that my projects were falling through one by one, he asked me: "Why don't you start your own orchestra? I will give you the money!" I took his offer literally, assuming that the bank would be my sponsor. Later, it turned out that what he meant was that he would give me a loan to get started.

But I was on cloud seven right then, two steps down from cloud nine, and decided to establish the Montreal Chamber Orchestra.

Chapter Thirty Three

THE MONTREAL CHAMBER ORCHESTRA

It is a well-known fact that conductors are a very competitive bunch and usually not much love is lost between them. Here are a couple of anecdotes which illustrate this. The great British conductors, Sir Thomas Beecham and Sir Malcolm Sargent, loathed each other. During the first Israeli-Arab war in 1948, Sir Thomas was having dinner in a restaurant. Somebody told him that the Arabs were shooting at the Jeep in which Sir Malcolm was riding. The reaction of Sir Thomas was: "Indeed? I never knew that the Arabs were so musical!"

Otto Klemperer, upon being told of the death of another prominent conductor, said, "What a good year for conductors." Such tales are apocryphal, but very believable for musicians.

In my effort to start my new orchestra, I ran into this attitude more than once. I will give a real example of this tug-of-war between conductors. After checking that the name "Montreal Chamber Orchestra" was available, I registered it. I still remember that this registration cost me ten dollars. At this time, I heard from a Hungarian violinist friend that another conductor (who shall be nameless) was also planning to start a chamber orchestra. My European background left me naïve in the ways of North American business, and I sent a message to my conductor colleague saying that perhaps we should get together to coordinate our plans to avoid a

Conducting the Montreal Chamber Orchestra, which I formed in 1959. This was another venue for me to show my skills.

programming or other type of conflict. At the very least we should be informed of what each of us was planning.

I received the following answer: "Tell him that he is a conductor and that I am a conductor. We have nothing in common to discuss!" This unfriendly statement cost him $10,000. It turned out that he had also had the brilliant idea to call his orchestra "The Montreal Chamber Orchestra". Unfortunately for him, I had already registered the name. He was sponsored by a rich friend of his, who had spent $10,000 dollars on a very elaborate advertising and publicity campaign. Posters, flyers, programs, and all the other accoutrements. If he had agreed to meet with me as I had proposed, I could have easily changed the name of my orchestra, since I had not yet had my publicity material printed. But I had the name and would not give it up. He had to junk all of his printed material; in the end, his silly behavior cost him dearly!

We did have something in common to discuss after all.

For the first concert of the Montreal Chamber Orchestra I decided to present an all-Bartok program: Divertimento for Strings, Sonata for two Pianos and Percussion, Music for Strings Percussion and Celesta. This was, for 1959, a very

L'ORCHESTRE DE CHAMBRE DE MONTRÉAL
THE MONTREAL CHAMBER ORCHESTRA

Fondateur et directeur musical LASZLO GATI Founder and Musical Director

1er concert MARDI, 13 OCTOBRE 1959 1ère saison
1st concert TUESDAY, OCTOBER 13, 1959 1st season

Président d'honneur WILFRID PELLETIER Honorary President

AUDITORIUM LE PLATEAU

Programme

BELA BARTOK
1 8 8 1 · 1 9 4 5

1. — DIVERTIMENTO pour orchestre d'instruments à cordes (1939)

I. Allegro non troppo
II. Molto adagio
III. Allegro assai

2. — SONATE POUR DEUX PIANOS ET PERCUSSION (1937)

I. Assai lento — Allegro molto
II. Lento ma non troppo
III. Allegro non troppo

| CHARLES REINER | pianos | ARMAS MAISTE |
| LOUIS CHARBONNEAU | percussion | GUY LACHAPELLE |

INTERMISSION

3. — MUSIQUE POUR INSTRUMENTS À CORDES, PERCUSSION ET
CELESTA (1936) *

I. Andante tranquillo
II. Allegro
III. Adagio
IV. Allegro molto

Première exécution à Montréal.   * First performance in Montreal

This is the all-Bartok program that I was warned not to do. It worked out perfectly. Bela Bartok is one of the greatest composers of the 20th century, and he ought to be played more often.

avant-garde program for Montreal audiences. Two of the pieces were Canadian Premieres and one was a North American Premiere.

Bartok composed these pieces near Lucerne, at the home of Swiss conductor and philanthropist Paul Sacher, who had commissioned Bartok to write these pieces for him. Several years ago, when I was last in Budapest, Paul Sacher came through with his orchestra doing exactly the same program. I actually gave him my autographed program from 1958 and he autographed his concert program for me.

The concert almost never took place because the tympanies (kettle drums) of the orchestra were somehow left behind in Vienna and his timpanist refused to play on any other instrument. The tympanies were sent later, and the concert did take place, one and a half hours late.

Conductor Igor Markevitch, the Music Director of the Montreal Symphony, berated me for choosing an all-Bartok program. "Why don't you do a 'regular' chamber orchestra program, like Bach, Handel, Haydn, and Mozart?" I answered, "Because everybody is doing the same thing. I want to be different."

Naturally, the estimated number of people who would show up to hear this avant-garde concert was a big question; and the next question was what would be the audience and critical reaction. My concert did take place in Plateau Hall, in front of an audience of about five hundred people. I knew that I would be losing a pile of money, but at that stage I could not turn back. The concert turned out to be a tremendous success. The reaction of the audience was wonderful and the critics gave us great write-ups as well. This Bartok Concert had a long-lasting influence on my conducting career, in spite of the temporary financial losses. In similar circumstances, I would do exactly the same again— it turned out to be the right choice of music.

Now I had some prominent conducting experience under my belt and my own small orchestra, but I still hadn't had my big break . . . yet!

Chapter Thirty Four

THE BIG BREAK

It is a well-known story that Toscanini, who was at the time, a cellist in an opera orchestra, took over the podium and conducted an opera from memory when the regular conductor became ill. This one chance established Toscanini, who went on to a hugely famous and rich career as a conductor. There is a joke amongst musicians (half-true), that half of the musicians of an orchestra keep a conducting baton in their instrument case, just in case. I was not one of them; I swear I did not have a baton packed with my violin!

In the fall of 1959 I was busy. I had conducted the Bartok concert with my Montreal Chamber Orchestra, and though I wasn't getting any conducting offers, I felt more in charge of my career than ever. I was rehearsing in the viola section for a performance of a French-language TV program called L'heures de Concert (The Concert Hour). Jean Deslaurier was the conductor. Just to demonstrate the challenge I faced, Mr. Deslauriers was not only the conductor, but also a health-insurance salesman; in fact, I bought my family's life insurance from him. The rehearsal was scheduled from 8 P.M. - 10:30 P.M. on a Saturday night. Around 9 P.M. he started to experience stomach cramps and asked me to take over the rehearsal. He made a point of asking me not to rehearse the arias, inasmuch as he would do them at Sunday morning's dress rehearsal. I filled in quite happily, had fun at the rehearsal, and arrived home at about 11 P.M.

I was awoken at 1 A.M. by a caller from Radio-Canada (the French language division of the CBC), asking me to conduct the entire concert the next day, due to the fact that

Conducting under the lights of the CBC in the late 1950's. Even afte my "Big Break", I had to work very hard to keep my name in people' minds My ambition still was that elusive Music Directorship.

Mr. Deslauriers had been taken to the hospital because of a heart attack. I accepted on one condition: that Mr. Deslaurier should still receive his honorarium for the concert. So I gave up my honorarium for being conductor and, since I wasn't playing my viola in the orchestra, I didn't receive my honorarium as musician either. I considered this a fine trade-off.

The concert went extremely well, and shortly afterward the CBC invited me to conduct the CBC Vancouver Chamber Orchestra in Vancouver and the CBC Symphony Orchestra in Toronto. I quickly became a regular on the French and English television and radio networks of the CBC. Many exceptional and fascinating musical experiences followed. For instance, I had the great good fortune to conduct the CBC Symphony Orchestra accompanying the outstanding Canadian violinist, Steven Staryk, performing Prokofiev's First Violin Concerto. I also conducted the North American Premiere of Kodaly's Symphony in C with them.

I received my Canadian citizenship in 1962, which opened up many more opportunities for me. However, up until the time I acquired Canadian citizenship, I would not travel to the Soviet Union. The Montreal Symphony Orchestra toured

Western Europe and I went along, but when they went to the oviet Union, I declined. This was the coldest era of the Cold Var, and I was a Hungarian refugee. Despite my Canadian anded Immigrant (Permanent Resident) status, there was no uarantee that the Soviet Union would recognize Canada's irisdiction over me. I had nightmares that government epresentatives would greet me at the airport saying, "Welcome ati! Welcome back! Welcome back for good!" Having had irect experience of totalitarian governments of both the Fascist

With Zoltan Kodaly in his Budapest home in 1964, while visiting on a Canada Council Grant. I travelled and studied in Europe for six months on the grant.

nd Communist variety, I did not share the naïve views of the ative-born Canadian musicians in the orchestra, who wanted ne to come along on those trips.

Canadian citizenship formally declared my ties to Canada, and he obligation of the Canadian government had to look after ny interests. So very soon after my big break, I was able to tart taking advantage of the privileged status of a Canadian assport.

One such instance occurred when the CBC asked me to conduct the North American premieres of Zoltan Kodaly's Symphony in C with the CBC Symphony Orchestra in Toronto. This was an interesting experience. The final score had not yet been published, so I had to make my own corrections to my copy of the score, hoping that the corrections matched the composer's intentions. When I returned to Budapest in 1964 for the first time since the 1956 Uprising, I visited Kodaly. I was anxious to hear the composer's opinion of my work. The only thing he said was that he liked my idea to go from the second to the third movement attacca (without interruption). I took this as high praise, inasmuch as Kodaly was a very taciturn person who preferred to speak in monosyllables; one had to take his silence as a compliment.

I studied Hungarian folk music with him, and when I talked to other musicians in Hungary I heard many jokes about him. At the time, Kodaly was the most famous living Hungarian composer and had quite a privileged position in Communist Hungary. As in all Communist states, everyone was equal, but some were more equal than others. In one joke, Kodaly is caught jaywalking across a busy Budapest street by a policeman ignorant of his identity. The policeman questioned Kodaly closely, getting his name, address, and much other information; when the policeman asked Kodaly for his annual income and Kodaly named an amount a hundred times more than the average Hungarian, he shouted, "Get out of here, old fool!"

Apart from conducting for the CBC in Montreal and Toronto I was also invited to conduct other radio orchestras in Halifax, Quebec, Winnipeg, and other cities coast to coast across Canada. With a fresh Canadian passport in my pocket, I felt the time had come to renew my old contacts in Europe and make a few new ones. I intended to gain guest-conducting work and position myself to take over a Music Directorship when one became available. Though I was, in fact, working as a conductor, I did not yet have a full-time conducting position with a single entity, which persisted in being my main ambition, regardless of my previous successes.

Chapter Thirty Five

EUROPE AND REUNIONS

In order to renew old contacts and make new ones, I decided to go on a European tour. In 1962, a passenger could stop in twenty-one cities without an extra charge on a single international plane ticket. My Canadian passport was welcome almost everywhere. The itinerary was to include London, Paris, Brussels, Oslo, Stockholm, Copenhagen, Helsinki, West Berlin, Munich, Zurich, Geneva, Lausanne, Vienna, Ankara, Istanbul, Athens, Tel Aviv, Jerusalem, Rome, and Milan. That is only twenty, but in the intervening forty-two years I have forgotten one. The pace was hectic, and the experience of waking up in a different hotel and going to a different office virtually every morning was very interesting.

In every city I visited, I had meetings with representatives of the local orchestras, radio broadcasters, and artistic management/promoting organizations. I had gone on the trip with very high hopes. Two invitations to conduct resulted from the trip: first, the RAI (Radio Italiana) Symphony Orchestra in Milan, and second, the Orchestre de Chambre de l'ORTF (Organisation de Radiodiffusion Television Francais). The latter engagement generated an invitation to conduct a concert with the Orchestre de Chambre de RDB (the Chamber Orchestra of the French section of Belgian Radio in Brussels). Besides, I had another reason to go; I wanted to catch up with my brothers.

I had caught up to Dodi in 1954, when he (then an attaché in the Israeli Diplomatic Service) had visited me in Budapest, and when he had helped me to escape from Hungary to Yugoslavia two years later. By the early 1960's he was a diplomat in Ankara, Turkey. I timed my visit to Ankara for Christmas week so I would not be able to do any business, even though the city had a fine Symphony Orchestra, and there might have been an opportunity for me. I had a pleasant visit with my brother and his family, and renewed acquaintances with my nieces and nephews.

Arranging things with Nandi was a bit more difficult. I had not seen my older half-brother since 1940, when he and Dodi had left for Israel. I didn't know how my half-brother was going to greet me. After all, it had been twenty-two years since we had seen each other, though we had, of course, exchanged letters and information over the years through our relatives. Nandi was living in Jerusalem and owned a small pastry/coffee shop; at first, I considered not informing him ahead of time and just dropping by his shop and asking for a bagel. Then I thought he might have a heart attack, so I gave him a phone call from Montreal to tell him of my schedule.

I was lucky that I called. Nandi got very upset and started yelling at me. Evidently, his wife had plans to visit Montreal to check out the possibility of moving their business there on the exact days I would be out of the country on my trip. Nandi insisted that it was a matter of life and death that I meet his wife. I had already set up all my appointments in all the other cities, so the only thing I could do was to delay my departure for a couple of days. Nandi's wife, it turned out, was already in New York, visiting her son from her first marriage, so I called her and told her that I could not wait any longer. Her response was quite cool. "I have survived for so long without seeing you, I can manage another few years!" And I had nearly disrupted my entire trip for this?

Naturally, after all this brouhaha, I had no idea what my reception in Jerusalem would be like. My brother had a lovely house, but just in case, I booked a room in a hotel. When I entered his store he was making change for a customer. He recognized me immediately; I was fourteen when he had left Romania twenty-two years earlier. He looked up for a moment and motioned me to sit down while he finished his transaction. The first reception was a bit chilly. He was still upset about my not meeting his wife. By the next day we began to warm to each other and he took me out to a Palestinian restaurant where I had falafel, hummus, kefir, and other Arab delicacies for the first time.

It had taken more than two decades, but finally all the family were back in contact, healthy, safe, and relatively prosperous.

What damage war does.

In 1964, after several years in the courts, I win my case against YAT in regards to the Munich air crash. I use the settlement money to buy a brand-new car for the first and only time in my life.

My girls at Niagra Falls.

Chapter Thirty Six

MUSICIAN ON THE MOVE

At the beginning of the Sixties, my career was getting busier and busier. Primarily, I was freelancing, playing violin and viola for radio, television, and film recordings, concerts with the Montreal Symphony, concerts with the Montreal Chamber Orchestra and with other organizations. At one point, I worked for six months performing every single day! Personally, I could handle the work, and I was making a good income for my family. But one day I looked at my income tax return and calculated that I was now turning over 40% of my income to the government. I had reached that high a tax bracket. I considered the return on my investment: if I took less work, I would make less money, but I would also pay less tax and have more time to spend with my daughters and wife.

Suzy and Kathy at a lake in the Gatineau Hills, one of our favourite family getaways.

So I cut back on my workload and made time to travel with my family. Usually we were able to go to Florida for a few days around my various engagements. Flying was out of the question due to the cost, time, and my family's previous experience. In order to make the trips as fast as possible I

Settled in our first apartment in Victoria. Both Suzy and Kathy learned piano and violin, though they chose not to become musicians.

told my wife that we should start driving every morning around 6 A.M., that way, we would have more time in Florida and fewer days on the road. Easier said than done, what with a wife and two daughters. We never left the motels before ten or even eleven o'clock!

The motels where we stayed usually had a pool. "Daddy, can we go swimming one more time?" my daughters would ask. Who could resist two charming ladies, especially if they are your own daughters? I decided that I would look for a small motor home which would allow me to drive while my three ladies were sleeping. Looking around, I realized that the only way I could afford one was if I built it myself.

I was planning to buy a step-van and equip it myself, and I had a good reason for this. I was conducting a small chamber orchestra of young musicians in Montreal when we won a competition. This meant that we had to go to Alexandria, New York for a radio recording. To transport the drums, two double basses and some musicians, we also needed a van. I thought I could serve my family and my professional needs simultaneously, a neat arrangement which pleased the engineer in me.

Then I came across a wonderful opportunity. A dress salesman in Quebec had a van custom built to his specifications. The body of the van was made of aluminum, not subject to the rust caused by the heavily salted roads in Quebec. It had three batteries, neon lighting, propane gas heating, shelves, a cleverly stored table on one wall, a full-length mirror, and everything else necessary for life on the road. It had cost him $10,000 in 1963, but I paid him only $3,000, which was just enough to get him out of his lease.

Before going to Alexandria, I had just enough time to rip out most of the shelving to create a storage space for the boxes containing the kettle drums. One musician came with me in the van and three other cars followed, creating a little 'musical caravan'. At the border, a US Customs officer entered the van and I had to explain to him who we were and where we were going. He asked me what we had in the boxes. I told him tympanies. "What is that?" he asked. "Kettle Drums." He didn't get that either. Not wanting to show his ignorance any longer, he waved us through. Six months later, when the van was fully equipped as a camper and me and my family were heading for Florida, the same customs officer greeted us at the U.S. border. He looked at me and said, "I know, you are the conductor. GO!"

In contrast to the rolling palaces we have nowadays, this little van seems a bit pokey. But it was comfortable, affordable, and useful.

The family around the dining table in the van. Efficient, yet friendly.

After using the van for the orchestra, I decided to adapt it entirely for my family's personal use. I had a vague idea of what I wanted, but I had no plan or knowledge of how to achieve it. I thought of building something along the lines of the European sleeping car coupes, which have a daytime use and a nighttime use. The only tools I owned were a hammer, some screwdrivers, and a half -inch drill with some attachments. I bought three sheets of 8' x 4' three-quarter-inch thick plywood, and one ½ inch thick plywood sheet. I also bought two piano hinges and got down to work. I improvised as I went along. The camper had a full-length mirror behind the driver's side door and a table which folded up and was stored on the wall. I planned to build two sofa-like contraptions facing each other.

The backs of these sofas were suspended from the ceiling. Behind them we had ample storage for the blankets, sheets, and pillows. The bottom part of the sofas flipped up on a piano hinge and revealed more storage. I added a support so the lids could be propped open.

During the daytime the two sofas provided ample seating space. This sometimes became very handy when we had guests, or when we would provide transportation in later years during rare snow storms in Victoria. Most of my neighbors in Victoria would have no idea how to drive in snow, but I had become a master after my ten years driving in the Montreal winters.

The backs of the sofa opened up and were suspended from the ceiling of the van to form the two bunk beds for my daughters. I cut three square pieces of 3/4 inch thick plywood to be placed between the two chesterfields facing each other. This way we had a six by six feet bed downstairs and a four by six feet bed upstairs. My wife made some very colourful coverings for our foam rubber mattresses.

Behind one sofa I built an icebox and shelves. On the other side we had hangers for clothes. We also had a curtain hung for privacy. I stored a two-burner propane gas stove on the side of the ice box. It was connected to the propane tank by an eighteen-foot long rubber hose. This way we were able to cook outside when we had good weather. I also built some shelves with sliding doors over the sofas. There was one small problem. I miscalculated how long it would take me to build the camper.

We already had the children out of school and ready to go. On this occasion, my free time did not quite correspond with the school holidays so I just took Suzy and Kathy out of school. After working 'overtime' for two days, I finally had the camper ready for the trip. I worked so hard finishing the job that my right arm and hand were hurting, and I was going to have to drive down to Florida with that arm in a sling. Luckily, the camper had an automatic transmission, so I managed.

We loaded the camper with food, utensils, clothes, games, books, and fishing rods. We left our apartment building, drove one and half blocks and parked in front of my bank. I put our stove on the folding table, and my wife prepared breakfast. We were already camping!

Exhausted, successful, and free to begin my vacation with my family. Never in my life had I had such good ham and eggs.

Les Préludes

Chapter Thirty Seven

MUSIC DIRECTOR AT LAST

In January 1967, Otto Werner Mueller, the Music Director of the Victoria Symphony Orchestra, invited me to be guest-conductor for a concert. He asked me to conduct Beethoven's Symphony Number 3, the Eroica. This invitation was the fruit of the long-term investment I had made back in 1958, when I borrowed money to take the six-week Pan-American Orchestra Conducting Course in Mexico City, under the direction of Igor Markevitch. At the finale of the course I had been asked to conduct the 2nd Movement, the Funeral March, of Beethoven's Eroica Symphony, an extremely challenging piece. For reasons explained in greater detail earlier, I conducted with great focus and a huge store of emotion. Otto Werner Mueller saw me do that, and I made a strong enough impression that he kept me in mind for a long time; he presented me with a plum conducting assignment fully nine years after he had seen my work.

The concert was a great success. Coming from sub-zero temperatures and three feet of snow in Montreal, I was pleasantly charmed with Victoria's beautiful setting on Vancouver Island and its balmy, springlike weather.

Only a couple of months after my visit to Victoria, Otto had a run-in with the Board of Directors and resigned in mid-season. The Symphony Orchestra was left without a conductor or a Music Director. They invited several guest conductors in to finish the season, who were also candidates for the position of Music Director. I was not invited, as I had recently conducted there, but I was considered for the position.

Signing on, Music Director with the Victoria Symphony Orchestra

It was just after 1 A.M. on an April morning in 1967, in Montreal, when I received a telephone call from John Meredith, the President of the Victoria Symphony Society, offering me the position of Music Director. He offered me $10,000 for the season. He was blunt on the telephone, probably because, with the time difference, it was after 10 P.M. in British Columbia. He said that if I accepted the position, I should come to Victoria to finalize the details, but that if I wanted more money, I should forget it. Mr. Meredith was a retired bureaucrat in the Ministry of Education and he still had the manners of a school principal. In spite of his scholarly attitude we later became very good friends. I told him that I would discuss the terms and conditions in person.

I went to Victoria a couple of weeks later and agreed with the Board on a salary of $12,000 and payment of my family's moving expenses. It was a good sum of money for the time, but I was already earning substantially more than that in Montreal as an orchestra musician, playing for the Montreal Symphony and for many other employers. I took the pay cut for a number of reasons. This was my chance to be a Music Director, and so conduct my own orchestra regularly and choose my own musical programs. The cultural situation in Montreal was becoming constricted as the new nationalism in Quebec restricted my ability to advance; I was neither a native-born Canadian, nor Quebecois, and ethnicity had become a greater factor in advancement than merit or artistic ability. This kind of cultural apartheid was anathema to me, having grown up under both casual and institutional anti-Semitism, and seen the corrosive effects of any kind of ethnic favouritism, especially government-sanctioned ethnic favouritism. I didn't want my daughters growing up in such an environment. So I took the job.

I was forty-two years old when I finally became Music Director of the Victoria Symphony Orchestra. This was my chance to put my twenty-one years experience in the various fields of the music business to good use. In 1967, The Victoria Symphony Orchestra was composed mostly of amateur musicians, especially in the string sections, and the majority of the wind section, both brass and woodwind, belonged to the Naden Band, a military band based in the Canadian Armed Forces military base in Esquimalt, north of Victoria.

The string players were mainly housewives, students and a few professionals. My predecessor, Otto Werner Mueller, was a formidable figure, more than six feet tall and had, according to his own accounts, acted many times like a policeman, directing the "civilians" in the orchestra in an authoritarian manner. Most of the amateur musicians were scared to death of him.

For the first few months of conducting, the musicians were very somber while they played, which frustrated me a great deal. I told them "You look like a very efficient forced labour camp!" I was trying to get them to smile and look happy. How could the audience enjoy a concert when they could see the musicians suffering on stage? Gradually, they lost their habits of fear and soon a sense of enjoyment took their place. Perhaps it was because they had so far to go that our honeymoon lasted the whole of the first four seasons.

While the Music Director is the focal point of practically all the activities of an orchestra, the position itself is very lonely. The Music Director cannot have personal friends among the musicians of the orchestra because some other musicians would resent you playing favourites. So I had friendly relations with most of the musicians, but could not be friends with any of them. Different positions in the orchestra have their idiosyncrasies, too. String players naturally play as a unit, and a conductor or music director can improve the quality of playing in whole string sections without giving too much individual attention. But the wind players are all individual soloists, so that section needs to be treated differently. And finally, in an orchestra, the player can either fulfill his/her role — soloist member of a section — or leave. And these difficult decisions, to train or to terminate, are all made by the Music Director.

I faced a number of such problems in the Victoria Symphony. For instance, my first clarinetist had intonation problems. He continually asked me to show him whether he was too high or too low in pitch — even during concerts! My first trumpet player was the kindest, nicest human being you could imagine; unfortunately, every time he had a solo passage to play, he lost his nerve and cracked notes.

By 1969, it had become obvious that I would have to make some changes in the orchestra. In the case of the wind section, the decision was not so hard. For most of these musicians, their main income came from their positions in the Naden Band. Playing in the Symphony Orchestra was more a question of prestige than of money for them. Their income from the orchestra was minimal. So, although it was very difficult for me to part company with some of the musicians, the knowledge that this would not jeopardize their livelihood eased my discomfort. Both musician and conductor sobbed when I had to let go first, my clarinetist and later, my first trumpet. However, this led to favourable outcomes for both of them. My clarinetist joined a jazz band, and my first trumpet ended up teaching music in the public school system. I had similar problems in the string section.

In the late Sixties, the Music Department of the University of Victoria, the Victoria Conservatory of Music, and the Victoria Symphony Orchestra did not have sufficient funds to import professors and musicians. I suggested that the three

THE VICTORIA SYMPHONY

Finally, not a guest, but the master, the maestro! I had arrived in Canada eleven years ago as a penniless refugee, and now I was Music Director in a Provincial Capital city!

organizations join forces, combine financial resources and engage musicians in joint practice. The musicians would both play for the orchestra and teach at the University and the Conservatory. The Orchestra would gain readily available, full-time, professional musicians, and the teaching institutions would gain instructors who wouldn't have to leave when offered orchestra positions.

This is how we imported our concertmaster from London, England; he doubled up as the head of the String Department at the Victoria Conservatory of Music. We spread our net over the world. We engaged our first bassoon, first horn and the leader of the second violin section from the U.S. Our first viola came from Calgary, and so on. Our audiences grew by leaps and bounds and I proposed to the Board of Directors that we double the number of concerts by performing each program twice. We went ahead with that, and in a short while we had sold out houses at both concerts. This helped immensely, but we were still financially constrained by our venue— the Royal Theatre, which had the very limited capacity of only 1200 seats.

To help with our finances, I went to speak to Mr. Gilmer in Vancouver, the CEO of Canadian Pacific Airlines and asked him to provide us with free airline passes for our soloists. This strategy won us air passes valued up to $4,000 per season, which meant we had $4,000 more for musicians and soloist fees. I also approached Air Canada, telling them of our arrangements with Canadian Pacific Airlines. Air Canada said that if they give us such support, they would have to give it to other orchestras as well. We ended up receiving $2,000 worth of passes per season, but other Canadian orchestras received such help too. My good friend Luis Finamore, the manager of the famous Empress Hotel in Victoria, provided free accommodation for our soloists. So the Victoria Symphony deducted the considerable expenses of transportation and accommodation from its budget for soloists. These indirect subsidies lessened our costs considerably.

I felt that by bringing these outstanding soloists to Victoria, we might as well take advantage of the opportunity to have them also perform in a recital on Wednesday evenings at the McPherson Playhouse. By doing so, we also reduced the per concert fees of our soloists. We ended up having a series of twelve pairs of symphony concerts and a recital series of eight concerts. We also performed concerts in Duncan and Campbell River, two small towns on Vancouver Island, and I remember engaging Narciso Yepez for a whole week, performing three concerts in Victoria and two up the Island.

The city of Victoria has the mildest climate in Canada. It is also a great tourist destination; in the seventies, it was estimated that Victoria had over two million visitors a year. I proposed to the Board to start a Music Festival of open air concerts. My proposal was turned down for two reasons. If people heard the orchestra in the summer they would not come to our regular concert season. And if my idea was a flop, they didn't want to be part of it.

Not to be denied, I asked the Board if they objected to me starting a Summer Festival on my own. They said no, go ahead. This was a great success for me personally and I devote a whole chapter to the interesting details.

I was very fortunate that during most of my tenure in Victoria the soloist fees were still reasonable. For instance, we had the great Russian cellist, Mstislav Rostropovich performing in two concerts, his fee being only $10,000. When I met him in Israel in the early nineties, he told me he was getting $50,000 US per concert. The famous "Three Tenors" would not even consider an engagement below $1,000,000 US.

Due to the still reasonable soloist fees and our arrangements with the airlines and the Empress Hotel, we were able to invite the best soloists in the world: Sir Yehudi Menuhin, Mstislav Rostropovich, Jean Pierre Rampal, Phillipe Entremont, Ida Haendel, Zara Nelsova, Nicanor Zabaleta, Narciso Yepez and many other notable performers.

The proportion of professional musicians in the Orchestra increased, and so did the quality of playing. Boyd Hood, a professor at the School of Music of the University of Victoria became my first trumpet. He was an excellent musician whose first love was performing. Several years later he ended up with the Los Angeles Philharmonic.

One season our concertmaster, who was British, suddenly had to return to England because of family reasons. The great soloist and concertmaster and my good friend Steven Staryk happened to be living in Vancouver, at the time, serving as a professor at the Vancouver Academy of Music. I explained our situation to him and he agreed to be our concertmaster for the rest of the season. This led to a very amusing situation.

We had a guest conductor doing a so-called "Pops" concert, who programmed an excerpt from Tchaikovsky's Swan Lake Ballet, which included a famous violin solo. In the intermission of the rehearsal the conductor came to me and said: "You have a very good concertmaster!" I told him, "I know. Before letting him come here, we let him be the concertmaster of the Royal Philharmonic Orchestra, the Concertgebow Orchestra of Amsterdam, and the Chicago Symphony among others!"

Unfortunately, my life was made miserable by certain board members who criticized my choices of "Pops" music. I invited Arthur Fiedler, of Boston Pops fame, as guest conductor. I thought that I would finally find out from the horse's mouth what they mean by "Pops" music. I asked him what is understood by the term Boston Pops. He said, "This is what it means. We serve champagne during the Pops concerts and the name came from the popping of the corks!"

So much for the definition of "Pop" music.

Chapter Thirty Eight

GUESTS OF THE VICTORIA SYMPHONY

During my tenure as Music Director of the Victoria Symphony Orchestra, I had the opportunity to invite some of the major artists of the period. At the time, even an orchestra of limited financial means, like the Victoria Symphony Orchestra, could afford them.

Today, due to the manipulations of some big artist management organizations, such as Columbia Artists Management among others, the fees of major soloists have gone totally out of sight. Some fees have increased five to tenfold! At these prices it is obvious that only a few major, well-endowed orchestras can afford to pay the $50 - 60,000 and more charged by major soloists. The motives of the managers, whether they manage musicians, actors, football players, baseball players and others, are understandable: 15% commission on $50,000 is more than 15% on $5,000.

CHRISTIAN FERRAS

During my first seasons with the Victoria Symphony Orchestra (1967-78), I was very fortunate to have as one of my soloists Christian Ferras, the great French violinist. At the time, Ferras was at the top of his career and his performance of the Brahms Violin Concerto was simply breathtaking. Herbert von Karajan recorded almost all of the violin concertos from Bach to Berg with Christian Ferras and the Berlin Philharmonic Orchestra for Deutsche Gramophone.

He reminded me very much of the great French violinist Ginette Neuveux. She was extremely masculine with a heavy neck like a male boxer and her playing was also very masculine. (She died unfortunately in a plane crash at a young age.)

It was an instantaneous musical and personal friendship with Christian. His autographed picture still means a lot to me. While he was in Victoria we played poker in the evenings at my home. One evening, after three to four hours of playing, I lost $4-5. The next evening he lost $4-5. But we had fun. We played often during his visits.

On his next visit he played the Sibelius Violin Concerto with me, which he had also recorded with Karajan. A gentleman came to talk to me before the concert telling me that he had came over from Vancouver just to hear Ferras play the harmonic passage in the Concerto. This is a difficult passage where the soloist has to play a passage of harmonics. By that time Ferras started to have problems with his health and private life. He had put on a lot of weight and started to have other physical problems. I don't know the exact nature of his family problems, but I understand that some of them were connected with his brother's gambling. To cut a long story short, he played again like God, but when it came to that particular passage of harmonics he simply stopped playing and resumed playing when it was over! I had a chuckle thinking of the poor fellow who came over from Vancouver mainly to hear that particular passage.

The last visit of Ferras to Victoria was the last in more than one way. I engaged him to play the Mendelssohn Violin Concerto and the Ravel Tzigane. Although I usually had only one rehearsal with my soloists, in this case we planned on two rehearsals because of the two works on the program. Ferras arrived sick and exhausted. He was fighting a bad flu and taking antibiotics. He had put on even more weight, was perspiring, coughing, and showing various other symptoms. I told him to rest and to skip the dress rehearsal Sunday morning, prior to the afternoon concert scheduled for 3 P.M. I promised to send my doctor to see him.

When I came home around 1 P.M. from the dress rehearsal, I phoned him at the Empress Hotel, but there was no answer. I thought that perhaps he was having lunch in the restaurant. A few minutes later, I received a call from my doctor telling me that Ferras was in the hospital with a heart attack. I had several emergency situations during my career, but this was perhaps the most harrowing one. I phoned my friend, Steven Staryk, telling him what happened and asked him not to tell me yes or no for the moment, but if I could arrange a plane and a taxi to get him to the concert, where he would play the Mendelssohn Violin Concerto at 3 P.M. with the Victoria Symphony Orchestra. I then put down the receiver, phoned a charter airline, chartered a plane for him, ordered a taxi to pick him up and than phoned him back. Steve said, "I was sitting in my dressing gown just doing my income taxes when you called, and besides, I haven't played the Mendelssohn piece for over a year!" I told him, "Never mind, you will have forty-five minutes in the plane to look at the music." I did not know at the time, however, that those small planes which fly by visual flight rules only are not even allowed to operate in inclement weather!

The sea between Vancouver and Victoria was under thick cloud cover, with dense patches of fog. The pilot flew practically at sea level between the islands and Steve had to warn him about what he saw on the right side of the plane while the pilot was looking out on the left side. Obviously, there was not much time for studying the music.

I had to replace the Ravel Tzigane; I could not do that piece without a rehearsal and it would have been unfair to ask Steve to play it. I phoned the librarian and asked her to hand the music for Sibelius' Finlandia to the musicians. We had performed this piece several weeks earlier in a different series. I started the concert five minutes after 3 P.M. I told the audience that Ferras had become ill, not mentioning the nature of his illness, and that Steven Staryk, "Who should be landing now . . ." would replace him. Steven was already well-known to our audiences.

Steve arrived on time. The Mendelssohn piece could not have been performed more perfectly if we had had ten rehearsals.

It was so good that we had offers to make a commercial recording out of the performance!

I visited Ferras at his home in Nice, the following year and we went for a walk with his dog. This was the last time I saw him alive. He died a few months later. It was like losing a close family member.

PHILLIPPE ENTREMONT

From the word "go", I became very good friends with Phillippe Entremont. I ended up inviting him as guest soloist three seasons in a row. In the first season he played a Beethoven concerto and de Falla's Nights in the Gardens of the Alhambra. For the second season I asked him to play the two Ravel Concertos for piano, as this was the Ravel Centenary. He told me later that he made a lot of money from my suggestion, as many other orchestras asked him to play the Ravel Concertos.

When it came to programming the third season I said jokingly, "Last year you played two concertos, so this time let's play three concertos." Some joke. We ended up performing a Mozart, a Beethoven and finally, the ever-popular Tchaikovsky piano concerto. When he became conductor of the Vienna Chamber Orchestra I told him: "If I could play the piano as well as you do, I would have never considered becoming a conductor."

Not speaking of Phillippe Entremont, whom I did not see conducting, I have in my career observed several great soloists attempt to take up conducting, thinking it is something very easy to do, compared to playing an instrument at the level of an international soloist. Sad to say, there is a little more to conducting than waving a baton, and very few soloists managed to bring their level of conducting up to the same level of prowess as their instrumental playing.

We saw each other last time at a reception, given by Van Cliburn in his gorgeous home in Fort Worth during the 1993 Van Cliburn International Piano Competition.

This portrait of the incomparable Yehudi Menuhin comes from the brush of the equally incomparable Myfanwy Pavelic. She is a Victoria born-and-raised artist, accomplished and respected internationally for the emotional depth and perceptivity of her work.

YEHUDI MENUHIN

I hated Yehudi Menuhin during my childhood. The Twenties and Thirties were times of the 'wunderkinder,' the child-prodigy, when Yehudi Menuhin at the age of nine had already performed with the Philadelphia Orchestra, and other gifted young children were performing with, or even conducting symphony orchestras. It was the dream of all middle-class Jewish mothers whose children were studying music, (especially violin), that their child should become another Menuhin — or better!

"You see," the mother would say to her child, "Yehudi Menuhin is only nine years old, and he is already playing with the Philadelphia Orchestra! You see what regular practice can do!?"

I was only nine and I was perhaps playing at the level of the Kreutzer etudes, and it took me ten more years to play some of the more common violin concertos half-way decently. My mother's impatience during those ten years was very hard to deal with. I am sure that the lives of many of my contemporaries who were studying the violin were made miserable by Menuhin's meteoric career.

If somebody had told me in 1938 that one day I would invite Yehudi Menuhin to be my soloist, I would have laughed for days. This reminds me of an aprocryphal story shared among musicians.

This supposedly happened when Eugene Ormandy, who was the Music Director of the Philadelphia Orchestra for more than forty years, and who was originally a violinist himself, came back to Hungary with Heifetz as his soloist. Apparently, Ormandy's mother told him: "You see my son. If you had just practiced, you could have been the soloist tonight!"

My first personal encounter with Yehudi Menuhin was in Budapest, during the 1946-47 season with the Fovarosi Szimfonikus Zenekar (The Symphony Orchestra of the Capital). I had joined the orchestra in the fall of 1946, and this was going to be my first professional job. Menuhin came with Antal Dorati, the Hungarian-born Music Director of the Minneapolis Symphony, to perform two works by Bela Bartok, the First Violin Concerto and the Concerto for Orchestra.

Menuhin and Dorati made a tremendous impression on all of us musicians. On top of playing with these supremely talented people, we performed the Hungarian premieres of perhaps one of Bela Bartok's greatest works. Bartok had just died in New York the previous year. All in all, it was an historic occasion.

My next encounter with Yehudi Menuhin was in the Erkel Theater in Budapest in the early Fifties. He was performing Mozart's Violin Concerto No. 5 and Beethoven's violin concerto. I was not aware that Yehudi had occasional muscular problems which affected his bowing arm. During the performance of the Mozart concerto these problems manifested themselves and we were all seated at the edge of our chairs, concerned that he wouldn't be able to finish the concerto. Then after the intermission he played the most heavenly Beethoven violin concerto! I remember that he played as an encore the Sonata for Solo Violin he had commissioned from Bela Bartok. He also played the Chaccone by J.S. Bach. It is not clear if he was just joking, but he started the Chaccone in D Major, playing an F sharp instead of an F natural. He stopped, smiled, and said, "Sorry," and started again in the proper key.

This concert played a great role in my life. In 1956, while working at The Symphonic and Chamber Music Department of the Hungarian Radio and the Musical Program Exchange Department, I arranged with Yehudi Menuhin to do the first videotape for the yet non-existent Hungarian Television. It was a Partita for solo violin by Johan Sebastian Bach.

In 1959, Yehudi came to perform with the Montreal Symphony Orchestra, where I was assistant solo viola. By that time, I had established the Montreal Chamber Orchestra and for our first concert, I had chosen an all-Bartok program. The concert was a great artistic success and we received very good reviews. Knowing Yehudi's interest in Bartok, I gave him the write-ups and the programs of the concert. A few weeks later, Yehudi wrote me a letter from England to congratulate me and to tell me that he hoped to invite me to his Bath Festival in England, or the one in Gstaadt, Switzerland. You can imagine how excited I was at this possibility, as I was just starting out on my Western conducting career.

Unfortunately, this invitation never materialized.

In the Sixties, I visited Yehudi in London, and even assisted at an orchestral rehearsal of Benjamin Britten's Variations on a Theme, by Frank Bridge. I remember giving him a little suggestion which he appreciated very much, in connection with a tricky glissando passage.

Fifteen years later, I was finally able to invite Yehudi Menuhin to be my soloist with the Victoria Symphony Orchestra. I asked him to play the same two concertos I heard him play more than twenty years earlier in Budapest, Mozart's Concerto No. 5 and Beethoven's Violin Concerto.

He played both concertos marvelously and played a Bach Gavotte as an encore.

Yehudi Menuhin was one of the most modest and most generous of persons I ever knew. He even agreed to give a lecture to the local Rotary Club.

The manager of the Empress Hotel went out of his way to give him a real royal reception and put him up in the Vice-Regal Suite, which had a large conference room, a dining room for ten people, two bedrooms and bathrooms and many other luxuries. Poor Yehudi felt very uncomfortable and was totally lost. I phoned up my very good friend, the well-known Canadian painter Myfanwy Pavelic, who had a gorgeous home, with a modern studio, an indoor heated swimming pool, and lovely guest quarters, and asked her if I could bring Yehudi along. She agreed, and sent a letter to Menuhin, inviting him to stay.

I took him there and it was love at first sight. It was an instant friendship which lasted to the day Yehudi died. Yehudi felt immediately at home, and practiced in her studio while she made drawings, paintings, even collages of Yehudi. A few years later, Yehudi even brought his sister Hepzibah to meet Myf. When the Royal Portrait Gallery in London wanted to have Sir Yehudi Menuhin's portrait, Yehudi chose Myfanwy Pavelic to paint him. In May, 1997, Yehudi conducted a concert with the Victoria Symphony Orchestra for the benefit of a charity chosen by Myf. She chose the Victoria Symphony Orchestra itself as the beneficiary.

JACK BENNY

One of the greatest American comedians of the Twentieth Century was Jack Benny; he was also one of its greatest humanists. He made millions by playing a Scrooge, an avaricious, miserly person, a person to whom money was the greatest and only value in life. In one of his sketches a robber held a gun to his back and shouted, "Your money or your life!" Benny characteristically held his right hand to his chin, his left arm crossing his chest and supporting the right arm and stood, pensive and silent. The robber asked, "What

I met Jack Benny in Toronto. Here he is showing me his Stradivarius. I cannot remember another man who was such a combination of culture, humour, humility, and generosity.

are you waiting for?" Benny replied, "I'm thinking it over."

This Scrooge was in fact one of the most generous people of his generation. At age of eighty-five, he embarked on a tour across Canada in order to raise funds for Canadian orchestras. I had the privilege to work with him when he did a fundraising concert for the Victoria Symphony Orchestra.

Somebody asked Isaac Stern, the great American violinist, how well Jack Benny played the violin. Stern said, "He plays it well enough for what he needs it for." Jack Benny was, in fact, a very accomplished violinist and had a beautiful, expensive Stradivarius violin. Although he could have been a renowned soloist and taken ostentatious pride in his skills, he used his violin instead as part of his act. He had quite a number of violin related jokes, including this one: Benny was late for a White House reception where he was supposed to perform. As he climbed the steps of the White House the security guard asked him, "What's in that violin case?" Benny decided to make a little joke. "A machine gun!" he replied. "Thank God," said the guard, "I was worried that you were bringing your violin!" This kind of self-deprecating joke made him both a multi-millionaire and personally admired by his audiences.

I went to Toronto to see his show, to get to know his routine and to talk to him regarding his forthcoming visit to B.C. The Toronto concert was preceded by a gala dinner at its new City Hall. We had a nice chat in his hotel room. He showed me his authentic Stradivarius, the violin which every serious violinist admires and aspires to own, and told me that he was looking forward to his visit. I told him how much everybody in Victoria was looking forward to him. I returned to Victoria where I found that, contrary to what I had promised him, the promotion of the concert and the sale of the tickets was going very poorly. Here was one of the most revered performers of the last sixty years, giving free of his time and talent (at the age of eighty-five) to raise funds for our orchestra, and we weren't going to fill the house. I was ashamed and angry.

One of Jack Benny's conditions to all of the fundraising concerts was that the tickets were to be priced at $100, a tremendous sum in the 1970's. At this time, George Harrison of the Beatles caused a scandal by charging the awful sum of $10 a ticket for his 1975 Vancouver concert. With proper promotion and effort by the individual board members it should not have been difficult to sell the 1,200 tickets and raise $120,000 for the Victoria Symphony.

Benny's arrival at the airport was organized in grand fashion. The Mayor of Victoria greeted him and he was driven to the Empress Hotel in downtown Victoria in a gorgeous, open Packard convertible that had previously belonged to Errol Flynn, courtesy of the Classic Car Museum.

The orchestra and I had great fun rehearsing his routine, which hinged on members of the orchestra performing in his comedy bits with exact timing. The difficulties here taught me how exceptional it is to be good at both comedy and music. In one routine he would start performing the Zigeuner Weisen of Sarasate, which has two cadenzas shortly after the start of the piece. A cadenza is a short variation on the musical piece, either improvised by the soloist, or written by the composer

Here I am at a Symphony Ball in Victoria. Yes, I was having fun!

or written by another composer. The routine was to go as
follows: When Benny reached the first cadenza the
concertmaster (the First Violin) was to interrupt him and start
playing it, assuming this mere comedian would not be able
to handle it. Benny was to come to me, the conductor,
gesticulating angrily that I should fire the concertmaster,
which I would. When it came to the second cadenza, the

assistant concertmaster would do the same thing, and again Benny would come to me in a temper and I would insist that the assistant concertmaster leave the stage. It was good and everything went fine at the rehearsal.

During the concert, however, when it came to the firing of the assistant concertmaster, she wouldn't leave the stage. In Benny's routine everything is figured out to the second. All the pauses and double-takes have to work within a set period of time for the bit to be funny. Benny glared at the assistant concertmaster. She remained in her seat. I made all kinds of signals for her to leave. Finally, she got up and left. Benny and I were both furious at her. When I saw her backstage and asked her what happened, she said that she wanted to show that she could stare at Benny just as long as the concertmaster did. I could have strangled her! She had no conception of comic timing, and she almost ruined the whole routine.

In another bit, Benny played the concertmaster of the orchestra in a performance of Tchaikovsky's Capriccio Italien. At one particular point the music speeds up and Benny would yell at me, "Slow down! Is this how you drive your car?", and other such non-sequiturs uncharacteristic of a serious orchestral performance. He told me later that he created this routine for his own pleasure — how else could he have had the chance to play the role of the concertmaster of the New York Philharmonic, the Chicago Symphony, and so many other orchestras? Naturally, he was also entertaining the audience on his own.

He would tell jokes and imitate how some famous violinists would hold their violins when they would come on stage. One almost dragged the violin on the floor, the other would hold it up over his head like a holy object, one would hold it under his arm like a newspaper...all jokes which a music-loving audience would appreciate. Personally, it was the experience of a lifetime to work with such a talented artist and memorable human being as Jack Benny. It is a tragedy that such unique individuals and philanthropists eventually have to leave the stage of life, following their colleagues into the history books.

Luckily, we have some videos of his work, so even future generations can enjoy his artistry.

THE FAMILY OF MUSIC AND MUSICIANS

The relationship between conductors, orchestra musicians and soloists is like that of an extended family. Everyone gets to know each other quite well, and often you get to know their families. Sometimes, lifetime friendships are established, based on one or two joint performances. I remember going to Dimitry Bashkirov's recital in Munich in 1992. This great Russian pianist had last performed with me about twenty years earlier in Victoria. When I went backstage to congratulate him, he immediately recognized me, embraced me and treated me like his long lost brother. The same thing happened with the wonderful Russian Cellist Karen Georgian. I met her in London about twenty years after our last performance in Victoria. Again, I received the same kind of warm greeting...as though we had seen each other only a couple of days ago.

Since 1958, I have been a regular guest conductor of the National Symphony Orchestra of Mexico. In the more than forty years of this collaboration, I had two, even three generations of musicians playing with me. I remember how touched I was when the first flutist of the Orchestra showed me his father's picture, telling me that his father used to play under my direction. The entire Diemecke family (Enrique Diemecke is the present Music Director of the National Symphony Orchestra of Mexico)— father, mother, brother and sister, all played under my baton in the Orquesta Sinfonica del Estado de Mexico.

Owing to the closeness of these relationships (which went beyond simple friendship), the loss of many great soloist friends of mine (Christian Ferras, Sir Yehudi Menuhin, Jean Pierre Rampal, Wytold Malkuczinsky, to name a few), and the loss of friends in the various orchestras with which I was associated, all affected me as much as if I had lost very close family members. That is the great sadness of an extended family, I suppose. When you are all young, it is wonderful, but the later years are darkened by one loss after the other.

It is fortunate that through the media of audio recordings, videotapes and film, that some performances of great artists are preserved for posterity. Naturally, this is not the same as knowing them in person, on and off the podium. Listening to past performances that I shared with my friends (since departed) brings back vivid memories of some of the unforgettable highlights of my career and, of course, some unforgettable friends.

Chapter Thirty Nine

OPINIONS - 1

THE AVANT-GARDE --
A "HOUSE IN DARKNESS"

In the Sixties and Seventies, the new "Avant-Garde" craze reached its apotheosis. Since Schoenberg, (dodecaphony-twelve tone, and other experiments), Webern and others, the search for new ways of writing and expressing new approaches to music became more and more a partisan affair of some composers. The horrible consequences of the First World War, Fascism, Stalin's Communism, the horrors of the Second World War and the atomic bomb, the factual decomposition of so-called Western Civilization, led to many art forms questioning the old values and the old ways of expression, including music.

From cubism on up and down the artistic spectrum, there was a search for a new way of expressing the realities of the Twentieth Century — for instance Picasso's Guernica, depicting the atrocities of the Spanish Civil War. There were the usual exceptions of some masterworks in the various new genres, but the majority of these experiments were short-lived and didn't leave a long-lasting impression or any real effect.

The majority of avant-garde composers ignored the audience more and more, discounting the necessity of human rapport between the composer-performers and the audience. They started to write more and more for each other, ignoring the listeners completely. Who can be more innovative? Who can write a score in a spiral form? Who can knock on the bottom of the piano?

Les Préludes

One of my many school lectures. I have always taken my responsibility to promote classical music, particularly to youth, very seriously.

I remember spending a whole afternoon with an avant-garde composer friend of mine, trying to produce unusual sounds on the violin and the viola. Putting a clothespin on the bridge of the violin, knocking on various parts of the instruments, and other non-musical techniques. The point was not that anything remotely valuable, musically, was produced; the point was that he experimented and was considered "avant-garde", creating a new "effect."

In the seventies, I attended a concert at Leonard Bernstein's Festival of Modern American Music with the New York Philharmonic Orchestra. The first half of the program consisted of Tchaikovsky's Symphony #6, the Pathetique. During the intermission half the audience left, obviously, caring little for the avant-garde pieces which were to come. Gradually, during the second half of the program, half of the remaining audience left. Only about twenty-five per cent of the original listeners stayed to the bitter end.

Among other works, they performed a composition of John Cage, written on some astronomical map. I had seen him conducting this piece years earlier during a Montreal Festival concert in the early Sixties. He started to direct by holding his right arm straight up, symbolizing 12 o'clock. As the arm (his arm) of the clock slowly moved, different sections of the orchestra were supposed to play or improvise.

This particular time, instead of "conducting" the piece, Cage had a black contraption going around like the hand of a clock. After the concert I went backstage to congratulate Bernstein. John Cage was also there. I grabbed Cage's hand and told him "Bravo Maestro, last time I saw you conduct this piece

**At the Banff School of Fine Arts, 1970's, directing a Youth Orchestra.
I always get tremendous pleasure working with young musicians.**

in Montreal. I must tell you that your conducting technique
has improved a lot!" He had a sense of humor, so he had a
good laugh.

Cage once gave a lecture at McGill University. The lecture
was about one hour long, and while he read his lecture, the
lecture was also played on a tape recorder. When the lecture
was over, Eric McLean, the music critic of The Montreal Star
said, "Mr. Cage, we couldn't understand one word of what
you said!" He answered, "This is how it was meant to be."

The spokespersons of the Avant-Garde movement officially
buried classical music with pronouncements like "Classical
music belongs in the museum," and similar statements. My
answer is then that breathing, the heartbeat, and the rest of
the metabolic processes belong in the museum. In my
opinion, the eighteenth and nineteenth centuries when
classical music reached its apotheosis have been the highest
achievement of the human spirit.

We as humans function within a space-time continuum.
We go from here to there. We return to the starting point.

Les Préludes

Everything has to relate to something else. Moreover, classical music's tonality, tonal centre, its increasing tension and resolution in harmony, melody, and dynamics all correspond directly to our human experience. Our heart functions like an internal combustion engine where an active action is followed by a rest period. If our heart did not have its regular rest periods, we would not live very long.

In the early Seventies, in order to find out what was really going on in the avant-garde circles, I travelled to Donaueschingen, West Germany, where every year an avant-garde music festival was held under the guidance of Pierre Boulez, avant-garde composer and former Music Director of the New York Philharmonic Orchestra. This turned out to be a real eye opener.

I distinctly remember a piece by an Israeli composer, called House in Darkness. Both the title and the work itself spoke volumes to me about the whole avant-garde scene. The Sudwestdeutcher Symphony Orchestra (based in Stuttgart) was in the centre of the stage. There were banks of loud speakers placed on both sides of the orchestra. The piece, which lasted about twenty minutes, consisted only of various sonorities and dynamics. It had no melody, no rhythm, and no tonality. At one point these sounds came from one bank of speakers and the orchestra provided competing sounds simultaneously. The sonorities went from soft to loud and vice versa, while commuting between the various sources of sound. In my opinion, it was not just the "House" which was in complete darkness, but also the audience. After a couple of minutes I, and most of the audience, lost interest in this composition, which I will not call music. I couldn't find a better definition of the present status of avant-garde music than the performance and the title of House in Darkness.

Quixotically, the "avant-garde" is a kind of tyranny — either "you are with us, or you are not 'au courant.'" This has led to avant-garde artists writing almost exclusively for each other. Fortunately, for the audience and for classical music, some very gifted young composers have begun to write again for the audience, writing tonal music and even bringing back some romantic elements.

Chapter Forty

THE VICTORIA SUMMER FESTIVAL 1972 - 1976

It was the spring of 1972, and things were going very well four years into my term as Music Director of the Victoria Symphony Orchestra. We were playing to nearly full houses, the musical standards of the orchestra had improved by leaps and bounds, we had wonderful international star soloists playing with us; and we were extending our concerts north up the length of Vancouver Island to smaller communities, which had never hosted full orchestral concerts.

Where could we go from here? In the late 1960's, Victoria attracted nearly two million visitors, most of whom came during the summer months. As I have alluded to in an earlier chapter of the book, I suggested to the Board that we start a Summer Festival. I was turned down. Not to be denied, I asked the Board if they had any objection to my creating a Summer Festival. The answer was no, and I took this as a green light.

We formed a small board consisting of people who would be actively involved in the Festival: John Di Castri, an architect, who was, at the time, the President of The Victoria Symphony Society; Myfanwy Pavelic, the great Canadian painter, who would be in charge of exhibitions and the visual arts aspects of the Festival, and Karl Spreitz who would be in charge of the film portion of the Festival. Many other prominent citizens joined in.

The University of Victoria had previously run the Victoria Festival Society so we added the word "summer" and shortly

Les Préludes

**Inaugrating the Victoria Summer Festival
with Victoria MayorPeter Pollen.**

thereafter the "Victoria Summer Festival Society" was incorporated as a non profit organization.

I worked fiendishly on three different budgets that were to be presented to City Council. One of the budgets presented a three week festival for $15,000, another one a four week festival for $25,000, and one a grand and ambitious five week celebration of art for $30,000.

Before I made my submission to the City Council, I got the Provincial Secretary and the Canada Council to promise that they would match any amount of money I could raise from the City of Victoria.

As well as money questions, there was the question of venues, particularly a venue for the orchestra. Where could they play which would be sufficiently public and scenic, close enough to the city centre, yet still have the opportunity for crowd control and ticket sales?

Centennial Square, in Victoria, is a lovely place, surrounded by the City Hall, the McPherson Playhouse, a restaurant, a four-story parking lot and some small stores and boutiques, including an Air Canada ticket office. It has a lovely fountain in the centre, with steps leading down from it to a little garden and the doors of the foyer of the McPherson Playhouse, forming a natural amphitheater. After office hours, this was one of the quietest places in downtown Victoria. Only occasionally would an elderly Chinese person wander through the square on his way to a senior citizen centre.

I planned to cordon off the square in the evening, set my orchestra in the middle of the amphitheatre and charge for the tickets. Everything was ready to present my plan to the Municipal Council. Finally, it was my turn. I told the Municipal Council about the commitment of the Provincial Government and The Canada Council to match the funds they would be willing to allocate for the Festival. I also presented the three versions of the budget depending on the available funds and the length of the Festival. I made points about the positive effects on tourism and the additional international prestige which Victoria would likely receive from hosting such a festival.

And the Council turned down my request.

The venue directly in front of the Provincial Museum was very popular with tourists.

With another politician in another outdoor concert venue of the Victoria Summer Festival.

Their chief argument was that Centennial Square is a public thoroughfare and can not be adequately cordoned off. One council member, who was running the 'London double-decker Tour buses, suggested, "Why don't you make the concerts free, then you don't have to cordon of Centennial Square in order to charge for the tickets?" Council Meetings are regularly attended by the media. When I was leaving the chambers, one reporter asked me "How does it feel to be turned down?" I answered him: "This is not the end, just the beginning!"

Next Monday, I was back at the Council Meeting. When my turn came, I told the Council that our Board decided to accept the Councilman's suggestion that we would not charge an entrance fee so we didn't have to cordon off Centennial Square. The Council accepted our proposition for a three-week festival with a budget of $15,000. They allocated $5,000 and named the alderman who suggested the free concerts to liaise with the Festival. I went to his home after the meeting and found him cursing up and down, calling me all kinds of names for being so shrewd and causing him to have another headache. He was joking...half-heartedly.

With the $5,000 from the City of Victoria, added to the $5,000 from the Provincial Government and the $5,000 from the Canada Council, the Festival had a grand total budget of $15,000, which was a very reasonable sum in 1972. Five years later, when I relinquished the Festival to the Victoria Symphony Orchestra, the budget had more than quintupled, to $85,000. All in all, the Victoria Summer Festival turned out to be one of the most rewarding experiences of my career

The format of the concerts was hectic, but very rewarding. Monday, Wednesday and Friday evenings the orchestra gave two one-hour concerts, each preceded by a half an hour rehearsal at the Heritage Court of the Provincial Museum. On Sunday afternoons, we performed either in the Band Shell in Beacon Hill Park, or in parks and halls in neighboring municipalities, in particular, Esquimalt, Saanich, and Oak Bay. These municipalities provided the extra funding needed to put on these performances.

Here is Market Square, also pictured on the previous page. I loved the intimacy and the informality of performing outside.

Conducting outside at the Festival

Before starting the actual concert series, we had six to eight rehearsals to prepare the basic repertory, which we varied every time, also adding new repertory with the half an hour rehearsals prior to each concert. Before each concert, we had some light classical music and announcements promoting the concerts on the PA system. In the Festival brochures, people were asked to bring their own chairs, pillows, and blankets to sit or lie on. It was also arranged, that in case of rain, the concerts would take place in alternative venues, in Victoria's case, in Christ Church Cathedral. This was prudent since the very first performance of the very first Summer Festival Concert did take place in the cathedral because of rain.

During the five years of the Festival, we fulfilled my greater goal, which was to bring symphonic music out of the concert hall and to a greater audience. Handicapped people in wheelchairs, children, babies, dogs, seniors, tourists, visitors, music lovers and all kinds of people were being exposed for

My family, about 1971, after my parents moved to Victoria. From left, Kathy, Agnes, my mother, Suzanne, me, and my father. Though my father never spoke very much, he attended all of my concerts and I knew he was proud of me and my accomplishments.

perhaps the first time in their lives to a symphony orchestra and symphonic music.

The atmosphere was simply magical. Not once did a baby cry or a dog bark while the orchestra was playing.

Naturally, in such uncontrolled surroundings, funny things happened. Victoria is a harbor city, and various transport ships, tugs, and ferries use the harbor. For the audience at such an open-air concert, the sight of a large seagoing ship passing silently behind the conductor and the orchestra would make the whole performance extra special.

I remember a performance of Beethoven's Leonore Overture No. 3 that took place on a lovely summer evening. To warm up, I told the audience a funny, true story. In the Leonore Overture a trumpet player is supposed to play a signal, out of sight, from back stage, to announce the arrival of the governor. At one performance, I continued, a fireman rudely stopped the backstage trumpeter from playing his piece, telling him that he could not play because there was a performance on the stage. The audience, naturally, had a good laugh and I turned to commence conducting the piece. We reached the spot in the overture when Boyd Hood, our First Trumpet, was supposed to play. At this very moment the horn of the Black Ball Ferry sounded. The audience, the musicians, and I all broke down laughing, and poor Boyd couldn't play. We had to start the overture all over again!

Outdoor concerts also had other challenges. The Heritage Court at the Provincial Museum, where the concerts took place during the week, was a real wind tunnel, and we quite often experienced windy conditions. Though it kept the sailors happy, the wind made it difficult for the musicians to keep the music on their music stands, and I had to buy special long wood-and-plastic clips to hold the music in place. In the early days I used my camper-van to shelter the musicians on at least one side from the wind, but soon the increasing popularity and importance of the Festival brought the Public Works Department of the Provincial Government onside, and they could not do enough to help us. To shelter us from the effects of the wind, they built a wooden barrier along the walkways above the orchestra. However, the barrier wasn't much help, so by the third year of the Festival, Public Works bought us a mobile stage with a built-in sound system for $48,000, the equivalent of the whole of the Festival's budget.

We decorated the stage with blue awnings and a blue "skirt" in front. It looked lovely and the new mobile stage provided the orchestra with some protection from the wind.

One summer, I was working with the Courtenay Youth Music Camp in Courtenay, a small logging and fishing community, about one hundred miles north of Victoria. We were preparing Mozart's Cosi fan Tutte with the producer and director of the Vancouver Opera. The audience was composed mainly of music students and teachers, family members and retired persons. The production was such a success that we took the whole thing to Victoria for the Summer Festival. For the performance in Victoria, we rented a hall in Oak Bay.

This is a great example of how arts activity benefits the community. For the performance, we had to upgrade the electricity in the hall to accommodate all our lighting needs. This was great for the hall because it could now take on other performers and performing troupes. In exchange for providing the upgrade, we asked for a discount on the rental.

During the Festival, I had a string quartet playing at noon in the Rotunda of the Provincial Legislature. You can imagine how impressed the tourists were, that we had such culturally enlightened politicians, having a string quartet playing in the legislature!

In the second year of the Festival we had an exhibition of some works of the Limners in the Provincial Archives Building. The Limners were a prominent group of Victoria painters, sculptors and other artists. A grand official opening took place.

An old building in downtown Victoria had been refurbished, very nicely, into a development called Harbour Square. It had all kinds of little boutiques, a bookstore, various food stores, including a little fish-stall, restaurant, and more. The building had one great problem, however: it had no customers. It was practically deserted.

When I visited the building for the first time, I realized the great potential that the courtyard had for concerts. I went to see the manager who turned out to be a young fellow managing the building for a Calgary real estate company. I told him that this building would serve as an ideal venue for concerts and that we could bring in thousands of people. I told him if he could give us $10,000, we could give them five concerts. I had the money the very next day.

Every year there was a grand official opening at the Provincial Archives Building with the Mayor of Victoria and other dignitaries attending. Our first concert at Harbour Square featuring the great jazz flutist, Paul Horn, was a great success. It attracted a couple of thousand people. Not only were people seated on the floor right in front of the orchestra, but they were also hanging from the landings two floors above the orchestra. We all got nice, yellow MARKET SQUARE T-shirts from the company and these concerts became an annual event for the duration of the Festival.

We made arrangements with the National Film Board of Canada to have regular film showings after the concerts in the Newcombe Auditorium of the Provincial Museum. We received some wonderful documentaries at no charge. In the last few years of the Festival, we established a close relationship with the J.J.Johanessen International Music School. Many of their outstanding artists performed with us: Ruggiero Ricci, Janos Starker, Lorand Fenyves, Gary Karr, and others. From 1972 through 1976, the Victoria Summer Festival became a fixture in Victoria's musical life and one of its major tourist attractions.

But during these five years, some members of the Victoria Symphony Board became jealous of the success and wanted to take over the Festival. They started to circulate ugly rumors that my wife and daughters were on the payroll of the Festival. I got so upset that I offered to sell the assets and the whole organization of The Victoria Summer Festival to the Victoria Symphony Society for $1, an offer which they graciously accepted.

By next season, the Victoria Festival was gone. Perhaps it was a symbolic gesture that the Provincial Government, soon after, sold the mobile sound stage that they originally bought for us.

Over and over in my career, I have witnessed people who were insignificant in regular life, but suddenly acted like "Big Shots" when they became board members of community cultural organizations. A good description of those people who go from board to board is that they are building their obituaries!

Nobody checks what these destructive egotists do on the boards of various organizations. How many organizations have been destroyed by these careerist board members? How many significant cultural events have been established and then pulled down? The recent scandals involving billions of dollars misplaced by various CEO's under the noses of their "experienced and knowledgeable" board members show the inherent weaknesses of board structure. These new scandals exposed corporate thieves of the highest order, but the criminals are little different from the egos which involve themselves at the community level. These are "community thieves". And they destroyed the Victoria Summer Festival.

In the end, I spent five years of hard work, reaped

tremendous rewards, contributed to the enhancement of the community, enjoyed a great deal of pleasure and came out with a grand profit of $1.

FINAL REPORT ON THE 1976 VICTORIA SUMMER FESTIVAL SUBMITTED TO THE CANADA COUNCIL

"I have the pleasure in submitting the final report of the 1976 Victoria Summer Festival which, this year, surpassed all our most optimistic expectations, in spite of rather unstable weather. The 1976 Festival drew an estimated audience of 90,000 people to the various programmes."

"During this 1976 season, the Festival Orchestra presented 47 concerts. The programmes consisted of 17 double concerts (back to back), held at Heritage Court and the Newcombe Auditorium of the Provincial Museum; 6 weekend concerts in various parks and auditoriums of Victoria, Saanich, and Oak Bay. A tremendously popular new series was presented in a downtown shopping area, Market Square, on five consecutive Thursday evenings, and one Sunday morning. This series was fully underwritten by Abacus Cities Limited, and the merchants of Market Square, and was one of the highlights of the season, attracting huge crowds (between 3,000 and 4,000 on the opening night alone). We were fortunate to present as soloists at these concerts Paul Horn, famous jazz flutist, Jack Rothstein, Concertmaster of the St-Martin-in-the-Fields Orchestra and other outstanding soloists."

"With the help of a student grant, we established a Festival String Quartet, which presented 27 noon hour concerts in the Parliament Buildings of B.C."

"The Department of Public Works had special signs made up, publicizing concerts in the Parliament Buildings and in the Museum, and also all the Guides were instructed to promote the concerts, which proved extremely popular with tourists and Victorians alike."

"We presented, for the fourth consecutive year, our Film Festival, which consisted of 15 film showings, following the Monday, Wednesday, and Friday concerts in the Newcombe Auditorium. The films also played to full houses."

"This year, we incorporated two exhibitions in the Festival shown at the Provincial Archives Building, "Into the Silent Land" – Survey of Photography in the Canadian West 1850 – 1900. A Public Archives of the Canada Travelling Exhibition was presented until August 11th, and the Japanese Canadian Centennial Exhibition from August 18th."

Les Préludes

"We presented excerpts from the Marriage of Figaro, with the cast of the Vancouver Island Operatic Society in the Cedar Hill Community Centre as part of a very successful all-Mozart programme."

"The Festival was officially opened by the Minister of Lands, Forests, and Water Resources, the Hon. T.M. Waterland, representing the Province of British Columbia, and Acting Mayor Alderman Hood, representing the City of Victoria."

"We had a very active promotion campaign this year, locally, nationally and internationally. The Festival was promoted through the B.C. Calendar of Events in the States, in the Victoria Visitors Guide, which appears in 250,000 copies and is distributed both in the States and Canada. The Arts Calendar of the Community Arts Council of Greater Victoria used the logo of the Festival on the cover of their Summer Issue for 1976, and gave extensive coverage to the activities and concerts. We ourselves printed 60,000 brochures which were distributed on the B.C. Ferries Service. The Read-o-gram of the B.C. Ferries at the Tsawassen Terminal featured details of the Summer Festival. The Downtown Business Association circulated their membership with Festival details, and displayed 300 posters in the City. 15,000 flyers were handed out on Government Street, and other downtown areas for the Market Square concerts. We had detailed ads in the weekend papers for the week's concerts, and daily ads in the Entertainment Section of the papers, also extensive public service radio coverage."

"As in the past, all events of the Victoria Summer Festival were free, including two concerts sponsored by the Music Performance Trust Fund through the Victoria Local of the AF of M."

"We presented twenty-eight soloists, some more than once, including such artists of international caliber, as Tsuyoshi Tsutsumi, Ruggierio Ricci, and Kajya Danczowska, Polish violinist (she and Ruggiero Ricci appeared with us courtesy of Shawnigan Summer School of the Arts). We enclose detailed lists of soloists, both instrumental and vocal."

"As soon as the audited financial statements are available, the usual copies will be forwarded to the Council. We expect to balance our books."

"The Directors of the Victoria Summer Festival wish to express their gratitude to the Canada Council for their generous support over the last five years of this unique Festival. We emphasized the role of the Canada Council in sponsoring the festival in all our promotional material, and in our advertising."

Yours sincerely,

J. Bristol Foster
President

And one year later, the Summer Festival was gone. It is now 2004, and neither Festival, nor anything like it has ever been presented in Victoria in the 28 years since I left it in the hands of the Board.

Les Préludes

Chapter Forty One

CONDUCTORS - 4

GREAT CONDUCTORS

What makes a great conductor? The musical performance. That is all. A conductor is great when the music lives every second, and when every second is a magical experience. All conductors experience a few great moments in a career. I call them "Holy Moments" because they take me out of this world and into a different existence. Great conductors produce these moments often.

In my opinion, at any one time in the world, there are only about five outstanding artists alive and working in each field. Five or so great violinists. Five or so great composers, and about five or so great conductors who stand far above the rest. In my opinion, from over seventy years of experience, the world is going through a significant down-time in terms of conductors. The overall standard is lower than it was fifty years ago.

Every great conductor's technique is unique to him. Some conductors coax fabulous music out of the tiniest motions of their baton. Others use the entire length of the arms through their whole range of motion in order to bring the audience into the performance. Some conductors use their hands and fingers delicately, and move their heads, lift their eyebrows, and use eye contact to direct the orchestra. Exceptional conductors are not limited to any particular technique; they have found something that works for them and them alone. Copying a great conductor's moves on the podium will not make a mediocre conductor good, or a good conductor great. It has been tried.

I really hate to say this: most great soloists do not make very good conductors. I have played with, been conducted by, and conducted with many of the greatest artists of the Twentieth century. Piano soloists, violin virtuosi, cello geniuses; I have been affected by their music, even said they played like gods in this very manuscript and meant every word. But instrumental virtuosity is no guarantee of virtuosity at the conductor's stand.

There is a little story about this. I had an interesting experience in the late Fifties when I was working as both an orchestra musician and conductor. Zubin Mehta had just started out on his conducting career as Music Director of the Montreal Symphony Orchestra, and he had a fairly limited repertoire and a lack of experience as a conductor. He was conducting Dvorak's New World Symphony at the Montreal Forum, which happened to be the home of the Montreal Canadiens hockey team. He wanted to hear the orchestra from the auditorium and asked me to conduct the Fourth movement of the symphony. I had a dilemma. In my opinion, he had conducted this movement much slower than it should be done. What should I do? Should I take his tempo or mine? I decided to take my tempo. I think he got the message because at the concert he took the movement much faster.

Being strong and healthy is good for any profession at any age, but I have witnessed some conductors not far from a mortal heart attack, but still able to make divine music. I had the privilege to be a musician working with Otto Klemperer in the late 1940's. By that time he was an old man and due to a brain tumor operation, he was partially paralyzed on his right side. He could not even hold a baton in his right hand, but this did not interfere with his ability to direct wonderful performances.

Only seventy years ago, there was not a single North American-born conductor, and many Europeans thought there never would be. Most conductors have been European because Europe was the cradle of classical music; it had the infrastructure of teachers, schools, composers, orchestras, and performances to nurture the class of conductors. Music and talent do not respect race or religion. What is important for a conductor is his musical insight and his ability to communicate this to both the orchestra and the audience. In the second half of the last century a number of outstanding Chinese, Japanese and Korean classical artists have emerged, including conductors. They have absorbed Western European music as their mother-tongue, demonstrating the universality of this music.

Once a conductor has been active and performed the standard classic repertoire for twenty or more years, and particularly if he has specialized in a certain area, he can often conduct from memory. But this memory comes not only from many performances, but from long and detailed study, and concentrated thought on the musical scores. Some conductors have a photographic memory. When an older conductor was asked his opinion about this phenomenon he said, "The problem is that they still have to turn the pages of the score and you can hear that." Memory alone does not make a great conductor.

The first ingredient of an exceptional conductor is a personal repertoire. Though any good conductor should be able to conduct anything in the classical canon, from Fifteenth to Twentieth Century music, most prominent conductors show their greatness in a particular area of music. It might be Baroque, or Romantic, two periods of music. Or it might be ethnicity, as was the case of Charles Munch, who was a fabulous conductor of French music; his performances of Debussy, Ravel, and other composers were beautiful. He was not as good in other kinds of classical music.

Noteworthy visual artists have superior visualization skills. They can look at a book and see a scene; they can look at a commonplace view and see within it a painting. Conductors are aural artists, so they must have superior auralization skills. A conductor can read a score the way a film director reads a book; a conductor calls it reading "below the score." The conductor creates a soundscape from the score which exists only in his mind. He builds this inner soundscape slowly, taking months, or even years. That is what great conductors do: they create a complete soundscape which reveals the true structure of the piece.

Now the conductor has to collaborate with the musicians and the audience. The conductor must, through psychology, and technique, get all three participants — himself, the musicians and the audience — on the same wavelength, breathing in unison, and holding themselves in anticipation at the same moment. As a musical guide, the conductor seems to say to the audience, "watch this beautiful scenery, see that beautiful mountain, this meadow, those flowers, that waterfall," through the soundscape he has imagined.

Great conductors can deal with stress. I mentioned before how just before a solo, an orchestral soloist's blood pressure can rise above two hundred. Multiply that pressure for a conductor. This person has the responsibility to honor the composer, direct the music, and respond to the audience (which he cannot see because they are behind his back). And he must place his soundscape at the mercy of the moment. Years of work will be expressed in an hour or less, never to be reproduced.

Conducting is a stressful job.

Listen to the following conductors, whom I consider some of the greatest of the Twentieth Century: Otto Klemperer, conducting Beethoven and Mozart; Charles Munch conducting French repertory; Toscanini conducting Verdi; Carlo Giulini, Erich and Carlos Kleiber in German repertory and Mario Rossi to name but a few. I am not going to describe their styles or effects or give them compliments. Words cannot describe music.

The listener is the only one who can provide that description.

Chapter Forty Two

THE PERFORMING ARTIST AND MANIC DEPRESSION - 1975

The higher an artist aims in his art, and especially if he does manage to reach some great highs, he must be prepared for long period of lows. This corresponds very much with the symptoms of manic depression. To reach those highs, the artist must be so goal-oriented that it borders on obsession, and the effort required to reach that goal looks like mania to those not similarly possessed. For instance, a performing artist might spend many hours a day for weeks, months, years and even decades studying a particular piece, developing his/her concept of the piece, working out the means of conveying this inner image to an audience which is being exposed to only a single hearing of this concept.

To leave a deep impression on the psyche of the audience, to burn an indelible memory of a certain passage, to shine a climax onto the retina of the inner eye, to penetrate and to touch the innermost being of the audience, all require an effort of incredible intensity. After a performance of such demands, and after the rewards of the standing ovations, bravos, and adulation, the artist finds himself alone in the dressing room.

After changing out of the perspiration-soaked formal dress, he or she most often heads home alone or to an empty hotel room. The sudden calm and silence seem almost deafening after the intensity of the music-making and the roar of the audience. The feeling of loneliness is overwhelming.

For myself, it takes several hours to come down from the high of a concert. I usually tape my concerts and upon returning home, I listen to the whole concert so that I can ease myself down, rather than crash from on high.

It was June 1975. I was at the Kennedy Airport in New York, on my way to Guatemala to fulfill a guest conducting engagement. I had already checked in for my flight, and purchased a bottle of scotch and some cigarettes for my friend, the music director of the orchestra in Guatemala. I can even remember carrying the music for Tchaikovsky's First Piano Concerto. I had made detailed plans for the trip. After my concerts in Guatemala, I would fly to Mexico City. There, I would rent a Volkswagen and commit suicide by hitting something, an embankment, or whatever on the Periferico, the circular highway around Mexico City.

The inner turmoil must have shown in my behavior and on my face. I slumped despondently in my seat on the shuttle bus during the ride between terminals. When we arrived the driver asked me, "Is anything wrong?" "No, nothing," I answered, and got off the bus. I had a long waiting period for my flight to Guatemala, and I was getting more and more distressed, agitated, and depressed. There are many types of depression. There is the depression which robs you of all energy and will. And then there is the depression which fills you with an intolerable bubbling misery, a pain which demands, screams for some action to resolve it. Finally, I phoned my wife in Victoria, British Columbia, telling her that I felt extremely depressed and I didn't think that I would be able to fulfill my obligations. Agnes was not aware of my suicide plans. She knew only that I was somewhat depressed when I had left Victoria hours ago.

Agnes promised to contact Dr. Solymar in Montreal; Dr. Solymar had been our family doctor when we lived in Montreal from 1957 - 1967 and he remained a close family friend. She would ask him for help and advice, and I was to call her back in an hour. It being Sunday, my chances of finding a solution to my immediate misery seemed very remote. When I phoned her back, she said, "I spoke to Doctor Solymar. He contacted his friend, a psychiatrist, named Dr. Solyom at the Allen Memorial Institute at the Royal Victoria

Hospital in Montreal. He made arrangements at the Hospital for you to be accepted as a patient."

It was quite a hassle to get my luggage back, which had already been checked for the flight to Guatemala. I had to cancel my duty-free purchases and my reservation for the flight, then I made a reservation for a flight to Montreal. I finally arrived at the Victoria Hospital in the late afternoon. Then I had to wait for more than an hour, until they found two young doctors who were doing their internship at the hospital, to admit me.

They questioned me at length and in great detail. By this time, I started to feel much better and wanted to continue my trip, although I had already phoned my friend in Guatemala from the Kennedy Airport to tell him that I was not coming.

Dr. Solyom was nowhere to be found and I was getting more and more despondent from wanting to continue my trip. In the meantime, it was getting quite late, and the young doctors convinced me to wait until next morning to speak with Dr. Solyom and decide then if I should go or not. Just in case, I phoned my friend in Guatemala, again telling him to hold fire and not to do anything until he heard from me.

The hospital didn't have any room available on the ward, since it was now after 10 P.M. They put a bed in a storage room, which was full of bedpans, sheets, and other hospital paraphernalia. I was given some sleeping pills and finally I managed to go to sleep. Next morning, I woke up full of beans and ready to go — as in leave. Again they could not find Dr. Solyom. At the time, I didn't know that I could have discharged myself from the hospital since I had come voluntarily and I was not committed. I became an expert on this subject later.

I phoned Guatemala again and told my friend to hang on until he heard from me — yet again. It was already noon when Dr. Solyom, a short, balding fellow, finally showed up. I told him that I felt fine and that I wanted to continue my trip and fulfill my obligations. He told me that my state of indecision, "now you feel depressed and you cannot go; now you feel fine and you want to go" is a typical symptom of manic- depressive illness. Eight years later at the Clark Institute in Toronto, this diagnosis was changed to hypomanic illness — a milder form of manic depression.

He said: "It is like having a green and red shirt. When you put on the green shirt you want to wear the red shirt. On the other hand, when you put on the red shirt, you want to wear the green shirt." I kept insisting that I felt fine, and that I wanted to go to Guatemala. Finally, we compromised. He would give me some antidepressants to take and, depending on how I felt the next day, we would decide whether I should go or stay.

As I still had a couple of days left before I was supposed to start rehearsing for my first concert in Guatemala, I phoned again my friend asking him not to make any move to replace me until the next day, when I would give him a definite answer.

Next day I felt medium-lousy and Dr. Solyom simply disappeared and was nowhere to be found. I walked aimlessly on the ward, visiting with some other patients, debating with myself whether I should go or not go. All day long, I kept asking the nurses to contact Dr. Solyom, but to no avail. Finally, I could not keep my friend, Jose Sarmientos, in Guatemala in suspense any longer. He needed time to find somebody to replace me, as he was supposed to be guest-conducting in Mexico while I would have been conducting his orchestra in Guatemala. I phoned him one last time to tell him that I was not coming.

The die was cast.

Dr. Solyom finally showed up the next day. In retrospect, I realize that he was deliberately "not to be found" when I tried desperately to contact him. He put me on an antidepressant called Nardil, and I was transferred from the closet to a proper room. I started to settle down to the routine of the ward. Pill time, feeding time, bed time, recreation time, TV time, etc. I had a very small, cell-like room whose ambience was not improved by the steel grates covering the window. There was hardly enough space to walk past the single, metal-framed bed and night table. I put my luggage in the steel closet. All in all, hardly the place for a severely depressed person, but much better and safer than being outside on my own.

It was summer in Montreal and the weather was extremely hot and humid. I had no air-conditioning in my room, so I slept naked. The first morning the Head Nurse discovered me; she gave me hell for doing this and insisted I dress properly. As I had my full-dress conducting outfit in my luggage, I dressed up, the very next evening in my white bow tie and nothing else. After that, they stopped complaining.

I "made the rounds" of the ward, visiting various rooms, talking to patients. I met a nice young girl of about fifteen in one of the rooms, who was also in the hospital for depression. I found her quite intelligent, with a good sense of humor. Six weeks later, when I left finally the hospital, she had become a "vegetable", totally unable to communicate. It was my first encounter with the "success" of some psychiatric treatments.

In another of the rooms, I found a chain-smoking patient. In the Seventies, smoking was still allowed in hospitals. He sat in an armchair, the ashtray full of cigarette butts, afraid even to leave his room. It turned out he was the manager of a branch of a trust company and he had developed a paralyzing fear complex. I visited him regularly and had nice conversations with him. First, I got him to come along with me for a stroll on the hospital grounds. A few weeks later when they let me leave the hospital on my own, I convinced him to come with me for a walk outside the hospital. He squeezed my arm tightly and trembled when we crossed the street. A few weeks later, he was allowed to go home to visit his wife and shortly afterwards he was discharged from the hospital. He was my first successfully treated "patient".

While I was kept on Nardil, nobody had advised me that one of the side effects of the drug was to make you high — really high! I felt elated, powerful, competent, ready to tackle the world, even grandiose. My mind bubbled, coming up with all kinds of crazy ideas. I even contacted the Johnny Carson Show, to invite me as a guest to his show on NBC. I offered to do funny things that many orchestra musicians and conductors would have liked to do, but could not, such as smashing a violin over a fellow musician's head, standing up and telling off the conductor, sharing with the audience how boring a concert actually was, and other such slapstick. Luckily, the NBC officials thought otherwise and chose not to invite me.

Over the weeks, as I was allowed more freedom, I was permitted to leave the hospital so I spent my time visiting old friends and old haunts from my decade in Montreal. One weekend I went to Val Morin in the Laurentians to the yoga camp of Swami Vishnuvenanda, where my daughters Suzanne and Kathy and my wife and I had spent some happy times ten years earlier. I thought that seeing some old friends there, meditating and doing some yoga asanas would do me good.

Back in the hospital, I tried out other means of treating manic-depression. I was on drugs, of course, but I tried psychotherapy, "talk therapy", and some other innovative approaches. In one experiment, my doctors put a biometric band on my head that was connected to a needle in some kind of instrument. You had to try to keep the needle steady by calming yourself and totally relaxing.

What I found very strange was that each psychiatrist was not only proposing his own unique treatment, but was actively denigrating the other doctors' methods of treatment. Those believing in chemical treatment, including my own doctor, dismissed psychotherapy, biofeedback, and most of the other tactics which were tried on me. The psychotherapists and psychoanalysts on the other hand, sneered at the chemical treatments my brain was soaking in.

I confronted our Head Nurse with this problem at one of our ward meetings. She stated that it was up to us, the patients, to choose the best treatment. It seemed to me that it bordered on the farcical to expect patients (in various degrees of depression) who considered the smallest decision a major task, to decide for themselves which treatment among the many offered was the most appropriate.

I stayed a total of six weeks at the hospital. During this time Dr. Solyom kept experimenting on me with different antidepressants with various results. Some drugs made me nauseated, some caused vertigo; some made me perspire heavily, or inspired flights of fancy. Finally, I left for Tarrytown, New York, where my wife joined me and where I was conducting a couple of concerts at a summer music festival. I did just fine, though I was to have a number of other depressive and suicidal episodes through the 1970's and 1980's.

After many years of being in and out of various hospitals and psychiatric wards, I have come to the conclusion that, besides trying to make it difficult, though not impossible for patients to commit suicide, most psychiatric wards are simply holding pens for the patients who mill around for days, weeks, months, and even years, while the psychiatrists try to find the 'magic bullet' to cure or at least diminish the symptoms of their depression.

Les Préludes

Chapter Forty Three

THE BOGOTA PHILHARMONIC ORCHESTRA - 1978

On the recommendation of my good friend Eduardo Rahn, the Music Director of the Maracaibo Symphony Orchestra of Venezuela, I was invited to be Principal Guest-Conductor of the Bogotá Philharmonic Orchestra for the 1978-1979 Season. As I had ended my eleven years of tenure as Music Director of the Victoria Symphony Orchestra at the end of the 1977-1978 Season, this invitation came at the perfect time. The position gave me an income without requiring me and my family to move to South America; I would travel to Columbia to rehearse and conduct the concerts, but otherwise I would reside in Canada while I looked for a long-term position, either in Canada or elsewhere.

Having spent the first twenty years of my life in Romania, which is basically a Latin country (though it is geographically in Eastern Europe), and having conducted quite regularly in Mexico and Venezuela since 1958, I always felt at home among Latin people. From my experiences I had found Latin American people to be warmhearted, loving and lovable, so I looked forward to this new assignment. The placement in Bogotá also gave me a good chance to perfect my Spanish.

The orchestra secured me a lovely apartment in a good section of the city, with excellent shops and restaurants within walking distance. Bogotá de Santa Fe, the capital of Colombia, is a major metropolis with a population of close to six million people. It is the industrial, educational and cultural centre of Colombia. Bogotá is situated at 2800 metres (about

8500 feet) above sea level. It took me some time to get acclimatized to the altitude. Even coming from Mexico City, which is 7500 feet high, I felt the difference in air density. Bogotá, like Caracas, Mexico City and most other Latin American cities, is a city of contrasts. Beautiful buildings, skyscrapers, modern homes and shanty towns share the urban landscape, where extremely rich people, foreign businessmen and diplomats live behind barricades and armed guards, while thousands of children are being born on the street, living and dying on the street

Bogotá had two symphonic orchestras at the time— the National Symphony Orchestra and the Bogotá Philharmonic Orchestra. The National Symphony Orchestra concentrated on regularly scheduled symphony concerts and opera performances. My new orchestra, the Bogotá Philharmonic Orchestra, gave its weekly concerts in the Convocation Centre of the National University of Colombia. We would also perform in weekly television concerts and travel through Columbia to perform in other cities. The Bogotá Philharmonic Orchestra had some excellent musicians and the standard of playing was quite high. They had a wide repertoire, from Bach to Schoenberg, Stravinsky and beyond. Musically speaking, my work with the orchestra was very rewarding.

Conducting is 90% psychology and only 10% music and musicianship. The conductor's 'instrument' is a 'hydra' with a hundred heads (the one hundred musicians of the orchestra). Getting these highly-trained, dedicated, proud professionals to follow your musical intentions without feeling coerced or pressured is a complex psychological game. As I have been for years both a conductor and an orchestra musician, I know that the greatest feeling an orchestral player can have is to feel that he is playing as he wants to play while he is actually following the conductor's directions. In this scenario there is effort, but no conflict between the two sides, and from there flow the best performances.

Conductors can easily establish a negative relationship with the orchestra by being constantly critical of the players. Now, criticism is a necessary part of the process of preparing, rehearsing, and performing demanding classical music.

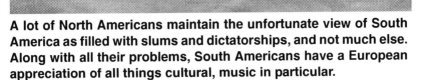

48 AÑOS DE SU FUNDACION

Sociedad

Orquesta Sinfónica Venezuela

TEMPORADA 1978   Viernes, 2 y Domingo 4 de Junio

TEATRO MUNICIPAL

Director: LASZLO GATI   Solistas: JAIME LAREDO (Violín)
SHARON ROBINSON (Cellista)

A lot of North Americans maintain the unfortunate view of South America as filled with slums and dictatorships, and not much else. Along with all their problems, South Americans have a European appreciation of all things cultural, music in particular.

Les Préludes

During the rehearsal of a symphony or other musical piece, the conductor will stop the orchestra in order to correct something or to request something from the players, perhaps a slightly different sound or a changed emphasis or twist in the phrasing. The conductor does not have the time to stop and praise one player or a section about their playing. And so the most frequently occurring aspect of the conductor or the orchestral relationship is the conductor's rebuke and the musicians' grumble. The conductor might be able to communicate through winks, smiles, and little gestures that the players did a good job, even during concerts, though this is not always possible.

Otto Klemperer was perhaps the greatest master in arousing the feelings of cooperation and collaboration with the players. In my experience, playing with Klemperer was for the musician akin to being served by a wonderful butler. This butler would make up your bed and all you (the musician) had to do was to lie down in it and play your heart out to the best of your ability. An orchestra player could spend many frustrating weeks, months and sometimes even years before finally having an uplifting experience like this with a skillful conductor or a talented soloist. Klemperer got the best out of us and was enormously popular with most musicians who worked under his direction.

I established a good working relationship with the musicians of the orchestra and our concerts and television programs were quite successful. I really enjoyed the whole ambiance and new friendships also outside of the orchestra. Though conductors cannot mix too much with musicians for the same reasons that professional sports coaches cannot mix socially with their athletes, I had the excuse of being a stranger in Bogotá, without a private network of friends and family. I accepted the invitation of a couple of musicians to a local spa, where I had a good massage, a steambath, and other pamperings; they also showed me much of the city, the places to go and the things to do. Perhaps these events and some of our trips with the orchestra to other cities were the times I experienced the closest camaraderie I had with them, and considerably closer than I had enjoyed with other orchestras.

Sometimes, when I had a free day I explored the Colombian countryside. At this time, the Cocaine Wars were not so bad so one could travel safely. One time, I visited an underground, full-size cathedral carved out from a former salt mine. The sculptures, carvings and ornaments looked totally realistic and authentic, like a real cathedral, although everything was carved out of salt!

I also found out more about South American culture in general. For instance, the Colombians are rightly proud of speaking the best Spanish in Latin America; by "best" the Colombians mean they speak the purest dialect of European Spanish, and have the best and most classical pronunciation of the language — in their own opinion. Our television producer's husband was a linguist, and he was pleased to bring my pronunciation of Spanish up to a more refined level.

In my career as a conductor, one of the funniest and one of the most rewarding experiences happened during this tenure as Principal Guest Conductor of the Bogotá Philharmonic Orchestra.

The orchestra performed the Shostakovich Piano Concerto several times with a wonderful Colombian pianist. The Concerto starts with a loud bass drum beat. When I came to the first rehearsal of the piece, I saw an interesting, intriguing sight. It was a huge bass-drum unlike anything I had seen. The drum was almost 6 feet high with skin on only one side, and it leant on one side supported by some metal legs. The young percussionist had a huge, metal mallet with a large, soft head, the size of an infant's cranium. The drum produced a wonderful sound and I worked with the percussionist to find the best spot to strike the drum and the best way to produce the ideal sound for the opening of the Shostakovich Concerto. This exceptional instrument produced a wonderful, audience-arresting B-O-O-M for the piece.

After performing the Shostakovich several times in Bogotá, the orchestra flew to Cali, a major city in Colombia, which is now, unfortunately, infamous for drug trafficking. After arriving in the morning and doing some sightseeing, I went to the theatre, changed into my formal wear and prepared for the performance. When I went on stage our famous bass drum was nowhere to be seen. Our young percussionist had only a small bass-drum tied to a chair with a string. He still had in his hand the huge, metal mallet, which of itself was about half the size of the little drum.

I had no idea what had happened and there was no time to find a replacement instrument. So I started the Shostakovich piece and gave a big upbeat for the bass drum. Our dear percussionist hit the tiny bass-drum with full force. The mallet went through both heads of the bass drum and stuck out the other side; worse, the destructive impact produced only a little "pluck."

The young player looked with surprise at the head of the mallet sticking out on the other side of the bass drum and slowly extricated it. The orchestra and I could not stop laughing. I conducted for about five minutes with my left hand in front of my face to cover up my paroxysms of laughter. In Spanish, bass drum is "bombo" and stupid is "loco." After this concert, our young percussionist acquired the nickname 'LOCO-BOMBO'.

I only learned what had happened after the concert. When the orchestra arrived at the airport it turned out that there was no way to get that huge bass drum into the small plane used in inter-city flights. It was just too big! There was no time to go back to the town to get the orchestra's regular bass-drum, so they decided to find one in Cali. Upon arrival, they began looking for a drum. After searching for hours, they finally found an ancient, fragile, tiny bass drum, probably something that the Conquistadores had left behind a few hundred years earlier. The skin of the drum was like totally dried out parchment, brittle and without strength. This is why it hardly produced any sound when the huge mallet went through both skins.

Even now, as I am writing about this episode, it is hard for me not to laugh!

Several times a week I went on early walks exploring various parts of Bogotá. Usually, I started out around six in the morning to avoid the heavy car traffic and air pollution. One morning, I saw a familiar looking statue in the distance. It turned out, as I approached, to be a statue of George

Washington, America's most famous founding father. Huddled around the lower rim of the statue there were six children, ages, perhaps five to twelve, and two dogs. Two of the children didn't have so much as a shirt and the shirts of the others were nothing but rags full of holes. Because of Bogotá's high elevation, the nights and early mornings were sometimes extremely cold, even in the summer. To keep warm, these urchins had supplemented their meagre body heat with various kind of papers laid over them...trash, we would call it. They had even made a little bonfire, the ashes of which discolored their feet. To see these children, starving, cold, and alone, lying at the feet of the great liberator of the American Revolution was to become aware of the bitterness of irony when expressed in this waste and outright destruction of human lives.

This scene speaks volumes of the politics and economics of Latin America. While the local corporations and foreigners, particularly Americans, siphon off the wealth of these countries, the majority of the population lives in abject poverty. One day, I saw a young boy whose 'cupboard' on the street was a little cubbyhole belonging to the water department where he kept his valuables. Travellers should visit the shantytowns, where there is no electricity, no running water, and 'houses' are built out of corrugated iron or cardboard. These shantytowns are slipshod, ramshackle and fragile, as well as filthy, and many are destroyed during the rainy season, when the rushing water washes away the meagre possessions of the poor.

Of course such poverty leads to extreme desperation. Theft, violence, and theft with violence are all too common. A friend of mine saw the following scene. An elegant lady wearing a golden necklace and earrings was walking on the street in broad daylight. Suddenly, three street urchins, ages six to eleven, jumped on her. One tore off her necklace, the two others ripped out her earrings with part of her ear and all three disappeared in a trice, leaving the elegant lady dazed and bleeding.

One day, I jumped on a city bus. As it was a warm day, after I got on I sat down near the open door. In the process of sitting down, somebody jumped into the stairwell, ripped off my Bulova Accutron wristwatch and disappeared! The whole scene took perhaps only a second. I didn't even see the thief's face. I yelled "Stop the bus," and jumped off, but the thief was nowhere to be seen and nobody saw anybody or anything. To this day, I don't know if the bus driver and the thief colluded, because the bus was moving slowly enough for the thief to jump on and off.

When I left Bogotá for the last time, I stopped at the duty free shop and bought a bilingual Seiko wristwatch which showed the days in English and Spanish. Twenty-five years later and many trips to South America later I am still wearing it. I can only assume that it is not as tempting as my golden Accutron.

One day, three young kids (one with a crutch) got onto my crowded bus. They pushed their way through the crowds, all the way to the back of the bus, even brushing against me. When I got off I realized that they had stolen my wallet with all my credit cards. Imagine the nuisance and time involved in replacing all your credit cards and identification. Now imagine doing it in Bogotá. I could write a couple of pages about how my platinum cufflinks disappeared, then reappeared, several times from the Hotel Tequendama before disappearing again completely.

One day, I was walking on the street and I saw three guys approaching me from the opposite direction. When they reached me, they surrounded me as though there were a big crowd around us. I checked my pockets and realized that a hand had slipped in and stolen my pocket diary from my inside pocket.

The longer I lived in Bogotá, the more I saw the techniques of theft advance and evolve as the haves and have-nots competed. Early on in my tenure, drivers were losing their wristwatches. When drivers stopped at a red light, their left arm resting casually on the windowsill, thieves would approach at a dead run and rip off the driver's wristwatch. The drivers responded by wearing their wristwatches on their right hand— the driving hand. The thieves' reaction was to escalate the conflict by running up and stabbing the left shoulders of the drivers, whose natural reaction was to grab the injured part with his right hand. Good-bye watch!

After several months of this, I told the musicians of the orchestra that the next time I returned, I would be in my underwear and bring only a conducting baton. I also told them that if they had a music school as good as their schools for criminals they would have the best orchestra in the world.

One day, as I was packing to go to the airport to fly back to Victoria, my phone rang. I was asked if I could take over a concert with Columbia's National Symphony Orchestra because their Music Director was tied up with another engagement. I accepted the invitation and postponed my trip home by a couple of days. On the program was a World Premiere of a work by a Colombian composer, as well as the Barber Violin Concerto and the Tchaikovsky Symphony No. Four. I had never conducted the Barber Concerto before, or the Colombian work.

I had a wonderful young Colombian violinist as my soloist for the Barber. He was studying at the time at the Moscow Conservatory and had come home for his holidays. At the first rehearsal we played through the Colombian work. The musicians' sheet music of the work was full of mistakes. As we had only two rehearsals for the concert, I had simply no time to correct the mistakes. I asked the librarian to collect the music from the musicians and asked the composer to correct the parts for next day's rehearsal, which he did. This sort of thing almost never works out; I was a strange conductor brought in on short notice to work with an unfamiliar orchestra; I was conducting a piece for the first time (the Barber), and conducting a new composition which hadn't even been completed.

The concert went extremely well, including the world premiere of the new Colombian work; my soloist played magnificently and it was a complete success.

Musical experiences like this made up for Bogotá's disturbing occurrence of violent crime. And before I left, I had one of the peak emotional, musical, and aesthetic events of my life, which I recount in the next chapter.

Les Préludes

The time for my final concert with the Bogotá Philharmonic arrived. At the last rehearsal with the orchestra, the musicians gave me a nice engraved silver memento of their friendship. I still keep it in a prominent place. Almost twenty years later, in 1997, the Bogotá Philharmonic Orchestra contacted me about the possibility of returning to Bogotá as a guest conductor. During our phone discussions, they mentioned that some members of the orchestra who played with me still have fond memories of my work with them in 1979. Although we could not sort out the financial, travel and scheduling matters and the project did not, in the end, materialize, I was very moved by the thought and the gesture.

I find the greatest satisfaction in life when I encounter musicians who remember what piece they played with me or under my direction, twenty, thirty, even forty years ago. As a former orchestra musician, I have great memories: Beethoven and Mozart symphonies with Otto Klemperer; Tchaikovsky's Fourth Symphony and a rehearsal of Beethoven's Ninth Symphony with Erich Kleiber. Ravel's Daphnis and Chloe and French repertoire, in general, with Charles Munch. Tchaikovsky's Manfred with Constantin Silvestri, and others. My life was enriched by those rare, sublime moments which occur in our journey from birth to death. These moments give us a chance to commune with the genius of the great masters, and I feel the greatest privilege is that I may have, at times, been a part of such moments for other musicians and audiences.

Chapter Forty Four

A PEAK IN COLUMBIA

One of the most rewarding musical performances of my career, and one of my most extraordinary experiences of human connection, happened in 1978 during my tenure with the Bogotá Philharmonic Orchestra. Because of its altitude and its closeness to the Equator, Bogotá is considered the city of eternal spring; it gets the intense tropical sunlight, but is rarely too hot. One nice summer day the orchestra left this pleasant altitude to descend, by bus, through the tropical heat of the jungle, to take part in the Tertulia del Rio Arts Festival. Tertulia del Rio was the highest point on the river that the Spanish ships were able to navigate. From there the local slaves had to carry the Spaniard's possessions, including their furniture, on their heads, up to Bogotá's 2800 metres.

The trip through the dense vegetation of the jungle was most interesting, except for the increasing humidity and heat. Our buses were not air conditioned and our discomfort grew as we approached the town. We had time to consider that the locals had never seen an orchestra before, and that our performance at this festival would be the first in this jungle town.

When we arrived we found that Tertulia lacked reliable common amenities. During the day the lights went out three times. Since their electrical system was not up to snuff, I asked one member of the local organizing committee to get candles for the musicians in case the lights went out during the concert. The candles never showed up.

The concert took place in a little church which could hold five hundred people. Fifteen hundred people showed up, most of whom somehow squeezed inside the place of worship while the others huddled in the open doorways. I had people sitting on my podium draped around my legs. You cannot imagine the heat in that church! The tropical heat outside exceeded 30 C. at very high humidity, which combined with the more than a thousand bodies and a thousand pairs of lungs in the small church to create a livid, suffocating heat.

Except that it was not suffocating.

This concert gave me one of the greatest rewards of my performing life. A holy atmosphere surrounded us, not only because we were in a church, but because the audience waited in an exalted state, as though expecting a miracle. And indeed a miracle had happened. Here, in the jungle town of Tertulia, the peasants and the farmers, the manual labourers and their wives and children were to experience for the first time a large-scale, live classical performance and the genius of Beethoven.

I ended the concert with Beethoven's Symphony No. Three, the Eroica. Before I began I told the audience about some aspects of the symphony; for instance, that the trumpet passage in the funeral march of the slow movement is where Man stands before God to hear the Last Judgement. Just before the final prestissimo (the very fast tempo ending of the Symphony), the lights went out and we had to stop playing. Naturally, the candles hadn't arrived and I had to handle the situation. First, I told the audience that we should sing something. This request was not met too favourably. How do you get fifteen-hundred strangers in the midst of darkness to agree on one tune? Then I said: "Vamos resar al Dios por un poco luz." ("We will pray to God for a little light" There was some hesitant, skeptical laughter since the residents of Tertulia had had many more years of experience with their utilities than I had. Then the lights came on. We resumed the prestissimo and ended the concert on a glorious note. The audience cried, laughed and cheered with delight and their love and joy flowed over us in the orchestra like a river, seemingly without end. I will never forget the joyful intensity on the faces of these people who were experiencing live, classical music for the first time in their lives.

After the applause died down, I went outside, took off my jacket, and wrung several litres of water out of it. This is how profusely I had perspired.

Whenever I hear people talk dismissively of classical music, saying that it is only a self-appointed "elite"" who can appreciate it, I remember the people of Tertulia, and I appreciate, again, the genius of the great composers, who speak with such eloquence over the passage of years, and across languages and cultures.

Les Préludes

Chapter Forty Five

WINDSOR MUSIC DIRECTOR - 1979

I was invited to be guest-conductor to the Thunder Bay Symphony Orchestra in January, 1979. It was a very cold morning in Thunder Bay, and I was preparing for my early morning walk when the phone rang. My wife had phoned from Victoria to tell me that Nandi, my older half-brother, had died in hospital during an operation. This totally unexpected and tragic event hit me very badly.

In 1979 Nandi was only sixty five years old. As a child, Nandi had broken his left leg badly and it had never healed properly. Hungarian doctors, at the time, had apparently broken his leg surgically in an effort to restore its natural function, but this did not work. His left leg remained stiff and unable to bend, and he limped for the rest of his life.

When he was young he had never let the leg be a handicap; he went dancing with my mother and other ladies, and, in all respects, led an active life. In 1939, at the end of August, we had even climbed the 2500 meter Mount Caraiman in Romania; the mountain of the infamous suicidal pack mules. But as he aged the leg bothered him more and more. In the last few years his leg had caused him greater and greater pain, and he had had to take up a cane for walking.

A doctor convinced him and his wife that it would be a minor operation to install an artificial joint in his left knee which would enable him to walk normally. The operation, apparently, was successful from a surgical standpoint, but his body insisted upon rejecting the foreign object. For two weeks, the doctors kept him on various antibiotics and other medications to cope with the reaction of his immune system, but none of their strategies worked. The doctors finally admitted defeat and scheduled a second operation to remove the artificial knee. During this operation, Nandi's heart gave out and he died.

While we were never too close (at one point not seeing each other for twenty-two years), his death affected me very badly. I remember walking that very cold morning on an icy, snowy road in the bright sunshine contemplating his life, our lives as brothers and life in general.

Irony followed me. From Thunder Bay, I flew to Windsor, to fulfill the guest-conducting engagement. The engagement was a job interview of sorts, as I was a finalist for the position of Music Director of the Windsor Symphony. The position had become vacant when the current Music Director had unexpectedly died in mid-season. One death was tragedy. One death was opportunity.

Maureen Forrester, the great Canadian contralto, was my soloist for this guest-conducting assignment. I knew Maureen and her husband, Eugene Kash, from my time in Montreal. Ms. Forrester had been one of the soloists when I had accompanied the Montreal Symphony Orchestra touring Europe in the 1960's. In Windsor, Maureen sang a modern composition by the well-known Canadian composer, Harry Sommers, and some Mahler songs. I finished the concert with the Dances of Galanta by Zoltan Kodaly. The concert was a great success and I had a wonderful reception. A couple of weeks later, I was offered and happily accepted the position of Music Director.

I had been awarded the post from a competition of over two hundred conductors and aspiring conductors. Winning this job was a big thing for me. I had acquired my Music Directorship in Victoria, in part, through an old personal connection, but I had resigned over the machinations of the Board of Directors and other problems.

Windsor is an industrial town— the Chrysler Corporation had a big plant there. Because of the industrial nature of the city, Windsor had attracted a very varied ethnic population including, large Italian, German, Serbian, Hungarian, Jewish,

"A gifted and sensitive musician...authoritative conductor"   Montreal Star

The Windsor Symphony announced my appointment with a bit of fanfare, including this very handsome and distinguished portrait of me on their year's program. I have never had any difficulities accepting or participating in the publicity necessary to run a successful symphony orchestra.

and Ukrainian populations. This turned out to be very useful during my tenure there.

Through a fluke of geography, Windsor is the only Canadian city which is located south of a major US metropolis. Windsorians traveling to Detroit drive north across the Canada-U.S. border. The proximity of Windsor and Detroit sometimes causes confusion for newcomers. I remember driving from Toronto to Windsor a few months before my engagement. I passed through London, Ontario, where most of the buildings were two to three stories high. As I was approaching Windsor, I saw some huge skyscrapers. Not until I reached the Detroit River did I realize that I was looking at Detroit's skyline looming over Windsor's modest buildings. It is a funny feeling when you start driving southwest from Toronto and end up driving north to Windsor and Detroit! I drove to New York several times, where Kathy, my younger daughter, was living and I always had the feeling that I was driving West instead of East!

At the time, the Windsor Symphony had only four hundred subscribers. Their home, the Cleary Auditorium, had only 1200 seats. I realized that I would have to do some drastic things to generate interest in the orchestra. We agreed with the local CBC (Canadian Broadcasting Corporation) television station to produce three commercials to attract the community's attention. In one commercial, I directed traffic with my baton in full dress, of course, at one of the busiest corners in Windsor. A police detachment was in control.

I organized a fundraising 'cabaret' concert for the benefit of the orchestra in the early summer of 1979, prior to the official commencement of my term which was in the fall. There, dinner was served at the concert and all of Windsor's who's-who, the Mayor and various officials and businesspeople attended. My wife and Kathy were also present. Among Strauss waltzes and other light selections, I also conducted the Toy Symphony of Haydn, with the participation of the Mayor and other dignitaries performing with the orchestra. It was a lot of fun. The Mayor presented my wife with a nice bouquet of flowers and Kathy received a nice corsage. After the concert, I sat down at a table and had something to eat, and an Italian grocery owner joined us.

When we were finally done, my wife pinched my arm so hard that it was black and blue for weeks. She told me that she was not willing to start all over and sit on the side and just watch me being the centre of attention. The beginning of my new job was to be the end of my marriage.

After the concert, my wife went back to Victoria and I took Kathy to New York where she planned to study ballet and acting. I arranged her accommodation with some good Venezuelan singer friends of mine. After New York, I returned to Windsor and rented a nice, two-bedroom apartment on the eighth floor of a riverside apartment, overlooking the Detroit River and skyline.

I went back to Victoria and got ready for the move to Windsor. I packed all my scores and some books. The only furniture I had shipped to Windsor were two single beds that we had bought in Montreal twenty-two years earlier.

I planned to drive my camper bus across the country to Windsor. My wife was supposed to come with me, at least part of the way, and fly back to Victoria from Calgary. My good old friend, the camper, broke down in Harrison Hot Springs and we returned to Victoria via tow truck. I wanted to leave Victoria, but Victoria did not seem to want me to leave.

My next attempt was to take a floatplane from Victoria harbour to downtown Vancouver and from there take the train across the country. I was already familiar with the beauty of the Rockies, but past Calgary the hundreds and hundreds of miles of unlimited view of the prairies lacked any variety. I had a little portable radio with me, but for several days, the only music was country and rock music. It was not actively unpleasant, but it was dreadfully dull.

The Windsor Symphony started the season with about eight hundred subscribers. My second season was sold out. I started to explore the possibility of giving concerts for the various ethnic groups in town. As a good Hungarian pianist friend told me, just before going on stage, "We are typical refugees!" I asked, "Why?" He replied, "Because we lost everything except our accents."

Whether refugees, immigrants or emigrants, we all carry our past, our national background, and our culture with us and anything reminding us of our previous background is cherished. I started to work with a very fine, Italian men's choir, all of whom were Chrysler employees. Over a period of three seasons, I lined up concerts for the German, Hungarian, Italian, Serbian and Jewish communities. Convincing the various groups about the importance of exposing their national culture and heritage was worth a little fund raising effort.

As far as my soloists and programs were concerned, I had difficulty with only two groups— the Hungarian and Jewish organizing committees. The Hungarians objected to my soloist, the wonderful Hungarian-Swiss pianist, Bela Siki. One member of the committee objected to him, especially, on the grounds that he was a communist. The funny part was that Siki had won the Geneva Piano Competition in 1946 and, shortly afterwards, was appointed to take over the cathedra of Dinu Lipatti at the Geneva Conservatory, who had died of leukemia at a very young age. The Communists took over in Hungary in 1948, and by that time Siki had been living in Switzerland for two years and had married a Swiss girl. I didn't know of his political persuasion, if any, but Siki was definitely not a communist.

I wanted to end the Jewish concert with the last movement of Beethoven's Ninth Symphony, based on Schiller's Ode to Joy, with a fine choir from Detroit. (We were also to perform a new oratorio written by a Jewish composer in the memory of the children lost in the Holocaust.) The Jewish committee objected to this because Beethoven was a German! Finally, I convinced them that they could not have a more uplifting message than this music.

Chapter Forty Six

THE MARACAIBO SYMPHONY ORCHESTRA AND "EL GAUCHO ELECTRONICO"

Besides The National Symphony Orchestra of Mexico, my longest artistic association as a guest-conductor was with the Maracaibo Symphony Orchestra of Venezuela. Over a period of about fifteen years (1969-1984) I conducted them every year, sometimes two or three times in a season.

In 1982, they did their first North American tour, which featured concerts in many important centres, one in New York's Carnegie Hall. We agreed with Maestro Eduardo Rahn (the Music Director of the Orchestra) that I would conduct them in Victoria, BC (where I had been Music Director of the VSO 1967-1978) and Windsor Ontario, in Canada, where I was the Music Director of the WSO at the time (1982).

During the spring of 1982, I conducted several concerts in Maracaibo, Venezuela. The programs included the works I was planning to conduct in the fall at their two concerts in Canada. They included Verdi's Il Forza del Destino Overture, Bartok's Concerto for Viola, Liszt's 2nd Piano Concerto, Scheherazade by Rimsky-Korsakov, and De Falla's 2nd Suite from the Three-Cornered hat. As an encore, I planned to perform Malambo from the Ballet Estancias by the Argentine composer, Ginastera.

Because Carlos Duarte, my piano soloist, had a broken arm at the time, we merely discussed with him the work and his interpretation, rather than rehearse. As our concerts in Victoria and Windsor were supposed to take place about six months later in the fall of 1982, we agreed that I would have one rehearsal with him and the orchestra in Victoria.

At the time, the Government of Venezuela was flush with oil revenues and generous with the arts. The orchestra chartered a plane for $85,000 (US) to fly them and their instruments from Tucson, Arizona to Victoria, BC, Canada.

All week long we had gorgeous weather in Victoria, but on the morning of the concert, there was thick fog at the Victoria International Airport and in Seattle and Vancouver as well. To cut a long story short, their charter landed in the morning in Spokane, Washington!

As the forecast said that there is a fair chance that the Vancouver International Airport would be open by early afternoon, I made arrangements to have two buses and a huge truck for the instruments waiting for them at the airport. I also reserved space with the BC Ferry Corporation for the buses and the truck. Just then, they phoned me from Spokane and told me that the pilot had announced that he was going to attempt a landing at Victoria International Airport, which was still closed. I rushed to the airport. I was very close to the runway, but you couldn't see a thing because of the fog.

I even heard the plane make two unsuccessful approaches before finally heading off to attempt a landing at the Vancouver Airport. Because of this exercise we lost another valuable hour. The local newspapers followed the story on their front pages and the local radio and TV gave regular progress reports. Some of the musicians told me later, that their French concertmaster and a few other musicians were scared and praying feverishly while the pilot made his unsuccessful landing attempts at the Victoria Airport.

When I realized that they would not arrive in time I had to cancel the concert. The orchestra arrived, finally, at 9 PM (the concert supposed to start at 8 P.M.). So we all sat around and drank 'Cuba Libres" (Rum and Coke) past two in the morning.

Our second Canadian concert was to take place in Windsor, Ontario two weeks later. This time around, they came by bus from Grand Rapids, Michigan via Detroit. You can cross the Detroit River through a tunnel or the Ambassador Bridge.

I advised the Canadian Immigration and Customs people that they would come through the tunnel (which was closest to the concert hall) and to have sufficient personnel there to handle them as fast as possible. I wanted to have at least a one hour rehearsal with them and my piano soloist.

About one hour before their arrival I had a phone call from them, saying that they have to come via the Ambassador Bridge, because their truck with the instruments was too big for the tunnel! I phoned my manager asking her to notify the customs people about the change (which she failed to do . . .). To be on the safe side, I went to the bridge myself. Finally, we managed to clear the orchestra and the instruments. It was a complicated process because the orchestra had a large number of musicians on a yearly contract from the Eastern Bloc countries and they didn't have Canadian visas.

I had to personally guarantee that they would leave Canada the next day! Finally, everything was more or less in place for our one hour rehearsal with Carlos Duarte, my soloist.

It turned out that about forty musicians in the orchestra had not only never played with me, but they had never even seen me conduct! For the tour, the Orchestra had engaged about twenty US musicians and the other twenty were newcomers from Eastern Europe. At the end of the rehearsal, some anxious musicians came to me asking what would I do in certain spots (especially in Scheherazade). All I could tell them was, "Watch me" and I jumped into my car to rush home, shower, change into my full dress and rush back to the Cleary Auditorium.

There is a spot in the Sheherazade where the first trombone plays an alarm signal and the first trumpet plays its echo. The trumpet player had played Scheherazade with me before and knew that I wanted an exciting alarm signal played fairly fast. The trombone player didn't know my intentions, which led to a very funny situation. When his turn came, the trombone player almost turned the alarm signal into a slow love song. Then came the trumpet players 'echo' almost twice as fast!

This happens twice in the piece and I couldn't do anything about it, except giggle together with the musicians who knew what was going on!

The concert was recorded by the CBC Television (Canadian Broadcasting Corporation) for later broadcast in Canada and Venezuela. Mr. Marc McGuigan, the minister of external affairs of Canada, Senor Peperoni, the Ambassador of Venezuela and the Venezuelan Consul General of Toronto attended the concert. Mr. McGuigan and Senor Peperoni addressed both the audience in the hall and the TV audience in Canada and Venezuela.

Beside 'Oh Canada' I had to conduct also the Anthem of Venezuela, which I had never even heard before. I put a first violin part on the floor in front of my podium and followed the orchestra. According to some Venezuelan musicians my 'performance' of the Anthem was 'almost authentic'.

It was in this concert that I received a new nickname, "El Gaucho Electronico." This arose from our performance of the encore piece that evening, "Malambo", from the Ballet Estancias by Ginastera. I had never conducted the piece, we had not rehearsed it, and I had never heard it played. So from my memory of the score, I led the players through a sprightly rendition. It was a pace which seemed appropriate to me, but the musicians told me afterwards that I had conducted it at nearly twice the pace as their own conductor back in Venezuela. The musicians enjoyed it though, and dubbed me, "El Gaucho Electronico."

In retrospect, this whole Maracaibo Symphony 'interlude' seemed to be jinxed. On top of all the problems listed above, the producer of the TV recording had his own unexpected problems. He had five cameras at his disposal, including one 'mobile camera', which he managed to get on loan from the CBC Station in London, Ontario. This was his most important camera as it could change positions; whereas, the other four cameras had fixed positions.

Based on the score of the work that is being recorded, the cameras are pre-programmed to take up positions prior to the next shot which the assistant producer calls out. For instance, "camera five take a close up of the first bassoon", etc. When the music reaches that point, the producer switches the cameras.

About thirty seconds into the recording of Verdi's La Forza del Destino (The Force of Destiny) overture, the mobile camera (#1) went dead and never recuperated. On the DVD of the concert you can even see the cameramen and his assistant trying frantically to fix the problem! This meant that the producer had to improvise every time camera #1 supposed to be in action. While this created big problems for him during the recording, it led to a new and innovative approach to recording an orchestral concert.

When editing the tape, he had the brilliant idea to cover up the segments he was unhappy with by superimposing text and pictures containing information about the composer, the composition, the performers and other such material. In my opinion, he had, inadvertently, found a new way of recording and transmitting an orchestral concert. While the audience receives interesting information visually, simultaneously, they can continue to hear the music.

How to turn a handicap into an asset!

Les Préludes

Chapter Forty Seven

TRANSITIONS

The seventies was a period of tremendous upheaval for me, personally as well as professionally. My marriage was to end, my parents were to retire, my children were to move out, and I was to give up my Musical Directorship and then win another. My professional life is covered in other chapters. I will talk about my family transitions here, which requires going back over some old ground.

The happiest period of my life was the first five years of my marriage to Agnes, culminating in the arrival of our first daughter, Suzanne, in 1955, the heady, relaxing year before the Hungarian Uprising in 1956, and our move into a new and spacious apartment to watch our baby grow.

Following this idyllic period, our collective nervous system (since Agnes and I were a physical, mental, and emotional collective, as are most married couples) was taxed to the limit.

First, we experienced the exciting times of humanized socialism, followed by the danger, violence and upheaval of the insurrection and the Soviet intervention. Then came the secret preparations for leaving the country, saying good-bye forever to all of our colleagues, friends, and family (particularly my wife's parents), and perhaps a good-bye to my career as well. The escape itself and the month of limbo in Yugoslavia were terribly stressful. The airplane crash almost killed us, and we cut our recovery short with a tempestuous crossing of the Atlantic to a new country and a new language. To cap this off, our first night with my parents in Montreal turned into instant, savage family warfare.

Add to all of this the fact that Agnes was still in ill health and pregnant with our second child, Kathleen. We were moving from one rented room to another. Agnes was doing alterations for ladies, kneeling in front of them for hours. I am sure that all these tremendous challenges contributed to a personality change in my wife.

After Kathleen's birth, we moved to our second apartment on Saint Kevin Street. As I was increasingly busy, Agnes spent most of her time being homebound with the two children. We had a neighbor who also had a daughter of Suzanne's age, and she and Agnes became good friends. I thought that developing her own circle of friends would be good for Agnes and would help her adjust to this new role, but it didn't always work out. During our second summer in Montreal, my wife and her friends took all their children to the Eastern Townships for several weeks' holiday. On their return my wife stopped talking to all of her holiday companions. I never found out what had happened.

Relations with my side of the family were very bad. After the fight in my parents' apartment in Montreal the night we arrived, the warfare between them and Agnes continued, with me taking punches from both sides. Any time I tried to calm the situation down, the effort was in vain and I ended up antagonizing both my parents and my wife. My mother would say, "Why don't you tell your wife that this is not how a daughter-in-law should treat her husband's parents?" My wife's response was to yell, "I don't want to see them! I don't want them to come to my home!"

This warfare subsided from time to time, such as when my parents bought us a crib and dresser for Kathleen's arrival, or when they would baby-sit their adored granddaughters. Once, in 1962, we left Suzanne and Kathleen with their grandparents while I combined a guest-conducting assignment in Calgary with a car trip through the Rockies to the Seattle World's Fair.

Later on, when I was the Music Director of the Victoria Symphony Orchestra and Executive Director of the Victoria Summer Festival, I was naturally very busy. Meanwhile, my wife was getting more and more moody and frustrated, staying home with the children, cooking, and gardening. I recognized this, and though we didn't need the second income, I suggested that she get a job in her line of expertise, such as a fashion consultant or saleswoman with one of the upscale fashion stores. I told her that having to dress, put on makeup, and commute to work with other people would give her a different and a wider perspective on life. The wife of the President of the University of Victoria had a little store specializing in wool, crocheting, pullovers, and other items. Agnes said that for her, the wife of the Music Director, to be working in such a store would be below her and below the community's expectations of her.

I thought that if she had more mobility she would feel more in charge of her life. I had tried to teach her how to drive years earlier in Montreal. We were in Westmount, a very tiny residential section of Montreal, and our daughters were in the back seat, without seat belts. There were no regulations in those days. I put her in the driver's seat and coached her through starting the car and putting it in gear. For a while we proceeded slowly and peacefully, when suddenly, not too far from the Bronfman residence, my wife stepped on the accelerator and the car swerved onto the manicured lawn of a beautiful home. In order to avoid driving right into the house, I reached my foot over my wife's foot and hit the power brake. We came to a stop just a few feet from the door. My unbelted daughters in the back seat made a sudden, elegant yoga headstand on the floor in the back of the car. I put the gearshift in park, changed places with my wife, and drove away in a hurry. This was the first and last driving lesson I gave my wife.

I told her that she should go to a driving school, that I was the wrong person to teach her. She refused in Montreal, and she refused in Victoria. So I had to drive her and the children everywhere, to shopping, to medical appointments, and so on. She stayed cooped up in her house partly by her own decision. She learned to drive only after our separation. When I moved to Windsor I left her both vehicles.

By 1975, my frustrations with some members of the Symphony Board, and later my tiffs with the Musician's Union took a toll on me which must have affected her. The Board Members of the Symphony were quite ineffective in running the show and especially in raising money. A group of my friends thought the solution would be to change the Board. They said, "We cannot get the community aroused by simply saying that the Board is not raising money, that they are not effective.", then they thought, "But if we say that they want to get rid of Gati, this would get the community moving!" And so they put this scheme in motion.

A local newspaper publisher was a part of the group. They printed a "pro-Gati/con-Gati" piece and rented a small mailbox where people could send their votes. They published the vote every day on the front page of the paper. I think the final tally was something like, 2,030 people for Gati and 40 against.

In the meantime, I had problems with a couple of American musicians who tried to create a revolution in the orchestra, taking actions and stances they wouldn't dream of doing in the United States. By that time, I was in a deep depression from all of this nonsense, and this obviously affected Agnes very badly. All of this happened during the 1975 - 1976 season. I didn't want to resign at the height of all this hugger-mugger so I gave my one year's notice at the end of the 1976 - 77 season, to be effective at the end of the 1977 - 78 season.

By this time, Suzie had moved to Vancouver, and Kathleen was studying ballet in Seattle. My wife was at home alone and gradually became more and more involved in Christian Science through a friend who was a practitioner.

After my resignation we had no concrete plans about our future. We had tentatively considered moving to London, England, where I would have many more opportunities to conduct and perhaps get a permanent appointment. We drove to Salt Lake City for an interview as a music professor at the Faculty of Music of the University of Utah. After the interview we continued, driving on to Palm Springs, California, to recuperate. A funny thing happened on the way.

Our car ran out of gas on the highway in the desert, just about midnight. It was a beautiful starlit night, blissfully silent, and we were in the middle of nowhere. Just as Agnes started to give me hell, a pickup truck stopped and the driver got out to offer us help. This turned into a very nice human experience. The truck driver took me to a small gas station. He woke up the lady owner who gave me a container full of gas, and then the fellow drove me back to my car. I put the gas in the tank, thanked him, and off he went. I drove to the gas station, where the sleepy lady was waiting, returned her container, filled the tank and continued our drive to Palm Springs.

Out of the blue I received the invitation to be principal guest conductor with the Bogotá Philharmonic Orchestra for the 1978 - 79 season. As there was the possibility to become the permanent Music Director of the orchestra, I took Agnes with me on one of my trips to see if she would like to live in Bogotá. I tried everything I could to make her feel comfortable in Colombia. We stayed at the Tequendama Hotel, at the time the best hotel in Bogotá, and went for a week at the seaside in Cartagena.

She hated everything.

She hated me for booking a hotel one block from the beach, and not on the beach itself. I changed hotels, but she remained in a bad mood for the rest of her stay. She clearly did not like the idea of living in Colombia. She had some language difficulties since she didn't speak Spanish. After this experience I took myself out of the running for the position and instead, in the late spring of 1979, I accepted the appointment as Music Director of the Windsor Symphony Orchestra.

To raise funds and to create interest in the Orchestra, I organized a Cabaret Concert. I have recounted in the last chapter that as we were leaving Agnes pinched me hard. She declared to me that she was not willing to start all over in a new city and have a life where I am constantly in the limelight and she is on the sidelines. I told her that, short of performing on the stage, the role of the Music Director's wife is to socialize, be part of the Ladies' Committee, and attend community functions.

After a day or two we talked over the situation and I suggested that she stay in Victoria for the first three months of the season to think over whether or not she wanted to come to Windsor. I would come back over the Christmas holidays and we would decide what to do. I thought we had come to terms, but we had not, at least in Agnes' eyes. Later that day we took Kathleen over to Detroit for a modeling appointment. While we were waiting for her, Agnes asked me if I still wanted her to stay in Victoria. I replied that waiting until I returned in December would give her time to think things over. She went into complete hysterics, screaming, yelling and trying to hit me. I had to hold her hands to protect myself.

Imagine what the publicity would have been in Windsor— the new Music Director beaten up by his wife in Detroit.

So I finished up my business in Windsor and went back to Victoria for the two months before the Windsor Symphony's season was to start. During this time we went to a marriage counsellor several times but to no avail. Each time, we ended up in a shouting match instead of reconciliation. Finally, it came time to go back to Windsor. Because I was carrying a lot of stuff with me, I wanted to drive the camper across Canada. Agnes decided to come with me as far as Calgary, then fly back to Victoria. We got as far as Harrison Hot Springs, a bit more than a hundred miles, when the camper broke down. We ended up returning to Victoria on the back of a tow-truck. A few days later I flew from Victoria to Vancouver and took the train to Toronto and Windsor. This was the last normal husband-wife contact we had.

On my return to Victoria in December, we had a meeting in the presence of her Christian Science friend. Again we ended up in a shouting match and even her friend came to the conclusion that our relationship was beyond repair.

After being legally separated for several years, we divorced.

There were transitions involving my parents, too. Shortly after our arrival in Montreal in 1956, I shamed them into moving to a more decent apartment on Park Avenue. They both carried on with their routine for several years. My mother worked in a factory, sewing, and my father got up at 2 am to go and do his part-time job in different bakeries. In 1968, one year after we moved to Victoria, my parents decided to retire and move to Victoria. My father was seventy-three and my mother sixty-eight.

They became regulars at my indoor and outdoor concerts. I think they were proud of me. My mother always introduced herself as "I am the mother of the conductor". After living in an apartment for one year they bought a small house. One day when I was visiting them I saw a green car in they driveway. I thought they had a visitor. I asked my mother, "Whose car is it?" She said, "Mine"!

At the age of seventy-three she learned to drive. We had a number of funny experiences connected with her driving. Victoria is more British than Britain. My mother was lost at one point and went into a small hotel to ask for directions. They replied, "On ne parle pas l'Anglais ici!" ("We don't speak English here!"). I have no idea how the hotel owners communicated with the uni-lingual American tourists who filled Victoria. My father, who all his life had been the driver, became the worst backseat driver, constantly telling my mother what to do, which way to turn, and at one point threatening her with his walking cane.

Because the house they had bought had no garage, they bought a bigger house, with a garage, basement storage room, laundry, and so on. They sold the car after couple of years mainly because of my mother's poor eyesight.

My public controversy with the Symphony Board affected them very badly. Just before I moved to Windsor, my father fell, broke his hip and was confined to a wheelchair. Used to a physically active life style, he could not take the confinement and physical restrictions. I came back to Victoria to see him at the Royal Victoria Hospital where he was hospitalized. He was confined to a bed, strapped down with gloves on his hands. I was told that he would scratch himself until he was bleeding. This was the last time I saw him. He died in 1980 at the age of eighty-five.

My mother started to have symptoms of senility in 1980 when she was eighty years old. Agnes and I had lunch with her. Suddenly, she asked, "When are they bringing the soup?" We said, "But you just had your soup!" "Not me", she answered. One day the Manager of the Safeway store, where she shopped for years, told me that she had filled up her shopping basket and left the store without paying. At one point she took out $5,000 from her bank account and hid it under the chesterfield for "safety reasons" and it was never to be found again. Then she hid a few thousand dollars in her washing machine and then gave the machine to a friend. We changed her account to a joint account so she could not access the money without my or my brother's signature. We also placed the house as a joint property so she could not transfer it to somebody else... and on and on. It is very interesting to see how first the short-term memory fails and gradually, we remember earlier and earlier memories. The year before she died (at age ninety-five) my mother was singing nursery songs from her childhood!

After short stays at a few old age homes, she ended up in a fairly decent one on Fairfield Road in Victoria. Normally, there were two nurses changing the bed-sheet and moving the patient. To save money they got a contraption to lift the patients out of the bed and move them around. Shortly afterward, an inexperienced nurse's aide dropped my mother on the concrete floor. Luckily there were no bones broken, but they had to take her to a hospital to put several stitches on her scalp.

Both my parents were cremated. My brother Dodi and I had a little ceremony before spreading my father's ashes in the Detroit River in Windsor, and my mother's ashes in the Pacific Ocean in Vancouver.

Chapter Forty Eight

AN "EXPLOSIVE" CONCERT

It was 1980. Now single, I threw myself completely into my new life. My tenure with the Windsor Symphony was, in general, very pleasurable. As Music Director I chose the music, found the soloists, conducted the concerts, and did all of the publicity and public education necessary to the position. It would be repetitious to give a list of well-known musicians who performed with us, or the community activities I participated in; as pleasurable as it was, it is much more of what I have already recounted. But my adventurousness did sometimes land me in a public imbroglio.

Every summer between July 1st (Canada Day) and July 4 (Independence Day), Detroit, Michigan, U.S.A. and Windsor, Ontario, Canada celebrated the 'Freedom Festival' together. There were many activities, like tugboat races, Keystone Cops chasing 'gangsters', re-enacting the rum-running between Windsor and Detroit during the Prohibition, and finally, a fireworks display launched from barges in the middle of the Detroit River. This finale culminated on the evening of July 4th.

The Windsor Symphony planned to give an open air concert prior to the fireworks. The last piece to be performed in the concert would be Tchaikovsky's 1812 Overture, a great and exciting crowd-pleaser which ends with sixteen cannon shots. In a concert hall these cannon shots would be created by the tympani. Since we were outside, and since the audience was prepared for the enormous noise of the fireworks to follow, we decided that these sixteen cannon shots would be produced by real explosions.

We hired a retired explosives expert from the city of Hamilton, Ontario, who specialized in producing mock bombing attacks and other such events. He also regularly produced the cannon shots of the 1812 Overture for The Toronto Symphony Orchestra and other orchestras. This expert also had an 'indoor' version of the effect. Dofasco, Hamilton's huge steel corporation, made sixteen little cannons which produced a marvelous set of booms! We used these little cannons the previous year when the orchestra played indoors. If it were to rain on the day of concert, the orchestra would move back into the Cleary Auditorium and use them.

The expert had a little keyboard, looking like an old typewriter with the sixteen keys, one key to a boom, and very simple to operate. Sometimes, celebrities would be invited to perform with the symphonies by producing the "booms" on the conductor's cue.

The Riverside in Detroit is partly industrial, with railway tracks and cars obstructing the view of the Detroit River. On the other hand, the Windsor side of the Detroit River had been developed into a proper riverside park. The city planners and various authorities had anticipated that hundreds of thousands of people from Detroit and Windsor would congregate on the Windsor side of the Detroit River for the festival and the fireworks. To be on the safe side, I organized a meeting at the site of the concert with the head of the Police Department, the head of the Fire Department, a representative of the City Hall and a representative of the Festival Board.

Our explosives expert showed up in a Volkswagen camper adorned with a mock five hundred pound bomb on its roof. We asked him to designate how much space he would need to set up his explosives and how they would work. First, they designated the area where the Parks Department set up a fence. Next, he explained how it would work. He then pushed sixteen wooden stakes into the earth within the enclosure, each stake topped with a small explosive charge. Fine wires from each explosive charge were wrapped around the stake and which lead to the keyboard, this having been placed at a safe distance from the explosives. Everybody seemed to be satisfied with the arrangements and we went our separate ways.

Because of the anticipated huge crowds, we had originally planned that the orchestra would perform on a barge tied to the shore. Unfortunately, our ladies in the orchestra with their celli and other instruments, and high heels could not negotiate the planks over the water, so we decided to stay on terra firma.

I went to the riverside early and parked my car at a safe distance from the park. I planned to hit the road as soon we finished the 1812 Overture and get out before the crowds started to disperse after the fireworks. Both the Detroit and the Windsor crowds started to congregate pretty early.

I tried to establish contact with the people doing the fireworks to coordinate our performance with the start of their fireworks. The fireworks technicians told me that they would start the fireworks at exactly ten o'clock and it would be up to me to coordinate with them. They assured me over and over that they would start at ten o'clock precisely. Naturally, I knew exactly how long it would take us to reach the point in the overture when the canon shots would be fired.

As more and more people squeezed into the area where the orchestra and the expert with his little field of explosives were to perform, I began to wish that we were on the barges. During the concert, I kept admonishing the crowd to get away from the fence, warning them about the loud explosions to come. It was a gorgeous evening, and the concert proceeded, accompanied by loud cheers from the celebratory, appreciative audience. Throughout the performance the crowds kept pushing in closer and closer, not just for the music, but also because our location was the closest to the fireworks.

Fruitlessly, I kept warning the audience to get away from the fenced enclosure! The time for our 1812 Overture arrived. The orchestra played very well and the audience seemed to be absorbed in the music. We were in the middle of the beautiful soft love motif, when suddenly, with a series of big explosions, the fireworks started — five minutes early! I had no choice but to continue. At the climax of the piece our cannon shots joined the noise of the fireworks; and immediately, we were accompanied by screams from the audience. There was a total mayhem.

As soon as I finished the last chord, I took off, heading toward my car. I had no idea what had happened, what with the darkness, the crowds, the intermittent flashes of light from the fireworks, and the general air of chaos. I remember at one point driving on the sidewalk just to get away as fast as possible. I finally got home, took a shower and had a drink. To relax, I turned on the TV.

"Thirty-five people hurt during the performance of Tchaikovsky's 1812 Overture!", "People threw Coca Cola cans in the enclosure which became shrapnel when the explosives went off!" These stories were broadcast not just on the CBC and US networks, but even in Europe.

I kept telling everybody that this 'performance' finally put Windsor on the international map. The next day I found out what had happened. I mentioned earlier that I kept warning the crowd to stay away from the enclosure because of the loud noises our explosives would produce; well, that was not the only danger. Apparently, when the explosives blow up, the wires are also blown to fine shreds. These shreds were embedded in the exposed skin, in the face, arms, and legs of a fair number of the people crowded around the enclosure. Luck prevailed, however, and nobody was seriously hurt, but because of the incredible size of the crowds, ambulances couldn't come in or get out.

The festival authorities ended up that night turning a school bus into an impromptu hospital ward where they treated the victims. Doctors, nurses, and other volunteers crouched over several dozen people plucking wires out of their flesh with small forceps. Though not in the least life-threatening, the procedures must have been quite painful.

This 'unforgettable' performance of the 1812 Overture was on the news for several days. I kept receiving legal notices from various lawyers for several months, stating that they planned to sue me and the Windsor Symphony for damages. I just forwarded these documents to the City Clerk as I was just a musician, and the experts from the City Fire and Police Departments, as well as our explosive expert, had assured us of the safety of the proceedings. I don't know of anybody who received any money out of this event.

There was an eventual good result. This little incident demonstrated to both the Windsor and Detroit authorities how dangerous it was to have such dense crowds assemble without arranging for proper access by law-enforcement or medical personnel, and a means of evacuation for persons hurt or in danger. It was only twenty years ago; looking back on it, I can hardly believe how naïve and unprepared we (the authorities and the participants) were. And I can only wonder, twenty years from now, what present naiveté we will look back upon in shock.

Les Préludes

Chapter Forty Nine

1985 - ANOTHER ENCOUNTER WITH DEPRESSION

In 1985, I had to resign from the post of Music Director due to my second major attack of depression. I have recounted this episode in the Prologue, but for those readers who skipped it, I present it again, in chronological order.

It was the spring of 1985, when I checked in for the second time that week to the Psychiatric Ward of the Hotel Dieu Hospital in Windsor, Ontario, Canada. I was depressed. This time I had a definite plan. The conditions seemed to be ideal. My room was quite far from the nurse's desk. My roommate had gone home for the weekend, and everything seemed to be quiet. The ward settled down for a peaceful night.

The day before I had asked my elder daughter, Suzanne, to bring in the hair-cutting gizmo I had bought in Nuremberg, West Germany, during our European trip in 1973. This was a double-sided comb that had two razor blades inside. Supposedly, it was invented by another Hungarian. Suzanne didn't know my secret plans. I had stripped the razor blades from the comb that afternoon.

The nurse brought in my evening dose of sedatives, which included Halcion. Halcion was very popular at the time for depressives such as me; later on they discovered it had a number of side-effects, including . . . suicidal urges. The nurse stayed around to make sure that I took all my pills. Finally, she left.

I realized that I could not wait too long to execute my plan. I had taken quite a heavy dose of sedatives and I had to hurry up before they took effect and caused me to fall safely asleep.

I thought myself both rational and considerate, so I decided to cut my arteries over the toilet bowl and not make a bloody mess. I took the chair which stood beside my bed into the bathroom, sat on it, leaned over the toilet bowl, and started to cut what I thought were the arteries in my arm, which I assumed to be the places that my nurses took their blood samples. Cio-Cio San's suicide aria from Madame Butterfly of Puccini sounded gloriously in my head; on the other hand, cutting myself was quite painful.

When I woke up the next morning, everything was peaceful. I was lying in bed. The chair was back in its place near the table. I felt quite normal. I looked at my left arm, and saw the sleeve of my green pajama crusted with dried blood. I realized immediately, that my suicide attempt had not been a dream. I got up and rang the bell for the nurse. When she came in, I pointed to my bloody pajama sleeve. She must have realized instantly what had happened. She hugged me and held me in her arms and I hugged her and held her in my arms.

I will never forget this moment, the feeling of her soft body in my arms, a feeling beyond personalities, beyond description.

I felt that I was embracing womanhood, life, peace, future...eternity.

Chapter Fifty

SUZUKI AND RECOVERY FROM DEPRESSION

After being hospitalized in Toronto for a month, I returned to Windsor. Although I attended a dinner gala concert of the Windsor Symphony Orchestra, a concert that I had originally planned, I had no official function. Because of my depression and my inability to handle all the duties of a Musical Director, I was no longer the conductor of the orchestra. I walked up and down the various streets of Windsor like a stranger visiting the city for the first time. I realized that besides visiting a psychiatrist once a week, I had to find some 'raison d'etre', a reason to BE, if I were to manage to avoid another suicidal depression. I made arrangements with the Director and owner of the Academie Ste. Cecile to teach Suzuki violin courses on an hourly basis.

What is the Suzuki Method?

The Suzuki Method of music education was begun in the middle of the twentieth century by Japanese violinist, Shinichi Suzuki. Suzuki believed that the best and most effective way to learn music is to be exposed to it from a very early age. He calls this the "mother tongue" method - young children learn to play an instrument in the same way that they learn their own language— by listening, absorbing, and copying.

In the beginning, the parent is given the first lessons on the instrument, while the child watches. In this way, the child's interest is aroused by its natural desire to copy the parent, and the parent learns how to coach the child at home. This also gives the parent an understanding of the technical difficulties that playing a musical instrument involves.

When the child begins learning, it is by ear - music reading is not taught till later. Again this ties in with the idea of the "mother tongue" — one could not imagine trying to teach an infant to read before it can speak. Similarly, the young musician does not learn to read music until he or she has begun to understand music aurally. In general, the age at which a child is taught to read music is the same as when he or she is learning to read books in their own language.

Here I am at a recital with one of my older Suzuki students

Suzuki's philosophy is one of "Talent Education": he does not believe that only certain people are born with "a gift," or "talent", rather that each child has infinite potential. He believes that in teaching the child music, he is, in fact, creating a medium for the emotional and spiritual growth of the child.

Suzuki's father had a violin factory in Japan. The joke about the Suzuki method is that he invented the method so his father could manufacture more violins in all sizes. According to the story of the origin of the 'Method', Suzuki and three of his brothers were playing chamber music. When Sinichi Suzuki suddenly stopped and said, "Do you realize that every Japanese child speaks Japanese?"" The brothers looked at him. He declared, "If they can learn Japanese, they can learn anything!"

On one of my trips to Mexico City, I attended a concert at the INBA (Instituto Nacional de Bellas Artes) given by Suzuki and twelve of his students, aged five to twelve years of age. The repertoire these kids were playing would have taken at least eight to ten years of study with the 'regular' method of studying the violin. At one point in the concert the kids were walking around the stage playing the Bach Double Concerto for Two Violins. When Suzuki gave them a cue, they switched from the first to the second violin and vice versa. Even accomplished soloists would have had great difficulty to do this.

The Suzuki Method actually starts before the child is born. The mother listens to a record (mainly the Vivaldi Violin Concerto in A minor.) When the child is born he/she already recognizes and reacts to the music heard in the womb! The children hear the same music played every day, so by the time they actually start studying the violin, they are already very familiar with a basic repertoire that they will study. Besides showing an example to the child, the mother of the child is taught some basic technical details (how to hold the violin, etc.), so she can practice at home with the child.

Suzuki students can be very young!

Working with the children was sheer pleasure. My youngest student was three years old, the oldest eight or nine. While the 'mother tongue' approach is totally logical and it works, I found that most Suzuki violin teachers don't have the proper training in solving the anatomical problems related to playing the violin. Perhaps this explains why out of the thousands and thousands of young children studying the Suzuki method all over the world, only a handful managed to become internationally acclaimed soloists.

During the summer school holiday, a couple of months after starting to work with the children, I went to Kingston, Ontario to take part in a Suzuki Symposium. We had master lecturers both in violin and piano from England and Canada. It was a very educational experience for me and I met some wonderful people. During my second school year I proposed to the Director to organize master classes in both piano and violin by inviting a master violin teacher from London, England and a pianist from Kingston, Ontario. I undertook to contact the Suzuki Centres in Montreal, Toronto, Hamilton and London, Ontario, and to organize a mini tour, thereby splitting the air fare costs and having each centre provide accommodation. I also sorted out with each centre who would greet the teacher at the Montreal International Airport and the different bus and train stations and who would transport her to the Toronto International Airport for the flight home. We managed to organize her trip and each Suzuki Centre, including ours, had a great experience. I also organized a recital at the Cleary Auditorium in Windsor, which was very successful

Besides my work at the Academy, I started to give Suzuki classes also at a Jewish Community Centre in Detroit. This turned out to be useful in more than one way.

Tamara Russo, a childhood violinist, colleague and friend of mine, was a member of the Beer Sheba orchestra in Israel. During one of my visits to Israel, I decided to visit her in Beer Sheba. We had a good time reminiscing about our childhood and careers. We exchanged addresses. In the winter of 1986, I got a phone call from her. It turned out that she was touring with the Beer Sheba Orchestra in the US. Due to some management problems they lost several bookings and she asked me if I could help them get a couple of engagements.

The tour of the orchestra was underwritten by the Israeli Government, so I didn't have to guarantee them a fee. I contacted the local Jewish Community Centre in Windsor and the Jewish Community Centre in Detroit where I was teaching. Briefly, I managed to organize the concerts in both places. I knew Mendi Rodan, the conductor of the Orchestra from Jerusalem where he was the Director of the Faculty of Music at the University of Jerusalem. He was also from Romania, which turned out to be a great icebreaker!

Their soloist was Gill Shahan, a wonderful young violinist who has made a great international career since then. Shortly before his concert in Windsor, he realized that he left his shoulder-pad in the hotel. I jumped in my car rushed home and got back with the shoulder-pad just in time.

Both concerts were well attended and very successful. The Orchestra and both organizing committees were very grateful to me for initiating these concerts.

Chapter Fifty One

RETURN TO THE WEST COAST

In 1989, my friend the graphologist, my confidante of many years, died of lung cancer, giving me one more reason to leave Windsor.

I was having once or twice a week sessions with my Freudian psychiatrist. Our sessions consisted of me talking and her listening for about fifty minutes. Finally, she would say, "See you next Thursday" (or whatever). After several months of 'treatment' I became angry. I told her that as I didn't receive any feedback from her, I would be better off talking into a tape-recorder — at least I could listen to what I was talking about.

This jolted her out of her 'Freudian torpor' and she actually talked! She suggested that I should buy new tires for my car for the long trip to the West Coast. She agreed with me that it was time to leave Windsor and make a new start in Vancouver.

I sold most of my scores for US $5,000 to a conductor in Detroit, and made arrangements to move some furniture into storage in Vancouver (not having yet an address in Vancouver and not knowing where I would live.)

I decided to drive through the States to the West Coast. I thought it might be less boring than driving through the prairies and also would give me the opportunity to visit some friends in Bismarck, North Dakota. It was mid December, but luckily there was not much snow and the roads were in fair condition, and there was practically no traffic on the highways. Most of the time I was by myself on the road. After visiting my friends in Bismarck I continued my trip.

After an hour or so, out of nowhere a police cruiser showed up and requested that I stop. The fellow from the North Dakota highway patrol came to my car and told me that I was speeding.

"But officer I was on cruise control how could I speed?"

"I don't care if you were flying, the fact is that you were speeding."

We 'negotiated' for a while back and forth, finally he gave me a $40 ticket for speeding. I had no intention of paying. Somehow they got hold of my address in Vancouver and kept sending threatening letters saying that if I ever show up in North Dakota I will be arrested. Finally, I gave in and paid.

One afternoon, I was having a late lunch in Coeur d'Alene, Idaho. I was reading the local paper and read of a sale of surplus military equipment at an air force base. I had heard so much about these 'surplus auctions' (you can buy a computer, a machine gun or even a tank for a few bucks), and as I was not in a hurry to get to Vancouver, I decided to go and see how this kind of thing works.

This was the final day of the sale, and it was closing at 5 PM. I asked how far it was to the air base and how to get there. Although I drove quite fast, it was fifteen minutes to five when I entered the base. The building where the sale was held was at a fair distance from the gate. I ended up driving behind a dump truck traveling at about ten miles an hour. At the first opportunity, I bypassed the truck on the narrow road. Suddenly, flashing lights behind me and a military police car forced me to stop on the side of the road. By that time, it was about five minutes to five so I knew that my bargain hunting ended right there and then. I explained to the officers that I wanted to catch the sale before it closed. They asked for my passport. When they realized that I was born in Romania they completely freaked out. One policeman drew his gun and stood in front of the car.

The other officer talked to his superiors on his radio in the patrol car. Finally, they escorted me off the base to make sure that I left the premises! Actually the situation was quite funny, other than that I made a total fool of myself.

When I arrived in Vancouver there was a great shortage of rental apartments; you had to make an application to rent an apartment and the landlords decided to whom to rent. I put in applications for three apartments, and decided to go over to Victoria and stay with friends for a couple of weeks until the apartment situation was sorted out.

I ended up renting a small apartment on the fifteenth floor, overlooking Stanley Park, the harbour and with a view of the mountains of North Vancouver. The apartment also had a nice balcony and I must confess when I became suicidal from time to time, I considered jumping from that fifteenth floor balcony. Speaking of suicidal thoughts, for many years this 'escape hatch' was on and off in the back of my mind. In some ways it was convenient to know that if nothing worked, if there was no more hope, I had this possibility to check out for good.

Is suicide a selfish act? Definitely! But when you reach the bottom psychologically, all you want to do is to end the torment, get it over with and get out! You don't think of children, or your wife, your parents, or even your friends who might be hurt. All you see is your hopeless situation and you wish to end it.

LITHIUM

After my first suicide attempt years ago, the nurse at the hospital who gave me my medication told me that I will have to take Lithium for the rest of my life. My reaction? Nobody can force me to take something for the rest of my life! I pretended to take my Lithium capsules, hiding them under my tongue or with the help of my tongue on one side of my mouth until the nurse left then I hid them in the night table. This went on for several days until they found the unused capsules.

Now if a doctor or anybody else had explained to me that Lithium does limit the range of ups and downs of manic-depression to a more moderate level (for reasons yet unexplained even to the medical profession), I would have cheerfully taken them!

To tell the patient that you have to take perhaps an addictive drug for the rest of your life, without explaining it in plain English, is simply not sufficient. Having been prescribed various anti depression drugs over the years, I realized that this is done on a hit or miss basis. You took the green pills so far? OK. Let's try the yellow pills, and so on ad nauseam. The patient is a guinea pig for the pharmaceutical industry. My last serious episode of depression occurred six years ago.

After spending a couple of weeks at the psychiatric ward of the St. Joseph Hospital in Vancouver, a new (at least for me!) psychiatrist came up with the idea of adding a 'booster' to my antidepressant, in the form of two Dexedrine tablets to my antidepressant Wellbutrin. I am also taking religiously my 900 mg. capsules of Lithium

In the last six years, I haven't had one episode of depression or a manic state! I am writing in detail about all this in case the reader or a relative or friend of the reader might find this information useful.

Throughout these periods of depressions and voluntary hospitalizations I carried on a fairly active life. On two occasions I went from a psychiatric ward to Mexico City, to conduct the National Symphony Orchestra of Mexico. Based on the success of the concerts I assume that I was OK!

DOLLAR CONCERTS OF THE PACIFIC

The Vancouver Sun, CKNW and the PNE
PRESENT:
Family Day at the Philharmonic
the 1st "Dollar Concert of the Pacific"
at the PACIFIC COLISEUM
Sunday, September 6, 1992 at 3 p.m.

On returning to the West Coast, I decided that I would resurrect somehow my concept of the Dollar Concerts. I incorporated the Dollar Concerts of the Pacific, and I tried to follow up every lead and every possible venue to turn my dream into reality. The first opportunity came when I was able to convince the Pacific National Exhibition's Board of Directors to present a Dollar Concert during the 1992 PNE. This plan materialized on September 6, 1992.

It was called "the 1st Dollar Concert of the Pacific" and the PNE gave it the title "Family Day at the Philharmonic" I engaged for the concert an orchestra composed of some of the best musicians in Vancouver and we called it 'The Pacific Philharmonic Orchestra'. (The concert was to take place in the Pacific Coliseum, capacity 16,000 people).

For the performance of Tchaikovsky's 1812 Overture Solenelle, I managed to obtain the services of the 'Band of the 15th Field Regiment of the Royal Canadian Artillery' whose conductor was Richard van Slyke. The program had great variety, from Brahms and Cimarosa, through Haydn, Mozart, Prokofiev, Puccini, Strauss Jr., to Tchaikovsky. Our soloists included the well known Jazz Flautist, Paul Horn, Li-Ping Zhang, a wonderful young Chinese soprano, Nancy di Nuovo, a virtuoso Canadian violinist, Joelle Rabu Canadian Chansoniere and her Pianist-Arranger J.Douglas Dodd, and Kevin Evans, (the Newscaster of the Canadian Broadcasting Corporation) was narrating Peter and the Wolf of Prokofiev. I also had a young girl from the audience 'conduct' Brahms Hungarian Dance No. 6, and we would have audience participation in Haydn's Toy Symphony, which is always great fun.

Although we had just a couple of thousand people in the audience, the concert was a great success. And I was determined that I will keep trying to organize some Dollar concerts along the successful formula of our concert in Windsor which was sponsored by The Windsor Star.

Two years passed until finally, it looked like I was successful to convince the powers to be at The Vancouver Star to sponsor the concerts. We planned three concerts. March 26, 1994, Tchaikovsky Favourites. May 1, Canada's Brightest Stars and June 5, 1994, The Best of Beethoven. We planned to charge only Eight Dollars for adults (and still only One Dollar for children). A family with four children could come in for twenty Dollars, less than four movie tickets.

Les Préludes

present

DOLLAR CONCERTS
AT THE PACIFIC COLISEUM

Come & have fun with us!

March 26, May 1, June 5, 1994

CHILDREN PAY ONLY $1!
(NO GST OR SERVICE CHARGE FOR CHILDREN!)

Popular Classical Concerts for the Whole Family!

❖ **TCHAIKOVSKY FAVORITES**
(Nutcracker, Romeo & Juliet, 1812)

❖ **CANADA'S BRIGHTEST STARS**
(Great Soloists)

❖ **THE BEST OF BEETHOVEN**
(Eroica, Fate, Fidelio, Emperor)

SUBSCRIBE NOW!
and have a chance to WIN:
• $35,000 towards a 3 year lease on the New 1994 Ford Aspire (no annual miles) • Two Tickets to New York, New Orleans or Orlando, Florida; • A Glorious Weekend for Two at the 5 Diamond Le Meridien Hotel in Vancouver, B.C. or • a chance to conduct a 100-piece Orchestra!

THE PACIFIC PHILHARMONIC ORCHESTRA
and the **Band of the 15th Field Regiment** of the **Royal Canadian Artillery**

*Conducted by **Maestro***
LASZLO GATI

Ford

SUBSCRIBE & SAVE UP TO 33% OVER SINGLE TICKET PRICES!

SUBSCRIPTIONS, INFORMATION AT

SPONSORED BY

TICKETMASTER
Telephone 280-4444

TOM LEE *Music*

▲ **DELTA AIR LINES**

MERIDIEN VANCOUVER

We had to have at least twelve thousand people to break even. To get this kind of crowd, I explained to the Editor of The Vancouver Sun, that we needed full page advertising on the Front Page and several other full page adds (as we got from The Windsor Star), editorials and additional promotional ideas.

Finally, I got the OK from him. The Editor told me: "LET'S GO AHEAD"!

You can imagine my feelings! I went ahead and got additional sponsors and contributions. Beside The Vancouver Sun, CKNW Radio and BCTV committed themselves to help promote the concerts. Delta Airlines, the Ford Motor Company, Tom Lee Music and Le Meridien Hotel joined in as sponsors. For subscribers to the concerts, we offered the chance to win $5.000 Dollars for a two year lease on a new 1994 Ford Aspire car. (Ford changed its mind and this car didn't go into production!) Delta airlines offered two tickets to New York, New Orleans or Orlando, Florida. A glorious weekend at the five Diamond Le Meridien Hotel in Vancouver, a chance to conduct a 100 piece Orchestra! In addition to the extremely low ticket prices, we also offered a 33% discount for subscribers.

I spent more than ten thousand dollars in having flyers and posters printed and making arrangements to be distributed, deposits on reserving the Pacific Coliseum, various insurance costs, the printing of the tickets, etc., etc. Everything was in place except for one, The Vancouver Sun!

In-spite of the commitment of the Editor to provide all the advertising and promotion the project needed, practically nothing materialized. We had a small ad (perhaps 6 x 6 inches) ON PAGE ELEVEN OF THE PAPER! I looked frantically for help at The Sun, going as high as I could, but to no avail. I had two options. Go ahead with the project on my own, and risk losing fifty-sixty thousand dollars, or cancel the whole project and loose 'ONLY' ten-thousand plus dollars!

As painful as it was, and all the wasted time and energy, I had no choice, I had to cancel the whole project! The situation reminded me of my experience in 1958, when Pepsi Cola made a commitment to me (in writing!) to sponsor eight open air concerts in the La Fontaine Park in Montreal. A salesman from the commercial department of the CBC (Canadian Broadcasting Corporation) managed to convince them to sponsor some hockey broadcasts instead.

If we are throwing the greatest achievements of Western Culture on the garbage dump and idolizing instead crass commercialism, the profit, the BOTTOM LINE!, what kind of inheritance are we leaving for future Generations? The Pyramids, the Taj Mahal, the Louvre, the Prado, Mozart's and Beethoven's music have no intrinsic commercial value per se, and millions and millions of people and several generations are admiring these summits of human achievements. Can you imagine, a hundred years from now, our future 'tourist generations' visiting The New York Stock Exchange as the greatest achievement of our present generation, where the Chairman managed to amass two hundred-fifty million dollars! (And other people managed to lose hundreds of millions of dollars . . .) Perhaps there will be guided tours to the producers of military paraphernalia like, Boeing, Raytheon, etc., which were producing, among others, the antiballistic missiles (which proved to be totally useless against box cutters!).

"What is better? To be sane in an insane society or to be insane in a sane society?" (Huxley, "Pala, The Island").

Chapter Fifty Two

1993 "THE PIANO SUMMIT"

I was always aware of the difficulties young musicians faced in establishing themselves as soloists, and the obstacles they faced in trying to move up the ranks. When I started my active conducting career, I made it a practice to engage young, unknown soloists, some of whom subsequently became very well known. I just had to be convinced that they were talented and able to offer a quality musical experience to the audience.

The monopolistic control of the classical concert scene in North America by a few major management companies such as Columbia Artists Management makes it practically impossible for young artists to 'break in', unless they have virtually unlimited funds. In January 1965, I was attending a course in Symphony Orchestra Management in New York, presented by the American Symphony Orchestra League at Steinway Hall, organized by Helen Thompson, the President of the ASOL at the time. One day, we had a visit by the representatives of the major managements companies— Columbia, Hurok, and others. In 1965 an artist had to put down $50,000 to be put on Columbia's Artist List! And for this amount of money there was no guarantee of even one concert. Furthermore, the artist had to pay for all the publicity materials, photographs, phone calls, and even stamps. This situation persisted for decades.

Finally in early Nineties, based on my many years of experience, I had another brilliant idea. At least at the time I thought it was brilliant . . .

Les Préludes

The accepted way for young soloists to get a break is to take part in various music competitions, like the Van Cliburn, the Queen Elizabeth of Belgium, the Queen Sofie of Norway, the Rubinstein Competition in Israel, the Montreal International Competition, the Leeds Competition, and the Tchaikovsky Competition in Moscow, the Geneva Competition, and others. I personally hate competitions. For every winner there might be hundreds more losers, and this offends my egalitarian sensibilities. In my experience, winning a competition hinges on so many factors, from being a student of one of the jury members, to having a jury which has a particular cultural, or even racial bias, to occasionally being an outstanding soloist and putting on a good performance on a particular night, that the First prize is not necessarily a true reflection of the abilities of the musicians. From this you may get the idea that competitions don't necessarily predict the future careers of its participants. Many times it happens that the person who did not win a First prize ends up having a great career while the First prize winner is a one-night-sensation.

There is also an additional problem. A management company will often agree to represent the ultimate winner of the competition. Because of the publicity value to representing the winner of such a prestigious competition, (for example, the Van Cliburn) this management company might book the winner for forty, even fifty concerts the first year. So here is a young pianist, who has previously performed perhaps three or four concerts a year, suddenly faced with an enormous challenge to their physical stamina, their mental toughness, their emotional maturity and their artistic integrity. And not every young artist is up to this challenge. For some young artists, winning a competition means a brief and intense period of work, followed by a breakdown and burnout from which they may never recover. I do not know how many promising musicians have had their careers ruined by early over-exploitation, but I suspect the number is considerable.

I decided to create an alternative venue for young musicians. Every year I received a catalogue from Geneva which listed all the competitions of the previous year, and all the winners and those who placed. I decided to select young pianists, not just the first prize winners, but those who had won different prizes in all sorts of different categories from a range of competitions The categories ranged from performing chamber music, playing the music of one composer, say, Stravinsky, or playing new pieces composed for a competition. My thought was that a young pianist who had won prizes at different competitions and in different categories had shown more talent than a pianist who had won a single first prize. I would choose four of whom I considered the most outstanding young pianists in the world, book a hall, and bring them to Vancouver.

I also thought, (wrongly, as it turned out) that audiences would break down the doors to have a chance to hear four of the best young pianists in the world. Vancouver audiences would otherwise have had to travel to Brussels, Moscow, Fort Worth, Leeds, or Geneva to hear these young talents, but thanks to me, they would be playing right here in Vancouver. The concert was to take place shortly after the US-Russia Summit Meeting between Presidents Clinton and Yeltsin which happened in Vancouver, and to drive home the concept that these are some of the best young pianists in the world, I named my concert "The Piano Summit."

I picked four pianists of different nationalities who had all won several, and different prizes at various competitions—one American, one Russian, one Italian and one Canadian, who was of Korean origin. When it turned out that two of my soloists (Simone Pedroni and the Russian, Ilia Itin), were chosen to participate at the 1993 Van Cliburn Competition, a very prestigious event which is held every four years, I decided to go down to Texas, where the competition was taking place, to pay Van Cliburn a visit. Van Cliburn had played with me and the Victoria Symphony Orchestra in the seventies and since then he had treated me like a brother. I met my future soloists and took some publicity pictures with them in front of the Van Cliburn Competition sign.

Van Cliburn invited me to the reception for the members of the jury prior to the beginning of the competition. The reception was held in his home, a very expensive residence surrounded by high walls in an exclusive suburb. I arrived early, so I decided to walk around for a while among the beautiful homes. I had started to take pictures, when out of nowhere a police car appeared. The policeman questioned me as to why I was taking pictures. After I explained to him who I was and the fact that I was trying to kill some time because I was early for the reception, he let me go, but warned me not to take any more pictures. Whenever something like this happens, I feel content again that I had decided so many years ago to move to Canada rather than the U.S., despite the fact that I would have had many more opportunities down south.

I returned to join the reception. I met several good friends who were members of the jury, among them, Philippe Entremont and Moura Lympany. I had a wonderful time sharing musical experiences and stories with this illustrious crowd. One member of the jury was a very well known lady pianist who had played the Saint Saens Second Piano Concerto with me about twenty years earlier, during my tenure with the Victoria Symphony Orchestra. The international classical music community is not really that large. Van Cliburn's mother was seated in a wheelchair in the middle of the room and was the centre of attention. I know what an important role she played in Van Cliburn's life. When he had played with me in Victoria, he was on the telephone continuously to his mother, getting reassurance, praise, and advice.

After several days at the competition I returned to Vancouver from Texas. I arranged with the Renaissance Hotel to provide free accommodation to my soloists and offered each pianist $3,000. The Renaissance also provided free accommodation for me and for my daughters, who came to Vancouver for the occasion from Los Angeles. I had major financial hurdles to overcome. I had to deposit $25,000 as a guarantee before the Vancouver Symphony would sign the contract, and I had to make a deposit for the Orpheum Concert Hall, pay insurance, have flyers and posters and tickets printed, etc.

THE PIANO SUMMIT

Simone Pedroni, Laszlo Gati, and Ilia Itin

Lucille Yoonhi Chung

Stephen Prutsman

JUNE 20, 1993 · 8:00 PM

AT THE

ORPHEUM THEATRE

So, am I naive to have believed that the population would come out to hear the best young pianists in the world? Were my publicity efforts not sufficient? Would slicker advertising have helped? Or was I pushing a lost cause? I can believe everything but the last statement.

MUSIC HISTORY IS MADE IN VANCOUVER!

"The Piano Summit!"

You can hear four sensational pianists, winners of major awards at some of the most prestigious music competitions, perform the:

PROKOFIEV, *CONCERTO* No. 3 in C Major
MOZART, *CONCERTO* No. 17 in G Major, K. 453
SAINT-SAËNS, *CONCERTO* No. 2 in G Minor, Op. 22
RACHMANINOV, *RHAPSODY* on a Theme of Paganini, Op. 43

WITH MEMBERS OF THE

VANCOUVER SYMPHONY ORCHESTRA
Conductor, LASZLO GATI
former Music Director-Conductor of the
Victoria and Windsor Symphony Orchestras.

IN AN EXTRAORDINARY CONCERT!
AT THE

ORPHEUM
SUNDAY, JUNE 20, 1993, at 8:00 p.m.
(Fathers' Day!)

SOLOISTS:
Stephen Prutsman (Baltimore, U.S.A.)
Simone Pedroni (Novara, Italy)
Lucille Yoonhi Chung (Montreal, Canada)
Ilia Itin (Sverdlovsk, Russia)

Tickets at TICKET MASTER, TEL.: 280-4444
Discounts for Seniors and Students
PROGRAMME AND SOLOISTS SUBJECT TO CHANGE

Our SPECIAL THANKS to TOM LEE MUSIC, for offering the choice of four NEW CONCERT
GRAND PIANOS to our SOLOISTS (STEINWAY, BÖSENDORFER, YAMAHA and PETROF).

The HOTEL MERIDIEN is the
"OFFICIAL HEADQUARTERS" of the
"PIANO SUMMIT"

This is a special presentation of Galiano Management, and the DOLLAR CONCERTS OF THE PACIFIC LTD.

Luckily, a friend of mine had just sold one of her houses and had disposable cash. Knowing the quality of the soloists, I did not want to make the tickets too cheap. And the price should also take into account that the audience did not have to travel to the various competitions, but could hear these great pianists right here in Vancouver.

I sent letters to sixty-two piano teachers offering them discounted tickets for their students. Only two answered. One asked for eleven tickets. The other one wanted just two tickets for herself and her husband, "but only in the Golden Circle"! If I was a piano teacher, I would have taken every student of mine to the concert, even if I had had to pay for their tickets to show them what it takes to be the best in the world.

Alas! Human nature can be funny some times.

Two days before the concert, I realized that we had sold only 800 seats out of 2800! I was looking at a potential deficit of more than $40,000. Alea Jacta est! I decided to just concentrate on the technical and musical aspects: securing a rehearsal hall and a new Steinway piano from Tom Lee (a great local music store), planning the rehearsals and arranging the newspaper interviews, photos, and publicity. I was in no position to cover the financial loss; I had left my last steady position eight years earlier, and I was living on my pension and some guest-conducting engagements. So I decided to postpone the financial worries until after the concert and just enjoy myself. Luckily, my younger daughter Kathy, a tremendous organizer, managed to mobilize about 1200 people to make the house look fairly full. She got disabled people, people from senior homes, and all kinds of others. And a wonderful and a very grateful audience they were.

Prior to the concert I had formed a business partnership with my friend. This was very fortunate. Due to my rather meagre income at the time, I could not deduct the losses from my income tax, but she could. It took three years to write off the losses. My daughters also contributed $5,000 each.

My system worked. I managed to choose Simone Pedroni, (who went on to win the Van Cliburn Competition out of hundreds of contestants), six weeks prior to actually winning the competition. He played with me and the Vancouver Symphony Orchestra only a week after winning the Van Cliburn competition. I had to smile when I heard that the following season it was advertised in Ontario that Simone Pedroni, the winner of the Van Cliburn Competition, would appear for the first time in Canada. This was about ten months after he played in Vancouver. The other performers were no slouches either. As I have previously written, all my soloists were first or second place winners in several competitions. Stephen Prutsman, the American, was the Second prize winner of the Queen Elizabeth Competition in Brussels. Lucille Chung, my Canadian soloist was the Second place winner of The Montreal International Piano Competition and a winner of several other competitions. Simone Pedroni, my Italian soloist, was the First place winner of the Queen Sofie Competition in Norway and several other competitions. Ilia Itin was a prize winner at the Tchaikovsky Competition in Moscow

To show you the calibre of these soloists I have to tell a little story. My Canadian soloist, Lucille Chung was studying at the Julliard School of Music in New York at the time. I gave all my soloists the option to choose whatever concerto or piece they wanted to play and which they felt comfortable with. When I invited Lucille, she didn't know what she wanted to play. Four weeks before the concert, she decided she wanted to learn (!) the Ravel Piano Concerto. After talking things over with her professor, she decided to learn (!) Saint Saens' Second Piano Concerto! It turned out, that not only did she learn the concerto inside-out by concert time, but she gave a magnificent performance. That is a fine musician.

In spite of all the financial problems I had to face, this concert will remain one of the most memorable of my career and one of the seminal highlights of my musical experiences. Every one of my soloists got a standing ovation — even from the paying members!

Long live the young generation!

Chapter Fifty Three

1994 - WINTER MUSINGS

Everybody is so busy with the day-to-day struggle, fighting the traffic, arranging daycare, making time to shop on the way to and from work, coping with the stresses of work (if one still has a job), attempting to filter the information overload blasting at us through TV, the Internet, advertising and computer technology, that very few people can enjoy the luxury of finding a breathing space to look at themselves, their lives, and life in general...for instance, musing lazily on a Sunday morning.

It is a good time to contemplate. Now that I am officially an old age pensioner, although I still am physically, mentally, and spiritually active, I can indulge myself in this kind of leisure time. I am listening to the Toronto Symphony Orchestra on the radio. They are playing Mussorgsky, Tchaikovsky, and Prokofiev's Romeo and Juliet. I look out the window at the trees, the gray sky, the falling leaves and contemplate the folly of human life.

My mother died at the age of 95 on September 23, 1994, almost three weeks after her birthday on September 5, and just a couple of days before my 69th Birthday on September 25, 1994.

While it is natural to expect that somebody might die at the ripe old age of 95, it is still a milestone in the life of the child. One has only one mother, and her passing drives home not just the finality of the event, but the finality of life itself, compounded by the realization that we children are next to depart, at least if the chronological order is to be maintained.

Les Préludes

Elections in the US have just concluded, and I am in a philosophical mood...

Last Tuesday, the US mid-term elections brought about a radical "open" swing to the right. The reason I use the word "open" is that, behind closed doors, there are as many right-wingers in the Democratic Party as there are in the Republican Party. It is a mystery how the mind works. How did I get from leisurely Sunday morning musings to the US elections? The "Southern Democrat" who jumped ship immediately after the elections "officially" joining the Republican Party, was as right wing as many of the other Southern Democrats — and right wing Republicans. I think the answer to the question, "What is the difference between a right-wing Republican or a right-wing Democrat?" is simply "location."

"Le plus ca change, le plus c'est la meme chose." (The more things change, the more they stay the same.) And if I were to use a more recent idiom, The Who wrote a song which includes the lyrics, "Come meet the new boss, same as the old boss . . . Oh, I won't get fooled again!"

I was born in Romania in 1925—in a virtually feudal country. Only a small segment of the economy could have qualified as "capitalistic." I grew up as a Jewish kid under increasing anti-Semitism and fascism, and I spent the five years of the war under the constant threat of being shipped out to Auschwitz or some other extermination camp. During the war, I also spent one and a half years in various kinds of forced labor and having the distinction at various times during the war of being bombed by the Americans, the British, the Russians and finally, even the Germans.

I spent ten years in Budapest, Hungary, from April 1946 to November 1956, during the rebuilding of the city and the takeover of the national government by the Communist Party. I witnessed the first years and the genuine enthusiasm of the "building of socialism", then the purges of the "spies of Tito", including the public hanging of Prime Minister Laszlo Rayk, whose name now graces the square in Budapest where he was executed. I experienced increasing disappointment with the process of "building communism" under the Stalinist system and the personality cult of Rakos, which culminated in the bloody October Uprising of 1956.

I have spent the past thirty-seven years in Canada, enjoying the positive aspects of so-called Western Capitalism and watching the portents of the disintegration of Canadian society turn to actual degradation. The actions of the present movers and shakers of the capitalist world are living proof that the careless nihilism of the "Apres moi la deluge" (After me the Flood) philosophy is still alive and well. It is unbelievable to see not just the unlimited greed, but particularly the shortsightedness, the utter blindness of these people, our so-called "leaders". With the present technology of computers and worldwide information available to them— they should have no problem in predicting the collapse of all of our economic, political, and ecological systems if the present course is maintained.

This contemplation takes me back to my birthplace, and my father's birthplace—Timisoara, Romania, called Temesvar, Austria-Hungary.

I always get a chuckle when I start a lecture saying that I was born in the same city as my father, but in a different country. For today's average American or Canadian, it is hard to understand that borders can change, for example, in the Balkans, where this happens quickly and frequently. North Americans should remind themselves that not so long ago Los Angeles, San Francisco, and in truth, all of California and Florida belonged to Mexico. The Mexicans have not forgotten this.

I was born in the same building in which Prince Eugen de Savoya had his headquarters during his campaign against the Turks in the early 1500's. There is even a plaque on the building commemorating this event. Perhaps after my departure from this earth, another plaque might commemorate the fact of my birth. So do I live with, and am part of, a long and complex history, something which our leaders are ignoring, to our great danger.

During my family's tour in Romania in 1973, we parked our Volvo on the other side of the street and from the open window of the car I took a picture of the house in which I was born, a house which seems not to have changed. I did this in order not to create suspicion by getting out of the car and taking a picture of a place of such "strategic importance". Such was the political climate in Romania at the time. During that car trip through Romania the most frequently seen highway sign was that of a camera crossed out by two red lines— the universal "forbidden" sign.

I will never forget how I scared the attendant at a gas station in Cluj when I took a picture of my wife and our two daughters standing in front of the Volvo while it was filled up. He gesticulated wildly to stop me, because even a gas station was considered an object of "strategic importance" by the paranoid Romanian government!

My earliest memory of childhood is that of standing on a small stool and looking out the window through a small opening between the large white pillows (the maid had put them by the window to air out). I still remember the worn-out wooden staircase. Although I don't have an actual recollection of the event, apparently, I familiarized myself in a rather dramatic way with that wooden staircase. A scar on my forehead still remains.

What happened was this: my Viennese Fraulein was going to take me for a walk in the park, so she put me in my baby carriage and left the carriage on the landing of the second floor of our house. She left me unattended for couple of minutes to pick up something from our apartment. I was quite a heavy baby and apparently, in my enthusiasm to go for a walk, I rocked vigorously back and forth. My momentum transferred to the carriage which moved across the landing and eventually tipped over the top step. The carriage and I tumbled down the staircase and I ended up with an opening in my skull — which is perhaps why my "third eye" seems to be fairly developed.

Looking at the present, increasingly insane world around us with all three eyes, I see the following: an explosive rise in "fundamentalist", reactionary thinking, whether it is Republican, Christian, Islamic, Jewish Orthodox, Protestant, or Catholic; a flourishing of ethnic wars such as those in Bosnia-Herzegovina, Chechnya, and the Sudan; a recurrence of genocide as policy, such as happened in Rwanda, and the threat of international terrorism on a level heretofore not imagined.

What a scenario for a peaceful future.

While this might sound very egoistic, at this moment I have to thank the heavens for being so old, in the hopes that I can check out before this whole crazy situation reaches its climax in a catastrophe, whether it be a world war, an economic collapse, or an ecological disintegration...or all three.

Les Préludes

Chapter Fifty Four

GAUDEAMUS IGITUR

My high school class was supposed to graduate together from high school in 1945. This graduation did not take place because some of us, after having been in different forced labour locations, had been dispersed widely after the war. To remedy this situation, some of my former classmates, presently based in Israel, decided to have a ceremony fifty years later in 1995 so that we could 'graduate' together. The former students came from Canada, the USA, Germany, Romania and, naturally, Israel. The reunion took place at the beautiful Carmel Gardens Hotel at Zichron Yaacov'close to Tel Aviv.

For me, it was an amazing feeling to be again with my classmates as if the fifty odd years of separation didn't exist! With four of my former classmates it was an instantaneous recognition of each other, as if we had seen each other just yesterday and not more than five decades ago! Alas, most of my former colleagues were total strangers — but after a few days together, some of them became vaguely familiar.

We heard and exchanged amazing stories, some funny, from our childhood, some serious, from our later years. One colleague told a story when they tied together the pictures on the wall of their classroom. When the teacher started the class, one of them pulled the string and moved the pictures back and forth. The kids yelled EARTHQUAKE! EARTHQUAKE! And ran out of the class. The teacher went over to the neighboring class and asked his colleague if he felt an earthquake? He answered no, but that day was April 1!

Here is a serious story. One colleague was captured by the Arabs during the Arab Israeli war in 1948. As they were taken to a prison camp some Arabs were shooting at them. He had a Bible in his backpack and a bullet lodged in his Bible, which saved his life. Suffice to say that he became an ultra-religious person.

We had identical twins in our class, Kallai Tibi and Vicki (their nicknames). They specialized in confusing our teachers by changing places with each other and answering questions directed to the other twin. Tibi came to pick me up from my brother's apartment in Tel Aviv and to take me to the Hotel. I was sorry to hear that Vicki died in November 1992. A friend of mine had this joke. You don't ask 'how is your wife', but 'who is your wife'. At our age, I think we should ask, 'is he/she still alive?'

To end our graduation ceremonies the organizers wanted for all of us to sing together the student song which is traditionally used at graduation. Using a tape recorder, they pre-programmed the spot in the Academic Festival Overture of Johannes Brahms where the melody occurs.

When the time came to sing it, they couldn't find the spot on the tape so they asked me to conduct them in a 'GREAT' performance of this well-known tune. It was a very moving feeling for me to conduct my childhood colleagues, their wives and some friends in a performance of this student song which had been delayed for fifty years.

Gaudeamus Igitur

Christian Wilhelm Kindleben (1748-1785)

"Gaudeamus" has been the traditional University student's song for two hundred years, and the tune is still played (and even sung along to, depending on the University) at graduation ceremonies today. Historically, it has also been the University student's traditional DRINKING song, and is regarded as the original embodiment of the free and easy student life.

HISTORY

Although Gaudeamus is regarded as being the oldest surviving student's song, claims that it was written as early as the 13th century are largely unfounded. A Latin manuscript dated 1267 does, indeed, contain the words to verses two and three of the modern Gaudeamus (as part of a poem entitled "Scribere Proposui"); however, it did not contain the words 'Gaudeamus Igitur' or, indeed, any of the modern first verse, and was set to music which bears no resemblance to the well-known modern melody.

The earliest known appearance of something close to the modern lyrics is in a handwritten student songbook from Germany dating between 1723 and 1750; these were picked up by C.W. Kindleben, but he made important changes to them before he published the resultant (modern) lyrics in his "Student lieder" in 1781 (the German origins of the modern lyrics explain the rather un-Latin word 'antiburschius' in the seventh verse, which is 'Latinised' German referring to student fraternities).

The melody, however, is of less certain origin; it was already quite well-known when C.W. Kindleben published his lyrics.

Translation of Gaudeamus Igitur

Gaudeamus igitur, iuvenes dum sumus
Post iucundam iuventutem
Post molestam senecutem
Our habebit humus
We delight as long as we are young
After a pleasant youth
After a painful old age
The ground will have us

Ubi sunt which handle our, in mundo fuere
Vadite AD superos
Forward AD inferos
Ubi iam fuere

Les Préludes

Where are those who were on the ground before us
They were towards the skies
They passed in the hells
Where they already were

Vita will nostra brevis is brevi finietur
Venit bit velociter
Raped our atrociter
Nemini parcetur
Our life is short, it will finish soon
 Death will come quickly
Our tears of atrocément
 By not saving anybody

Cheer Academia, alive Professores
Cheer membrum quodlibet
Live will membra quaelibet
Semper sint in flora
Live the school, live the professors
That each member lives
That all the members live
How they are always flourishing!

Living omnes virgines, easy, formosae
Living and mulieres
Tenerae, amabiles
Bonae, laboriosae!
What lives all the virgins, easy, beautiful
The women live
Tender, pleasant
Good, hard-working!

Cheer and respublica and which illam regit
Cheer will nostra civitas
Maecenatum caritas
Quae our difficulty protegit
Live the State and that which directs
Live our city
And the generosity of the patrons
 Who protects us here

Pereat tristitia, pereant osores
Pereat diabolus
Fatherland maledictus
Atque irrisores!
That from go away sadness, the troubles
That from the devil goes away
Damned by the fatherland
And others

Les Préludes

Chapter Fifty Five

THE LECTURER

To fight my loneliness in Vancouver, I joined one of the best Toastmaster Clubs in Vancouver. The standard of the club was high, with some excellent speakers and a good atmosphere of camaraderie. After the meetings we usually went to a nearby pub, had a beer and some lively discussions. At a later date, I visited various other clubs making many friends, some friendships lasting fifteen years up to this day. Because the routine of the meetings is always the same (naturally, the quality of speakers varies) after a while attending the weekly meetings became boring. Once in a while I might visit different clubs.

In the summer of 1989, I visited my daughter Suzanne in Los Angeles. With a friend of hers we went to see the Pritikin Institute in Santa Monica and have a 'vegetarian' lunch there. (Since then, the building has been turned into a high class hotel.) It turned out that Suzanne's friend specialized in memory training classes and he did this also on various cruise ships. This was music to my ears. I asked him if he could tell me whom to contact to enquire about the possibility of giving lectures on ships. He said that most cruise companies work through an agency and he would mail me a list of addresses.

Several weeks later, he sent me a list of forty (!) Cruise lines and agencies. I wrote to all of them! I had a slightly positive answer from three agencies, one (working for Cunard) asking to send her a video tape of one of my lectures. I sent her the video in May.

June. July, August, September, October, nothing, just silence. For the fun of it I phoned her up asking if she had received the tape. "Oh yes!" was the answer, followed immediately by, "Could you join a cruise next week on the QE2 from Southampton to New York?"

I said, "I have been waiting six months to hear from you and now you want me to go on less than a week's notice? When is the next cruise?" She said in two weeks. That would be fine, I said. As I could take a travelling companion with me, I asked my daughters to decide amongst themselves who would like to join me on this trip. This time it was Suzanne. As she was flying from Los Angeles and me from Vancouver, we decided to meet in London at the bus terminal in front of Victoria Station, where the busses stop.

Our train to Southampton was leaving in a couple of hours, so we looked around in Victoria Station. I have a picture of Suzanne in a candy shop which was filled wall to wall with huge glass cylinders filled with all kind of candies in various colours! We came across a string quartet, composed of young students performing in one of the passageways. We listened for a while than I asked the violinists and the viola player, "Who wants a rest" I replaced the viola player and had some fun playing with them for about fifteen minutes.

The special cruise train stopped right at the dockside in Southampton. As you know, my last crossing of the Atlantic was in the 8.000 ton Arosa Star. The Queen Elizabeth 2 is 62.000 tons, almost eight times bigger than that little ship.

The QE2 is very luxurious, with several dining rooms, a theatre for the nightly shows, a casino, a movie, a library, etc. If you didn't feel like eating in the formal dining rooms, you can always have a buffet breakfast or lunch on the deck, at the rear of the ship. The ship is not only a floating hotel but also a shopping centre where you can find all kind of expensive items. For people who are more interested in practical activities, there is even a large computer room where computer classes are given.

You don't have to satisfy yourself with simply eating and shopping. There are many possibilities for physical exercise. You can walk or jog on the promenade deck for miles. There are tennis courts, exercise room, putting green, basketball court, outdoor and indoor pools, and so on.

After several cruises I became familiar with the hierarchy

of a cruise ship. Naturally, the 'supreme commander' of the ship is the captain reigning over his officers and crew. He is responsible for the safety of the ship, to maintain the ship engines and all the technical aspects in order, keep up the schedule as planned, and so on.

The Hotel Director looks after the accommodation and comfort of the passengers. He is in charge of a number of officers who help him with all the problems related to the passengers, planning excursions on the shore, looking after the luggage delivery to the proper cabins and unloading them on arrival. Finally, there is the catering director who is in charge of the seating arrangements in the various dining rooms, the feeding of 3000-4,000 people, three-times a day, the kitchens, etc. We had a guided tour through the kitchen of the QE2. It is like a huge factory.

Some trainers from the Golden Door Spa in California were running exercise programs on the ship. I got to know the leader of the group which led later to a one week stay at the Golden Door spa in California and a one week stay at the Rancho la Puerta spa in Mexico, giving lectures in both places.

I think the Atlantic is allergic to me (or I am allergic to it). On this crossing I was in a major storm yet again. The prow of the ship must be about six to eight-stories high. Much of the five days crossing of the Atlantic, you couldn't see it because it was covered by the huge waves! Six of us were sitting at a round table in the dinning room having lunch. From a sudden jolt caused by a huge wave, the table cloth including dishes, cutlery flower decorations, and everything else, went flying. We were told later that they lost a large quantity of dishes during this trip.

There was a grand piano in the dining room; at one point this large, heavy instrument started to move towards us. Luckily it was chained to the floor; otherwise, it could have been a catastrophe. Suzanne was seasick all the time walking around with seasickness patches. This didn't stop her from going disco dancing every night!

I was expected to give two one-hour lectures during the trip. To see the location and circumstances of the lectures I decided to attend a lecture myself, it was a lucky break! The ship was rolling so badly that the lecturer performed a kind of ballet hanging on for dear life to the microphone stand!

I decided that I would give my lecture seated behind the microphone stand and save myself and the audience from an improvised ballet performance. Because of the storm, (and a lot of seasickness) there were not too many people at my first lecture, but the situation improved by the second lecture.

Upon arrival to New York City we visited Kathleen, my younger daughter, who was living there at the time. After a couple of days, I returned to Vancouver and Suzie to Los Angeles.

In Vancouver, and Vancouver Island, I started to give lectures, from the Vancouver School Board's Adult Education program, through various colleges including at UBC (the University of British Columbia.). At one point, I was giving lectures at the Vancouver School Board adult education programs, the Capilano College, Kwantlen College, Vancouver College, Camosun College in Victoria, the Pearson College and Malaspina College on Vancouver Island and the University of British Columbia.

After a while, I realized that there was a scheduling problem especially with the colleges. You make a time commitment to them, but they don't make it to you. Whether a program is presented or not depends on the number of participants. If the numbers are too small, they simply cancel the lectures. I remember one year when I was booked for the whole month of February, which meant I reserved my whole month for them. Then, a few days before the starting time of the lectures they cancelled them one by one. Based on this experience I decided to concentrate on the cruise lectures.

My next assignment for Cunard was a twenty-eight-day cruise from Los Angeles to Vancouver, Vancouver to Anchorage, Alaska, and Anchorage to Vancouver. It was a very interesting, educational and wonderful experience. I learned several things. Normally, people travelled one way, Vancouver to Anchorage and flying back to Vancouver, or flying to Anchorage and returning with the Saga fjord to Vancouver. So far so good. But how about the weather?

Going North from Vancouver we had miserable weather,

freezing rain, fog, the visibility was limited to the immediate vicinity of the ship whether on the sea or in a harbour. Suzanne was with me on this cruise and got so disgusted with the cold and unfriendly weather that she jumped ship and returned to Los Angeles from Ketchikan, Alaska. Coming back from Anchorage to Vancouver we had the most gorgeous weather. From Glacier Bay up and down we realized what the poor northbound passengers missed! They had to go home and report: "We were in Alaska!" "But what did you see?" "Nothing."

Another interesting aspect of cruise life is the constant change of passengers. As a conductor, I am used to see the changing personnel of an orchestra over a period of five, ten, twenty years. On a cruise ship this happens every five, ten days! Just when you start to be familiar with certain people sitting at a certain table in the dining room, suddenly, somebody else is sitting there! I realized how frustrating this must be for the waiters serving their tables, losing a group of people with whom they established a certain rapport and starting all over practically every week.

Although I just witnessed three changes of new groups of passengers, I felt a loss when the familiar faces suddenly disappeared.

I was privileged to take part on some very interesting cruises. For instance, a Scandinavian cruise from London-Tilbury to Saint Petersburg. We were fortunate to catch at the Hermitage the exhibition of paintings the Soviet troops seized in Europe during the Second World War. Willy-nilly you felt history all around you. Leningrad-Saint Petersburg itself, the Hermitage, the beautiful palaces, the Aurora battleship, its gun giving the signal for the start of the Great October Revolution, the Winter Palace, the Admiralty, and others too numerous to mention.

In the courtyard of one of the palaces there was a military band dressed in some old dilapidated Tsarist uniforms playing for the tourists and collecting donations (in Western style). I felt sorry for them and the great Russian people. How many more dictators and tragedies they will have to go through?

Our tourist guide told us a joke in the tour bus, "Who is

multilingual?" We answered "Somebody who speaks several languages," "Who is bilingual?" he asked. We said "Somebody who speaks two languages." He asked "who is unilingual?" This time he answered "The Americans!" Unfortunately, this is not just a joke, it is the American Tragedy. As English became the practical Esperanto of the World the Americans never did and do not now bother to learn the languages (and cultures, customs, history, etc.) of other nations.

With American troops stationed in more than hundred-twenty countries and the US flexing its muscles as the only World Power, the advocates of the New American Empire would do well to catch up and learn at least a couple of other languages (like Arabic) before they will go through a few more Vietnams!

I went on several cruises in the Caribbean, once as far as Trinidad. The same pattern repeated itself over and over. These little islands were run over by millions of tourists. American and international 'duty free stores' on the main streets. Besides serving customers in shops, the native-born are limited to being taxi drivers, policemen and street cleaners!

The profits are 'downloaded offshore' and the locals don't benefit at all from the tremendous wealth and live in abject poverty. Naturally, this situation leads to tremendous frustration and political upheavals. We couldn't even land on one island because an emergency had been declared!

Another interesting cruise was going from Auckland-New Zealand to Tahiti, visiting a number of fanciful Polynesian islands like Bora Bora, Suva the capital of Fiji, New Guinea, New Caledonia, Solomon Islands, Tonga, and Moorea. We had an interesting experience one day when we crossed the International Date Line twice, going from Wednesday to Thursday, back and forth.

The Caribbean pattern was repeated on all these islands. Extreme wealth siphoned off to far distant offshore tax free heavens and extreme poverty for the natives. Naturally, the well to do (mainly American) tourists couldn't care less. They want to have fun with their dollars.

I mentioned earlier that on the QE2 I met some people from The Golden Door Spa in Southern California. Some of the group came to my lecture and a few months later I received an invitation for a one week stay at The Golden Door and (the hard task) to give two one hour lectures during that week.

At the time, one week at The Golden Door cost $5,000 dollars. Now, (in 2004) it is only $6,400. The Golden Door is a beautiful spa built in Japanese style with Japanese gardens, ponds with goldfish pools, exercise rooms, and various kinds of relaxation areas. I received the full treatment as the paying guests. As I was trying to lose weight, I was put on a 1200 calorie vegetarian diet, which was served up beautifully. Pizza made with roasted red pepper instead of meat and other tasty amendments to regular (fattening) cuisine.

I had my personal physical exercise trainers who developed a special routine for strengthening my weak points. When I left the spa I was given a special video showing the exercises I should practice at home. I had massage therapy, aromatherapy, and mud wrapping; I took part in water exercises and volleyball, participated in Tai Chi classes with a visiting master, went for early morning walks in the hills with the other guests — all in all a week that was worth every penny.

Next year I was invited to the Rancho la Puerta, situated just inside the Mexican border. The spa is located there because Edmund Szekely, the Hungarian health guru who established the spa, couldn't get a US visa at the time and this was the closest location they could find to the Hungarian Jewish colony of Hollywood, their future clientele. The spa has beautiful surroundings and is built and organized in a different fashion from The Golden Door. Everybody has their own individual chalets built in different styles. There are nice walkways through the lovely grounds to get from one end of the spa to the other. This spa is less pricey than The Golden Door (in the $3,000 per week range instead of $6,000). The whole atmosphere is less formal and less structured. I had a great time and I hope they enjoyed my lectures.

Les Préludes

Chapter Fifty Six

POLITICAL ACTIVISM

Having experienced directly (and sometimes escaped from) the positives and negatives of all of the dominant political systems of the Twentieth Century, I have developed a number of strong political and economic opinions. I was never tempted by political office, but I never backed away from expressing my views or from participating in Canadian politics at the municipal, provincial, or federal level. Most of my participation was in the form of presenting my views strongly and clearly when I mixed, as I often did, with politicians and business and education leaders. As my conducting career wound down, I ended up speaking at public hearings on important political matters, municipal, provincial, and federal.

My views are most elegantly and succinctly expressed by a transcript of the following presentation which I made in 1996, at public hearings which the government of British Columbia held on the MAI, the Multilateral Agreement on Investment. As a Canadian citizen and a member of the Council of Canadians, I felt deeply compelled to present a case against this violent, imperialistic, abusive, and regressive piece of corporate statism.

LASZLO GATI'S PRESENTATION AT THE BC GOVERNMENT'S HEARINGS ON THE MAI
(Multinational Agreement on Investment)

L. Gati: By the way, my name is Laszlo Gati, for those who think I'm a lady.

Les Préludes

Your Honour, ladies and gentlemen, first of all, I wish to congratulate the government of British Columbia for holding these public hearings on the MAI, and I thank you for the opportunity to address this illustrious panel. I am appearing in front of you as a concerned citizen, one of almost thirty million in Canada and close to six billion worldwide. While I am not appointed officially to be a spokesperson for anybody or everybody, many of my concerns are universal, and they affect most people.

Before addressing some of the issues connected with the MAI, let me tell you a little bit about myself. My name is Laszlo Gati, and I am an orchestra conductor. I was born in the same city as my father, but in a different country. When he was born, our city was called Temesvar and belonged to Austria-Hungary. By the time I was born, it belonged to Romania, and it was named Timisoara. At the time, Romania was practically a feudal kingdom. I grew up under increasing Fascism and anti-Semitism and spent the war years under a Fascist military dictatorship. I spent one and a half years in various forced labour camps and had many harrowing experiences during the war, narrowly escaping a pogrom, several air raids and bombing attacks by the Americans, British, Soviet and Germans at one time or another.

After the war, I went to Budapest, Hungary, to continue my musical studies. I stayed there until November 1956. I saw the building of so-called socialism, with its many positive and its many increasingly negative aspects, the growing personality cult, the power struggles — which included the public hanging of Hungary's Prime Minister, Laszlo Rajk,- and finally the Hungarian Uprising and Soviet military intervention. We left Hungary in November of 1956, heading in a taxi towards the Yugoslav border and finally ending up in Belgrade. On our way to Canada, we survived a plane crash near Munich, Germany, and spent three months in hospital. We finally arrived in Montreal in April of 1957, where my parents were living at that time.

During my 42 years in Canada, I participated in, watched and enjoyed the increasing welfare and cultural development of our country. Unfortunately, after about fifteen years, I watched with dismay the gradual deterioration in every sector: economic, political, cultural, welfare, etc. This threat accelerated especially since the signing of first, the Free Trade Agreement, and then NAFTA, and now we are living under the Damocles sword of the MAI, which darkens the horizons even more.

I mentioned earlier that I am a musician. Actually, I am a symphony conductor, former Music Director of the Victoria and Windsor Symphony Orchestras, the Montreal Chamber Orchestra, etc. I was guest-conductor and principal guest conductor of more than fifty orchestras on four continents. I am also an Honorary Citizen of the City of Victoria. These extensive travels gave me an opportunity to realize how people live in various countries, and I have watched the gradual deterioration practically everywhere over the years, from Latin America to Eastern Europe.

There is an Israeli joke. "How can you make a small fortune in Israel? You have to go there with a big fortune." I could paraphrase this joke and ask, "How can you turn a first-class industrialized nation into a Third World pariah? Leave it to the shadowy powers of the U.S. and multinational corporate military complex. They know how to do it.

Some of you perhaps remember when President Eisenhower warned of the dangers of the military-industrial complex. In its drive for globalizing its interests and acquiring natural resources and the cheapest labour markets, the U.S. has been practically deindustrialized — except for the arms industry, which is flourishing. While in the last century the slogan was, "Bring in the coolies to do the work," now the slogan seems to be, "Export the work and the jobs to the coolies" — prison labour, child labour, forced labour, etc., whatever is the cheapest. They use the availability of this cheap labour to eliminate the well-paying unionized jobs at home because they have to compete in the global market, which the same corporations created.

The U.S. is projecting a more and more belligerent attitude worldwide, acting as the only superpower in the world, whose corporations and military forces can dictate whatever they want to the whole world. Can we still speak of democracy in

Canada, the U.S. and some other former democracies? I don't think so. In view of the fact that economic and political decisions are not made anymore by the elected representatives of the people, but are made in secret backroom negotiations between the various corporate power brokers, democracy as we knew it is finished. The role of our elected politicians has been reduced to rubber-stamping those decisions, sadly without any public discourse — at least at the federal level.

British Columbia seems to be the "Last Mohican" in this dismal picture, as the present hearings attest. Clearly in the United States and increasingly in Canada, the major corporations and billionaires and millionaires are the ones paying the bill for the election of certain individuals and political parties. Naturally, as citizens of a democratic country, we are allowed to vote for those parties and politicians. After the elections, it is not surprising that they will serve the same corporations and millionaires that paid their bills and not the people who actually elected them. The one who pays the piper calls the tune.

Brian Mulroney declared that making a free trade agreement between the United States and Canada would be like going to bed with an elephant: you can be crushed. Then he proceeded to do exactly that. John Turner, the former head of the Liberal Party in the Canadian Parliament called the Free Trade Agreement the "Sale of Canada Act." The Hon. Jean Chrétien stated before the elections in '93 that if elected, he would not sign the agreement unless he could renegotiate it. After the election, he rushed over to the United States to sign the unaltered Free Trade Agreement. As you know, he also promised to abolish the GST (Goods and Services Tax) before the '96 elections. After the elections, he became a "musician" and just wanted to harmonize the GST, not abolish it.

We've already lost our independence and national sovereignty under the Free Trade Agreement and NAFTA. Do you remember when the former NDP government in Ontario wanted to introduce provincial car insurance? Allstate, the U.S. insurance giant, threatened the Ontario government with a multi-billion dollar lawsuit for loss of potential revenues. The NDP government had to abandon the idea. We know of the Ethyl claim and now the potential claim against B.C. connected with water, etc. As you know, all these past, present and future claims are adjudicated not by Canada's Parliament or Judiciary, but by extraterritorial organs whose decision is and will be binding on the formerly sovereign Canada.

I recommend very highly to all of you to read the book written by a Saskatchewan farmer, a former leadership candidate for the Progressive Conservative Party, David Orchard, entitled The Fight for Canada: Four Centuries of Resistance to American Expansionism. By the way, I just saw it in front of the door.

In a recent interview, John Turner gave about ten years for Canada to be absorbed completely by the United States. From an economic point of view, we are practically there. The Liberal government of Jean Chrétien is having a fire sale of Canada and Canada's assets, into which Canadian taxpayers invested billions of dollars. It is enough to mention the privatization of the Canadian National Railways, the port of Churchill, etc.

Where is Prime Minister Trudeau's NEP, the National Energy Program? Where did the body which is supposed to screen investments in Canada disappear to? Canadian politicians from Preston Manning up and down are falling over each other in the effort to dismantle Canada.

Not long ago we had a more or less free press in Canada and in most of the western democracies. Now practically eighty percent of our daily newspapers are in the hands of one individual, one company, which pursues not national but corporate goals.

What I find really disturbing is that apparently, Mr. Marchi and his Canadian negotiating team are acting as a battering ram in pushing through the MAI. Is it just stupidity, coercion, corruption, all of that — or what — that turns these elected and non-elected representatives of Canada, to sell out their country and its people as fast as possible?

I am sure you are aware that France opted out of the MAI negotiations, finding the MAI incompatible with France's national interests. Does it take a Canadian Einstein to figure out that we should do likewise, as the MAI is also incompatible with Canada's national interests?

During the APEC conference, as you know, pepper spray was used against peaceful demonstrators in order not to embarrass the mass-killer Suharto. During a recent visit of Jean Chrétien to Vancouver, baseball bats were used to bloody some peaceful demonstrators. Are we far from the water cannons, tear gas, rubber bullets and, finally, real bullets habitually used by fascist military dictatorships? I am afraid that we are much closer than you think.

Let me end with some excerpts from a State of the Union address by one of the great Presidents of the United States:

'We cannot be content, no matter how high the general standard of living may be, if some fraction of our people — whether it be one-third or one-fifth or one-tenth — is ill-fed, ill-clothed, ill-housed and insecure.'

'This republic had its beginning and grew to its present strength under the protection of certain inalienable rights — among them the rights of free speech, free press, free worship, trial by jury, freedom from unreasonable searches and seizures. They were our rights to life and liberty.'

'As our nation has grown in size and stature, however, as our industrial economy expanded, these political rights proved inadequate to assure us equality in the pursuit of happiness. We have come to a clear realization of the fact that true individual freedom cannot exist without economic security and independence. 'Necessitous men are not free men. . . .'

'In our day, these economic rules have become accepted as self-evident. We have accepted, so to speak, a second Bill of Rights under which a new basis for security and prosperity can be established for all, regardless of station, race or creed. Among these are: the right to a useful and remunerative job in the industries or shops or farms or mines of the nation; the right to earn enough to provide adequate food and clothing and recreation; the right of every farmer to raise and sell his products at a return which will give him and his family a decent living; the right of every businessman, large or small, to trade in an atmosphere of freedom from unfair competition and domination by monopolies at home and abroad — how about that? — the right of every family to a decent home; the right to adequate medical care and the opportunity to achieve and enjoy good health; the right to adequate protection from the economic fears of old age, sickness, accident and unemployment; and the right to good education.'

'America's rightful place in the world depends in large part upon how fully these and similar rights have been carried into practice for our citizens, for unless there is security here at home, there cannot be lasting peace in the world. . . There are grave dangers of riotous action in this nation. If such action should develop, then it is certain that even though we shall have conquered our enemies abroad, we shall have yielded to the spirit of Fascism at home.'

This excerpt is from the 1944 State of the Union Address given by U.S. President Franklin Delano Roosevelt.

S. Orcherton: That was a good presentation.

Speaking from the present day, I can say that, much to my shock and delight, the MAI failed. Too many countries perceived how bad it was. But the corporatists will not stop. Even now, my prediction of an increasingly-belligerent America stands proven by the invasion and occupation of Iraq, and the theft of Iraqi's oil. I keep up the good fight by remembering Hume's admonition, "All that is necessary for evil to triumph is that good men do nothing."

I do not concern myself only with national issues. Every responsible citizen should involve him or herself in local issues, too. In Vancouver in 2004, there was a grand debate on whether or not to spend more than $3 billion on an overpriced subway line to the Vancouver International Airport. In my opinion, and the opinion of many others, the cost was prohibitive, and the effect would be to cripple transit in the rest of the metropolitan area. I spoke more than once at the public hearings. My address is below.

RAV REVISITED JUNE 18, 2004

Mr. Chairman,

Last night as I was walking home I saw the following sign: "FIGHT CRIME, JAIL A LIBERAL." (The Liberals is the name taken by the current governing party in British Columbia)

At first I found the sign quite funny.

After reading in yesterday's Vancouver Sun the various statements, research, generous offers, name calling and so on, I find it less funny.

I expected to see here this morning a couple of armed bulldozers to take care of any remaining opposition to this magnificent plan concocted in heaven (or some back rooms out of the sight of the paying customers.)

Where to start? As you know, the Vancouver Board of Trade commissioned Ipsos-Reid to conduct a research regarding the existing support for the RAV in the Greater Vancouver Area. Sampling the opinion of 800 people (out of more than two million inhabitants) they came to the conclusion that there is "overwhelming" support for this project in several communities.

Either they used some brilliant new algorithm in coming to this conclusion, (that even Einstein would have been proud of), or they simply supported the paying customer's preconceived notions.

It is common knowledge, that the present Provincial Government is hell bent for privatizing and outsourcing everything in sight, whether it makes economic sense or not.

Just think of Healthcare, outsourcing part of BC Hydro to an offshore corporation for fifty or fifty-five years and now the RAV.

I read Premier Campbell's "generous" financial offer in the name of the Provincial Government. I see a little problem with this, namely the fact that the Provincial Government doesn't have one penny to spend.

What they have is your money, my money, our money and the money of future generations they are so generously offering.

If it is our money, then we should have a say in how it is spent.

Why is it kept in secret what is the financial guarantee, the commitment of the population of BC for thirty-five years to the yet unknown corporation? One Hundred million, five hundred million dollars? Why is it secret?

All we hear about is the generosity of this corporation to invest 300 million dollars in this project. Obviously, they wouldn't do this if they were not guaranteed a substantial profit.

Beside the financial aspects of this very convoluted proposition there is the right of municipal governments to run your own affairs, without Provincial or Federal interference.

Why is this incredible pressure to ram down our throat this project when experts are telling you that there are cheaper and better solutions?

Ladies and Gentlemen. You, the Mayors and representatives of the various municipalities are the last line of defence against the interference of the Provincial and Federal Governments in your affairs.

You are representing the population of your municipalities and I hope your decision will be in their interest and not the interests of a foreign corporation represented by the Provincial Government.

I understand that the Vancouver City Council passed resolutions on several occasions to stop Federal and Provincial interference in the City's affairs.

You have two choices. You can simply throw in the towel and let the Provincial Government take over your duties, and go home.

Or, you can stand up for your right to represent the best interests of the community.

This is your last opportunity to reject the RAV and stop the interference of the Provincial Government in your affairs.

Les Préludes

I am sure that your committee will find a saner and cheaper solution, by rejecting the RAV altogether.

Thank you.

Chapter Fifty Seven

OPINIONS - 2

FROM BOOM-BOXES TO
BRAIN-BUSTERS

Once upon a time, people lived in small, secluded villages and developed their own language, habits, music, dances, arts, and crafts...in short, their culture. Some of them communicated with the neighboring villages through smoke signals or drumbeats. Face-to-face transactions were handled through sign language, the "silent trading" developed by the Phoenicians, or, in the worst case, through warfare. The relative isolation of these secluded small entities led to the development of folk music or native music, and associated folklore and artifacts. Depending on the conveniences of location and the development of mobility technology (the horse, the wheel) and improved communication, bigger entities developed and soon we were able to speak of a region's folklore, a common history.

This was the incredible, creative, fertile background from with each nation developed its own distinct art forms, including music. From the Sixteenth to the Twentieth Century, the development of classical music in Europe reached its pinnacle, and other centres across the globe followed. Most of this music was based on or enriched by the folk music of various regions. Dvorak's Slavonic Dances or Brahms's Hungarian Dances are, naturally, obvious examples. From Mozart through Beethoven, Brahms, Mahler, and beyond we will find various folk music snippets appearing in diverse compositions— the way each region had its own customs, language folk art, so was their music.

With the advent of recordings and the gramophone, people were able to hear music from other regions or countries. With the advent of the radio, gradually, continents and even the whole globe could hear music from the different regions of the world and be influenced by them.

In the last thirty years or so, in the Western World, especially the US and Britain, a new type of music developed, a priori based on a 'universal' beat. This beat, this rhythm, consisted mainly of an anapestic beat (when the accents fall on two and four 1, *2*, 3, *4*, instead of the more natural *1*, 2, *3*, 4, and mainly 60 beats in a minute. What made this 'tumpus uninteruptus' (constant beat) even more 'efficient' was the advance of electronic technology which could deliver this 'music' at a 110-120 decibel level of loudness — the threshold of pain.

Many people are familiar with the so-called Chinese Water Torture. Drops of water fall at regular intervals on the head of the condemned man for an indefinite time, driving him insane. Not many people are familiar with the fact that Pavlov, the Russian scientist of the 'conditional reflex' fame, induced artificial neurosis in dogs, exposing them to a constant rhythm of 60 beats per minute.

In classical music and even in most of folk music, the space between two notes is flexible; it can expand as needed and the space could be best described as having the trajectory of a free-swinging pendulum. This flexibility corresponds to our breathing, to our heartbeat, in fact, to our whole metabolic process. I call a good classical music concert an inner psycho-physiological massage. A divine Mozart or Beethoven symphony can bring us into a totally different realm and uplift our spirits.

Aldous Huxley asks in his book, Heaven and Hell, The Doors of Perception:

"What is God? The blue of the sky, the expanse of the ocean, THE SPACE BETWEEN TWO MUSICAL NOTES!" (My emphasis.) Several other people came also to this conclusion.

In rock music, the space between two notes is shortened. The second and fourth notes 'arrive' sooner than they should. This gives a constant jolt to the listener. At rock concerts we have these tremendous noise levels and thousands of listeners moving together to the beat, many of them also under the influence of alcohol and /or narcotics. The hypnotic effect is also enhanced by strobe lights, fireworks, and other paraphernalia of theatre.

Now, through the medium of radio and especially television, you can have an audience of hundreds of thousands or even more than a million people listening to the same music and moving to the same beat. In my opinion, all this is causing a mass psychosis, even mass brainwashing.

Do you remember the Boom-Boxes of ten – twenty years ago? Kids were running around with those huge monsters on their shoulders, driving the neighborhoods crazy with their loud music.

Nowadays, the ambiance of the street is almost silent as far as music goes, except for some overzealous young drivers who drive around with open windows showing off their expensive stereo equipment and the range of noise they can produce. This could be seen as an improvement, but for the reality.

What happened to the Boom-Box? Courtesy of the Sony Walkman and other similar gadgets, the music formerly played on the Boom-Boxes is still being blasted at one hundred twenty or more decibels, but is now blasted directly into the ear and brain of the listener from an inch or two away via the ear buds to the Personal Stereo. The Personal Stereo has freed the neighbors, but enslaved the children. Adolescents and young adults are listening hours and hours every day to this physically abusive attack on their brains.

They listen easily to 20 or more hours a week, 80 to 100 hours a month, 1,000 to 1,200 hours per year, and many thousands of hours over the years. To assume for a moment that this has no effect on the listener, besides the increasing deafness due to the high decibel level, is total nonsense.

First of all, they become immune to any other kind of music or even rhythm. Can you visualize a pleasant, sensual Strauss Waltz in the middle of the sound-orgy of a rock concert? The audience would go berserk — or become comatose. Zubin Mehta tried to combine a rock group with the Los Angeles Philharmonic Orchestra in a sports stadium. It was a total flop. It is like combining fire with water. Classical music needs the total flexibility and freedom that music will allow, and rock music needs the rigidity of the unrelenting beat. Unfortunately, for the tens of millions of people addicted to rock, classical music, folk music or even good old-fashioned jazz simply doesn't exist.

Unfortunately, this mass offensive is obliterating wonderful and colourful folk-music all over the world. Rock or the misnamed "World Beat" is a musical bulldozer flattening and destroying everything in its path. It is the McDonald's of the music world, an efficient industrial machine which lacks past, future, or respect for other music. McDonald's philosophy of fast food destroys a lot of local eating habits, and McRock does the same thing to the listening habits of the local population.

Unfortunately, we are living in the era of mass production and mass psychosis. (I will not address the TV commercials, the subliminal suggestions and the various propaganda we are constantly exposed to through visual media.) By now, two or even three generations are totally 'hooked' on the 'beat' delivered by the 'Brain Busters (as I call them), and are 'immune' to classical music, folk music, or jazz.

Now that most of the world drinks Coca-Cola, eats McDonald hamburgers, shops at Wal-Mart and listens for hours and hours to the same beat, our uniform 'civilization' is assured, and so is the obliteration of hundreds of years of musical, cultural and culinary achievements.

Only another Orwell could describe this future of music, culture and of humanity itself.

I feel I must relieve myself of yet another opinion, expressed in a letter to Andante. Andante is a wonderful web location (www.andante.com) where one can listen to classical music, order records and CD's, and exchange opinions with other lovers of classical music. I am responding to an article posted by another member of the Andante forums.

Re "Is better education really the Way to Save Classical Music?" By Bernard Holland

First of all, I would like to congratulate Mr. Holland for his insightful article. After an active performing career as a conductor, a violinist, a violist and (sometimes a teacher) for the last fifty years or so, very few things upset me more than the so called 'music appreciation' courses.

They try to install an unholy fear in their students that unless they know "what it is all about", they cannot enjoy the music. The opposite is true. Unless at the moment of performance they manage to get rid of their preconceived notions, they don't even hear the music.

"Toscanini took it much faster," "the horns were too loud," "The orchestra was too loud you couldn't hear the singer" (sometimes this is true . . .), etc., etc.

How can a gynecologist make love to his wife or lover, unless he can forget all he knows about human anatomy at the important moment? How can a music critic listen 'objectively' to a performance, unless at the moment of the performance he is able to forget all his preconceived notions, even knowledge of the piece?

I think by now it is common knowledge that music is a right brain function and all the theories (even about music) are functions of the left brain. For every outstanding performer we have four-five 'experts' who cannot perform, but who can talk about the performance and performer.

We in Europe were fortunate to grow up surrounded by classical music both as listeners and as performers. Unfortunately in North America, by now we have two-three generations who were not exposed to classical music. Naturally, their children are exposed even less. From early childhood they are exposed to rock 'music' and its variants.

Who is in charge in programming the music on the commercial radio and TV stations? The most knowledgeable musicians? No. It is the advertising companies who decide what kind of music and program will sell their product, and it is definitely not classical music, of which these people are totally ignorant.

Thank God for PBS, NPR, CBC and few other stations which are still programming classical music. Compared to the total musical programming, we can speak perhaps of three to five percent classical music programs in the sea of rock and so called pop music.

It is not commonly realized that rock music is the opposite of classical music and even human nature. In classical music we have a constant interchange of tension-relaxation, of soft-loud, slow-fast, harmonic and melodic tension etc.

From Debussy to Aldous Huxley, many people came to the important conclusion that the most critical element in music is the space between two notes.

In classical music, this space is flexible it expands when needed as a German Maestro said "Ausklingen lassen, aussingen lassen." (Let it ring out, let it sing out.) In rock music this space is shortened, not speaking of the anapestic beat (accents falling on 2-4 instead of 1-3 in a 4x4 bar.).

The audience literally gets a shock between two notes, like when Foucault's free swinging pendulum would be stopped prematurely at both ends of the free swing, or if a child's swing would be obstructed at both ends. If one adds to this the high decibel level, the hours per day, the weeks, months, years children (and adults) are being exposed to this assault, combined with other stimuli, they become 'immune' to classical music. They need the "Tumpus Uninteruptus", the constant 'beat'.

When one reads about one orchestra folding after another, the auctioning of their assets, the dwindling audiences, it is hard to remain optimistic. When will the powers to be realize that "BACK TO BASICS" in education should be back to music, and the arts in general.

Apparently, we learn 60% of what we will learn during a lifetime from one to six years, another 20% from six to eighteen, and another 20% the rest of our life. The present education system ignores totally the most important period when the child learns the largest amount of knowledge, walking, talking, languages, etc.

Except for some small exceptions, (the Montessori schools, the Suzuki, the Kodaly, the Orff method) here and there in few places, this most important period is totally ignored by the standard educational system.

Let me say few words about the Kodaly method. Zoltan Kodaly the well-known Hungarian composer and educator was a pioneer in music education. The so called 'Kodaly Method' taught the children to sight read in two three voices. Kodaly wrote every year the Bicinia and Tricinia Hungarica test pieces for the children's exam.

I was a witness in Quebec City when Elizabeth Szonyi (at the time Kodaly's assistant) tried to get a group of music teachers to sight read some of the material that 8-10 year-old children read regularly in Hungary. They were unable to do so.

On the initiative of Kodaly, special schools were established; where music was at the centre of the curriculum, up to eight hours per week. These children did 40 to 80% better in all other subject matters. Critics said that this was due to the fact that these children were very gifted.

The same program was introduced in regular public schools with exactly the same result! We know what kind of outstanding achievement the Suzuki and Orff Method produced. The fact that children are singing individually and collectively in choirs, gives them a tremendous foundation. If we would expose children to early music education and expose them regularly to classical music in the form of being listeners and especially performers, there would be some hope left. Unfortunately, the 'basics' in education for our politicians and educators exclude music and the arts at this time

Laszlo Gati

Former Music Director of
The Victoria and Windsor Symphony Orchestras

Les Préludes

Chapter Fifty Eight

DEPRESSION REDUX 1997

In my opinion, my depressions and depressions in general are usually triggered by an outside shock and a chemical imbalance which, combined, lead to a major episode of depression several weeks after the initial shock.

In the spring of 1997, I started to get more and more depressed. On the invitation of a good friend, I went to Little Rock, Arkansas to spend a couple of weeks there with friends. I started to feel more and more lousy while I was there. By the time I returned I was in the grip of a full depression. I had nightmares and various suicidal thoughts. I entertained plans to jump from the Second Narrows Bridge, on a major commuter route in Vancouver. I considered committing suicide by attaching the tube of the CPAP (Continuous Positive Air Pressure) machine that I use for my sleep apnea to the exhaust pipe of my car. As in my other suicide attempts I even figured out where I would do it — at Cypress Bowl, a beautiful recreation area in the mountains north of Vancouver.

When I told my family doctor all of this, he told me: "If you are suicidal, go to the emergency room of a hospital. They will take away your shaver and two days later they will kick you out." Having heard that the Psychiatric Ward of the Shaughnessy Hospital, a facility where I had spent a few months on and off years ago, was closed, I took it for granted that they had closed all the psychiatric wards in Vancouver. Frantic telephone calls to my brother in Tel Aviv, and to both my older daughter in Santa Monica and my younger daughter in Budapest, ensued.

Naturally, Los Angeles was out of the question due to the horribly expensive medical bills. Kathy told me that they have good psychiatrists in Budapest, and that the medical expenses are quite reasonable, so I decided to go there. My brother sent me some money and I left for Budapest. Kathy arranged for me to see a psychiatrist the day after my arrival and the next day she left for New York for ten days. I saw the psychiatrist twice a week. According to the psychiatrist I was even joking at the first visit, but as time went by I started to feel more and more lousy. I stayed in an apartment on the opposite side of the street where Kathy lived, and Kathy arranged for somebody to stay with me. I was getting so suicidal that around three o'clock in the morning I sneaked out of the apartment and went over to the apartment building where my daughter lived, used her key to let myself in, took the elevator to the fourth floor, and for about half an hour contemplated jumping.

I concluded, finally, that I could not do this to my daughter, to burden her with committing my suicide in her home. I cannot describe meaningfully the tremendous strain and the deep struggle of looking down into the abyss of the darkened courtyard preparing to jump, then pulling back. In a tremendously exhausted state, I returned to my building, sneaked back to my apartment and tried to go to sleep. By the time Kathy came back from New York, Dr, Lust recommended that I should be hospitalized.

He recommended a psychiatrist at the National Psychological and Neurological Institute who agreed to accept me in his department. Kathy helped me pack a few items, including several rolls of toilet paper, and we took the tram to the hospital.

The Institute is a huge complex with several psychological wards, but also surgical wards, an epidemiology section, and other wards. This institute used to be called 'Lipot Mezö' (Lipot Field) and was known as Hungary's largest insane asylum. Imagine my state of mind when I became an inmate there. The ward where I ended up was quite dark and filthy. There were four people in each room and the rooms had no doors. Nurses, doctors, visitors, and inmates could move from room to room without impediment. I took some sedatives in the evening and went into a deep sleep.

When I woke up in the morning, my cherished toilet papers were unrolled all over the floor of our room and several other rooms. It was obvious that some of the other inmates had visited my luggage. The toilets were quite dirty, and had no toilet seats. All this just contributed to my depression, instead of getting me out of it. The next night I had horrible nightmares. I was in a big courtyard where some kind of committee was holding court to decide who would remain forever in the hospital. I was one of the 'chosen' ones and was incarcerated in a cage with some violently insane inmates. I begged my daughter and her boyfriend to get me out of there.

They were successful in having me transferred to a much more elegant and 'sophisticated' ward. The building almost looked like a sanatorium. It even had a swimming pool (without any water). It had well groomed surroundings in a park-like setting. Here, instead of the Head of Department making the rounds visiting the patients, we, the patients had to line up in front of his office every morning. After a lengthy wait in the line-up, we could exchange a couple of words with him and his assistant and then leave with a prescription and advice . . . or not. I shared my room with an elderly gentleman who was in his last stages of prostate cancer. It was obvious that he had some special arrangements to be hospitalized with prostate cancer in a psychiatric ward.

Even within this 'sanatorium' there were different classes of people and services. One day they had a party for some foreign medical delegation and I saw various pastries and delicacies that were normally unavailable not just in the hospital, but even in Budapest. In the meantime, my depression was deepening. I became suicidal again. A main thoroughfare with heavy bus and car traffic was nearby and I decided to commit suicide by throwing myself in front of a bus or a car. I stood for hours on the side of the road trying to build up enough courage to jump in front of one of the moving vehicles. While it was obvious that my chances of being killed would be better if I threw myself in front of a bus, I was concerned that several people riding in the bus might be hurt if it stopped suddenly. While these discussions went on in my mind, I sweated profusely, trembling and considering each approaching car or bus as the 'target'.

Finally, totally exhausted, I returned to my ward. Apparently, my absence from the ward had been noticed and a search had been mounted. My doctor ordered that they should take away my civilian clothes and I was forced to appear in the dining room in my pajamas. Following this episode, I spent practically a whole week in bed 'hiding' under the bedcover and only going to the dining room to have my meals. Once again I asked my daughter and her friend to get me out of there. Finally I managed to be discharged from that ward, ending up at my 'final' destination in this same hospital.

The ward was a little less 'elegant' than my last one. Once again I shared a room with three other people. Besides the 'average' patients with mental illness, a corner of the huge common room was partitioned off for patients who had some serious illnesses besides their mental problems.

I was extremely fortunate that both the head of this department, Dr. Riemer, and his assistant were very well prepared and conscientious doctors who knew what they were doing, and whose main concern was the welfare of their patients. They told me that they had available all the latest drugs from all over the world. They put me on various drugs, including Zoloft which at the time was new, even in America. That was only one of the treatments. Dr. Riemer was very fond of sleep deprivation treatment to fight depression.

You went to sleep around eight PM. They woke you up at one AM and you had to stay awake twenty-four hours. We had a huge common room where those undergoing sleep deprivation paced up and down hour after hour. I cannot tell how efficient this treatment was in successfully treating my depression or what role it actually played in my getting gradually better.

One of my 'colleagues' introduced me to the exercise room not too far from our ward. We went there together to exercise on the various machines. After many weeks I got permission to leave the hospital for several hours and went to town to visit my daughter and friends.

After a few more weeks I was finally released.

Chapter Fifty Nine

75! SEVENTY-FIVE YEARS!

September 25 1925-
September 25, 2000

It always bothered me that beside someone's date of birth there was only a dash. It gives me a feeling of unfinished business. Beside my name it would read Laszlo Gati, born September 25, 1925 - . What have I not finished?

Today is my 75th Birthday and from this vantage point I can almost see what will inevitably follow that fatal dash. Obviously it is not what, but when will it happen. As a child, I had been taken to several funerals and I remember a segment of the sermon dealing with various things happening in a lifetime, including the fact that there is "a time to die."

When I think of Mozart and Schubert, both of whose lives were cut short when each was barely thirty years old, I am ashamed of myself having lived already two and a half times longer and having achieved perhaps only a tiny fraction of their output.

Naturally, I realize that we all have our preordained trajectory to follow and it has to be right for our circumstances, talent and opportunity and cannot be compared to anybody of lesser or higher standing. We can only assess our own achievements as they relate to our own abilities, aspirations, circumstances, and not compare them to the achievements of others. There will always be people who will have achieved much more than you and you will always find people who achieved much less.

It is no use to try to 'get a feel' of how much time we have left. It is much more important to do the most and the best of our 'useful' time, while we are still active, in relatively good physical shape, and still have most of our mental faculties before Alzheimer's, senility or the other multiple frailties of old age take over.

It is incredible how our concept of time changes over a lifetime. As children, time has no meaning and seems to be limitless. As a teenager I remember that during the War years we had the impression that time had stopped, and that the War would never end. During my great love affairs I tried to stop time, to cherish every moment. Unfortunately time has no feelings. When we would like it to slow down, it seems to speed up, and when we would like it to speed up, it slows down to nothing.

I keep the following quote on my refrigerator:

TODAY!!!

LOOK TO THIS DAY:
FOR IT IS LIFE, THE VERY LIFE OF
LIFE.
IN ITS BRIEF COURSE
LIE ALL THE VERITIES AND REALITIES
 OF EXISTENCE:
THE BLISS OF GROWTH
THE GLORY OF ACTION,
FOR YESTERDAY IS BUT A DREAM
AND TOMORROW IS ONLY A VISION.
BUT TODAY WELL-LIVED
MAKES EVERY YESTERDAY A DREAM OF
HAPPINESS,
AND EVERY TOMORROW A VISION OF
HOPE.
LOOK WELL, THEREFORE, TO THIS
DAY:
SUCH IS THE SALUTATION TO THE
DAWN.

-Kalidasa

I find this quote inspiring and true. But how many of us are really living our life TODAY, on the principle of 'CARPE

DIEM' (Seize the Day)? Most of us are living either in the past or in the future, not realizing that all we have is TODAY! We say, "I will be happy when . . ." "I will be content when . . ." "Where did the happy times of my youth disappear?" and in doing so, we forget to LIVE IN THE MOMENT.

When fully healthy, we function on three levels simultaneously. We carry our past with us, good or bad; we plan for the future, and all the while living in the present and facing day to day necessities. It is interesting to note that when one is suicidal all one wants to do is to get out, to get it over with, to end it all. When one is in a more or less 'normal' state, the feeling that the inevitable end is getting closer and closer is suddenly looming larger and larger on the horizon. I remember that I found it totally ridiculous when the life insurance salesman used to describe in glowing terms how happy and satisfied everybody would be when I was gone. I felt like telling him: "I'll be dead and I won't care if they will be happy or not."

By now, many family members, many friends, and many colleagues have passed on. Just yesterday walking on the street, I noticed that the trees are growing, sprouting new leaves, or shedding old ones. The busses are running as usual, the political situation is getting worse— as though nothing at all had happened since the day I was born. I want to shout in anger, "Don't you realize that my wife is dead, and my father and mother too, and my good friend died as well! What right has the world to continue on so impassively?"

I think we elders have to go so that the billions who will inherit the mess we leave behind will have a chance to suffer or enjoy life more or less as we did. Sometimes I have the impression that I could put my whole life in a thimble and not find it. If the past 75 years passed so quickly, how fast will the remaining one, two, five, ten, or fifteen years come and go?

Bela Bartok, the great Hungarian composer, said just before dying of leukemia, "It is difficult to leave when one's backpack is still full of goods (ideas)." Not being a creative artist (except for my attempts at painting) perhaps my contributions to the history of humanity will be so small that only my daughters and some friends who attended some of my concerts or have some of my DVD's, CD's, videos, and tapes will remember me for a while.

I am always amazed when some great artist, writer, or musician, who had a fifty, sixty or even seventy-year career passes away, and they are remembered in the media for one day or two at most. Luckily, now through the medium of recordings and videos, posterity has a chance, at least, to see and hear some of these great artists.

As one gets older, birthdays become less and less celebrations and more and more milestones on the highway, measuring the distance to the final destination, which is in this case really the end of our present journey.

Chapter Sixty

CONDUCTORS - 5

"FEET ON THE GROUND, HEAD IN THE CLOUDS"

"Everything flows out and in; everything has its tides; all things rise and fall; the pendulum swing manifests in everything; the measure of the swing to the right is the measure of the swing to the left; rhythm compensates."

The Kybalion -Hermetic Philosophy

"Everything you know about conducting and everything you have read in this book, you must forget at the moment of performance and simply let go."

Laszlo Gati

Did you ever see a child 'conducting' along with an orchestra or with music emanating from the radio, the record player, TV or whatever? Of course you have. In one way, conducting is child's play: any child can do it. On the other hand, it is such a difficult art that very few conductors have truly mastered it.

Conducting is not merely technique; there are a myriad of other problems connected with conducting, some of which I have already addressed. Among the hundreds of conductors

I performed with over my seventeen years as an orchestra musician, in my opinion there was only one whose conducting technique was flawless — and he wasn't even a conductor!

This great exemplar is Carlo Zecchi. Zecchi was a great Italian pianist. I recorded some Mozart sonatas with him and the Belgian violinist, Andre Grumieux at Hungarian Radio in 1950's. A few months after this engagement, Zecchi broke his arm. His limb was insured for several hundred thousand dollars, and the insurance company would give him the payout, allowing him to live during the recovery, only on the provision that he not play the piano for several years. Entirely reasonable from the insurance company's point of view, but for Zecchi . . .

What torture! For a pianist not to play the piano!

Zecchi used some of the money to hire an orchestra in Rome and he learned how to conduct. When he came back to Budapest as a conductor for a single concert, he had such a tremendous success that he was immediately hired to conduct a second concert. His repertory was so small that he had to repeat some pieces from his first concert. I still remember some of the works he conducted: Schubert Symphony Number Seven in C Major, Tchaikovsky, Romeo and Juliet, Vivaldi's, Concerto Echo in Lontano. Zecchi was a wonderful musician, a great pianist and now a great conductor who had developed a wonderful and unique conducting technique.

He later established a summer school for conductors in Italy, but not enough conductors followed his example. In my opinion, Zecchi's technique should not be considered unique or exceptional, but should be considered the norm.

It is impossible to describe music by the spoken or written word, because music has its own language. It is similarly difficult to describe Zecchi's conducting technique unless you see it and experience it in person, but I will try to explain at least some aspects of his technique.

First and foremost, was his mastery of the motions of a free swinging pendulum, which gave him total liberty and natural motions in whatever he conducted. His approach, style and logic in conducting Tchaikovsky's Romeo and Juliet was an eye opener. His approach was totally different from the approach of most conductors and when you analyze his reasons for conducting it the way he did, it turns out that he conducted the music that was in the score, instead of conducting Romeo and Juliet the same way he might conduct the music of, say, Haydn.

For instance, most conductors conduct the whole first part in four (Four beats to a bar). Zecchi starts conducting in four, but switches to two beats in a bar when there are half notes— when the melody requires it. Suddenly the whole music and technique are in harmony.

He is alternating between two and four, again as the music requires. For instance, he conducts the harp arpeggios in four, cutting off the winds on the fourth beat which gives a chance for the orchestra and the audience to breathe! (I am not the only one who noticed that the audience and the musicians have to breathe sometimes.)

During the four bar accelerando (speeding up) to the Allegro (the duel motif), he does a very interesting thing. If you run out of breath because you are running or upon hearing bad news or whatever, your inhalations get shorter. Try it! The four bars of the accelerando consist of half-notes (half-note strings, half-note winds). Again he is conducting the piece in two beats, not four. Most conductors accelerate by bringing in the downbeat (exhalation) sooner, while the logical way should be to shorten the inhalation (the upbeat).

This is exactly what Zecchi did. Let's see if I can demonstrate this in words.

Oooone-Twoooo/ Oooone -Twooo/ Ooone-Twoo-Oone-Two// One tacata and so on Allegro in four_.

To show the freedom of his conducting style, he twice did a funny thing later in the work. It was in an allegro passage in four beats. Normally four beats are conducted by moving the baton so: One-down, Two-left, Three-right and Four-up. This is the 'angular' conducting technique. Because in that particular bar there was a bass drum beat on the third beat and a cymbal on the fourth beat, Zecchi made it descriptive. He conducted the second beat to the right (instead of left), the third beat down (for the bass drum hit), instead of to the right, and the fourth beat up for the cymbal clash. Although this was against the 'rules' it made complete sense and a wonderful surprise effect for the orchestra and audience. The only way for you, the reader, to visualize this properly is to put on Romeo and Juliet and try conducting it yourself.

I must confess that after this experience with Zecchi, I cannot visualize conducting Romeo and Juliet in any other way.

Very early in my career I was disturbed by the so called 'German School of conducting', in which the conductor is a half-beat ahead of the orchestra. The audience and even the musicians in the orchestra are disoriented by seeing actions which are not in time with what they are hearing. Zecchi's technique has the conductor conducting exactly one beat ahead of the orchestra; this one change makes it much more likely that the musicians and the audience will synchronize their breathing and their anticipation of the changes in the musical piece.

I was also disturbed by the 'angular' style of many conductors. By 'angular' style I mean a style in which the conductor holds and moves the baton in abrupt, straight lines which are at sharp angles to one another. The difference in angles between strokes is, of course, what visually marks the beats of the music for the musicians. This is moderately good for setting a metronomic pace, but leaves very little flexibility for the conductor to speed up or moderate the tempo of the piece, which is crucial, particularly when an orchestra is accompanying soloists.

Furthermore, when using the 'angular' style, most conductors speed up the motion of the baton as they come to beat, and this results in the notes being 'attacked', rather than 'played.' That seems confusing, but I can explain it with a simple real-world illustration.

In my opinion, every future conductor should spend hours, possibly weeks, even months watching a Foucault Pendulum and practice the motions of a free swinging pendulum at home until he can replicate the motions of a free swinging pendulum. A Foucault Pendulum is a large pendulum which hangs down from its pivot; when it swings to the end of its range of motion, it is rising, and as it rises, it slows down.

And when it reaches either of its peaks, the pendulum slows to a definite stop, then starts back, at first slowly, then faster, reaching its greatest speed at the midpoint, the lowest point of its range of motion, before beginning to climb again and slow down.

Whether we like it or not, the Universe has its unchangeable laws, and we have the choice to act in harmony with them and use them, or be in constant conflict with them and so make our task more difficult or even impossible. If we reach the stage when we can incorporate the motion of a free swinging pendulum in our conducting, then we connect not just with the inner logic of the music, but we can establish a 'logical' connection with the audience and the orchestra who will all function on the same wavelength, even breathing in unison!

As the wheels of a car turn exactly the same way whether the car goes slowly or fast, so the free swinging pendulum motion has to be present whether the music is slow or fast. This gives tremendous flexibility to the conductor by 'lengthening' the period of the 'pendulum' as needed.

There are many advantages to using this technique in conducting. One advantage is that speeding up or slowing down requires only a small change in the amplitude of the swing. A longer swing slows down the pendulum (and the beat), and a shorter swing speeds it up. But unlike the 'angular' style, where the conductor has to use more muscles and greater effort to speed up the beat, speeding up the tempo using the pendulum principle requires very little effort.

Another advantage comes directly from this lesser effort. With lesser effort going into maintaining or changing the beat, the conductor can put more attention and effort into the other controls he exercises over the orchestra — emphasizing certain phrases, bringing sections in after a rest period, and so on.

I remember accompanying Shura Cherkassky performing the Second Piano Concerto of Chopin, in Mexico City with the National Symphony Orchestra of Mexico. He played so freely, that is, with changes in tempo, dramatic pauses and such, that the musicians had a problem hiding their smiles.

Just before going on stage at our second concert, he turned to me and said, "If you don't mind I feel like playing more freely tonight." I told him, "Go ahead." I had no problem whatsoever. By lengthening the arc of the pendulum, I was able to wait for him as needed without any problem. If I had had an 'angular' beat it would have been a catastrophe.

Now that I have shared the Great Secret, there is still the question of what I am like as a conductor, what advantages and what strengths I have demonstrated over my career, and how I rank. These are big questions. My life has been music, and conducting in particular, and any revelations of my conducting will also reveal me — maybe more than I have revealed to you so far.

I am a very sensitive person. Perhaps I have not revealed this too much in this book, this writing; for I have recounted even the deaths of friends and colleagues and acquaintances without many flourishes of emotion. But I am sensitive, and this sensitivity is what allows me to read a score and to present a composer's work to an audience in a way that I believe is closest to the composer's original intention. This is not all positive. This sensitivity given great heights of emotion and fulfillment; but, as I have noted, it has also led to deep lows and harsh depressions. So be it. This is one of my strengths as a conductor.

I have, I believe, a larger repertoire of pieces that I can conduct well than many other conductors. This comes directly from the great variety of my musical experience. I have played and been a soloist on the violin and the viola, played the piano, and have studied intensely several of the other instruments in the orchestra, in addition to all of my conducting experience.

When I am asked, "Who is your favourite composer to conduct?" I always reply, "Whoever I am conducting right now.", but having given my opinions on the strengths of various conductors in different repertoire, I must come at least a little clean about my own strengths. I did just say that I had a wider repertoire than many conductors, but I believe I am most simpatico with the Romantic composers,

Tchaikovsky among them. But, and there is a "but" here. I also have another strength— Mozart.

In my mind, there are only two composers of classical music— Mozart, and everybody else. This does not denigrate all of those fine composers who are not Mozart; it just shows how far separated from everyone else Mozart is. Conducting Mozart is like flying an airplane. When I took flying lessons for a while, I learned a most interesting thing: you, the pilot, are not actually in full control of the airplane. The laws of physics are in control, and keeping the airplane in the air is all a matter of the pilot very carefully negotiating within the laws of physics. The easiest way to illustrate this is to describe the takeoff. When a plane is taxiing down the runaway it gradually increases speed, and at some point the laws of physics take over, lift exceeds drag, and airplane lifts into the air automatically. The pilot has nothing to do with it; once the magic speed is reached, the plane takes off on its own. Mozart's music is a lot like that. It is exquisitely tuned and balanced, and when the conductor hits just the right tempo or speed, the music, the orchestra, the conductor, and the audience all "take off" effortlessly. And I can do that; when I conduct Mozart I can find that tempo, that speed which lifts musical performance into something else.

My ability to sight-read (developed over the years of experience I just mentioned), helps me in my conducting. I can read a score and compare it to what my musicians have just played and make judgments and corrections quickly.

I have also developed an acute sense of justice, equality and fair play. I showed this early on in school, when I stood up against bullies for the other students, and when I stood up to the Communist authorities in Hungary to improve radio programming. This affected my conducting most deeply in my relations with the musicians I played with and conducted. Though as a conductor I had to maintain a certain distance, I believe I had excellent relations with musicians because I treated them with respect and I treated them as musical partners, collaborators, rather than as extensions of my own ego. I offer as proof my over forty years of connection with the musicians and organizations in Latin America, and the

My daughter, Suzanne Gati

fact that the children of musicians I conducted are now musicians who tell me their parents remembered me fondly.

My adventurism. I have conducted inside concert halls and outside in shopping precincts, inside ballrooms and on beaches, conducted with special effects and cannons, conducted Pops concerts, and classical corps de ballets. I have conducted for politicians, business leaders, and religious authorities, and for peasants and aboriginals in their own communities. I kept with me always my sense of pride and joy in the attainments and intrinsic worth of classical music and classical performance and shared that with all my audiences.

I have always been ambitious and creative, whether or not this was driven somewhat by my occasional manic episodes. The Victoria Summer Festival, the Piano Summit, the Dollar concerts, and many of my other activities, regardless of their financial success, have always been a source of pride for me.

Performing beside, with, and for the greatest personalities and talents in music over the fifty years has enriched my life immensely. Every

My daughter, Kathleen Gati

moment of joy in listening to or participating in those great performances remains fresh and continues as a source of both comfort and inspiration. And these accomplished people, by their example, and sometimes by their teaching, expanded my horizons of music appreciation and skill. I always opened myself to these experiences— retaining, as in the case of the Avant-garde, the privilege to judge some things as less than worthy. What is the use of experiencing the heights of achievement if one cannot compare them to the depths, and, knowing the difference, apply it to your life?

My care for children. Even when a recent immigrant in Montreal, a mere player and not a conductor, I spoke at schools and anywhere else they would have me, addressing the need for culture, beauty, and accomplishment in the arts to elementary and secondary school students, to teachers and administrators, and to the parents. I sometimes feel broken-hearted when I consider the vicious and short-sighted program cuts which are denying so many children the joys and advantages of music education and performance.

My general activism and promotion of democracy and respect for the community and those within it. I have maintained my sensitivity to the plight of the greater number of people: from the poor peasants of Romania who would give city visitors to the countryside the food off their plates and the shirts off their backs, to the idealists of the Hungarian Uprising, who tried to maintain socialist ideals and provision of the greatest good to the greatest number, with a humane political and social structure; to the CBC, the schools, and local community orchestras of Canada, for which I worked and promoted tirelessly, and to Canada's political mosaic, where I joined the Council of Canadians, and have stood, and continued to stand for the strengths and accomplishments

Suzy, Papa, Kathy

of Canada's political culture.

*****

I feel guilty in not spending sufficient space and time writing about the importance of my wife and daughters in my achievements and indeed, in my life. There are no

Me visting Slava Rostropovich backstage at the Orpheum Theatre, Vancouver, 2002

adequate words to describe their contributions.

They provided me not only with some of the happiest periods of my life, but they were my greatest supporters and admirers throughout. This admiration was mutual. I watched my daughters develop into wonderful mature, loving, sensitive human beings. And I am grateful for all the happy times spent with my wife and my children over the many years.

Unfortunately, none of us are perfect and blameless when our actions, whether purposeful or inadvertent, hurt other people. How many times have I wished I could go back in time and react differently to a situation or change an action I took! This is not possible. The most I can do is to ask forgiveness from everybody whom I offended or hurt in any way, shape or form during my lifetime.

I must confess that I was not very successful in forgiving others who hurt me more than I hurt them! I wish I could go back and give seminars on the 'Art of Forgiveness'! I have read books on the subject, attended seminars, discussed it with friends and foes, but I still have not mastered it completely.

As LaMartin says, "Life is a series of preludes . . ."

At the beginning of this book I set out as my main aim to describe those sixty years between hearing Liszt's 'Les Preludes' for the first time at the age of nine and conducting it in Budapest at the age of sixty-nine. Naturally, these sixty years were preceded by nine years and followed by another ten.

I am approaching the end of my preludes "to the unknown song of which Death intones the first note". I hope that my passage through life contributed happiness and pleasure to the life of people I was fortunate enough to affect, whether through my love, friendship, my music making or even by this book.

Shortly this 'unfinished symphony' will be finished and a new cycle will begin.

Lazlo Gati
August, 2004

Les Préludes

.

EPILOGUE

LES PRELUDES 1995

In the Preface I described my first encounter with Franz Liszt's great Symphonic Poem, Les Preludes, at the age of nine, and its lasting effect on my life and career. Les Preludes continued to manifest itself through the Nineties. Several times since my escape from Hungary as a refugee of the 1956 Uprising, I had returned to Budapest and had discussions with the Opera and various orchestras about the possibility of guest-conducting. When one orchestra manager told me they were already booked for the next four years, I told him, no problem: "As I have already waited thirty-five years, four more years won't matter." Obviously, a return to Hungary and notably to the Franz Liszt Academy was of great emotional importance to me. I could almost consider it as a book-end to a sixty year saga between the two performances of Les Preludes.

At my Piano Summit Concert in 1993, one of my soloists was the wonderful pianist, Lucille Chung. In the two years since our concert, she had had a great career, playing in many different countries to great acclaim and respect, but her sentimental wish was to perform the Liszt First Piano Concerto with me in the Great Hall of the Franz Liszt Academy in Budapest. Lucille had some relatives and Korean friends in Budapest, among them the owners of a Korean factory, making, among other things, instant noodles. They were willing to underwrite the concert. To make the concert possible, both Lucille and I happily agreed to forego our honoraria.

Fortunately, my younger daughter Kathleen was living in Budapest at the time. Showing the same organizational skills as at the Piano Summit, Kathy undertook to contract the orchestra, book the hall, have the tickets printed, look after the advertising and promotion, liaise with the sponsors, and do all the other scut work. Hungarian Radio agreed to record and broadcast the concert in Hungary and through its International Service and the European Broadcasting Union, which reached several European countries. I managed to obtain a $5,000 grant from an arts foundation to pay for the filming of the concert for a subsequent television broadcast. After several frantic weeks, everything was ready for my professional return to Hungary.

On March 25, 1995, almost exactly sixty years to the day when I heard, for the first time, Franz Liszt's Les Preludes , I would be conducting it in the Great Hall of the Franz Liszt Academy in Budapest, where I had spent ten years (1946 to 1956) studying and performing as a violinist and conductor.

On arriving in Budapest I had to give several newspaper interviews and interviews for Hungarian Radio and Television. Lucille and I did some joint interviews in English; the rest were in Hungarian.

During my earlier visits to Budapest I refrained from contacting my old friends and colleagues, in order to protect them from associating with a former-dissident foreigner. This time it was different: I had lunch with my old friend Dr. Kecskemeti Istvan a couple of times. It was he who was boarding with my family at the end of the war, and I boarded with him and his mother in 1946 when I came to Budapest to continue my musical studies. We would go to the artists' club called Feszek (Nest) together.

Several former musician colleagues from my time with the Hungarian State Concert Orchestra came to see me, including Laszlo Hara, bassoon professor at the Music Academy and Imre Kovacs, Flute Professor. I was really moved by Kovacs, whose student was my first flutist. He came to every rehearsal to coach her! My 'Gang' from Hungarian Radio, composed of my former recording engineers, program planners, technicians, headed by my composer friend, Decsenyi Istvan, all invited me to a joint dinner where we talked about our happy and unhappy old times together at Hungarian Radio.

Usually we had our 'business' meetings with Kathy, her boyfriend and various associates at the beautiful Muvesz Espresso (Artist Espresso) near the Opera on Andrasy Ut. Kathy organized a well-attended press conference at the Building of the Writer's Union before I even started rehearsing. In the midst of all these activities I felt compelled to see an important person from my previous life.

When I established the Musical Program Exchange Department, I engaged a wonderful secretary. Her nickname was Cica (Kitty). She was the former wife of one of my composition teachers and well-known composers, Pal Jardanyi. At the time she was a gorgeous, tall woman.

Now she lived in an old age home. She must have told the other inhabitants that I was coming. I had to, quite literally, go through a reception line before getting to her room. Cica lived in a small crowded room, thick with cigarette smoke. She was a chain smoker and kept the window closed.

I would have never recognized the young woman in this old person, with her wrinkled face and trembling hands. I debated with myself whether it was right to visit her and see her in her present state, instead of remembering my gorgeous and effective young secretary. I concluded that for her sake, it was the right thing to do. She was grateful that I came to see her. My visit gave her a moment of importance, almost a moment of 'glory' among the residents of that old age home. A conductor from Canada had come all the way to visit her! Due to the smoke I had to cut my visit short.

During an early morning walk, I took the street car to the Margaret Bridge, got off at the station in the middle of the bridge, and walked through Margaret Island all the way to the Great Hotel, where I usually had breakfast. Margaret Island, with its manicured parks and gardens, swimming pools, and spas, all in the middle of the Danube, is a real gem. It also has an open air venue for about five thousand people where we used to perform Shakespeare's A Midsummer Night's Dream, with incidental music by Felix Mendelssohn, conducted by Otto Klemperer.

Those nights were unforgettable. I don't know in how many performances I took part during those three summers from 1948 through 1951. I also remember a funny situation during the Youth Festival in 1949.

It was advertised that members of the Bolshoi Ballet would be performing with the State Philharmonic Orchestra. Five thousand people were waiting and waiting, but due to some mix-up there was no ballet dancer to be seen, and the audience started to get restless. Finally, they found some dancers, who showed up accompanied by Mstislav Rostropovich. He already liked women at this early age! As I was considered the linguist in the Orchestra, Rostropovich and the accompanist informed me of their program and who would be performing what; that it would be half in German, and half in Russian. In order to cut down the overall length of the proceedings, I decided to make the announcements myself, instead of translating the information for the official announcer.

As I was reading the program and the names of composers and performer, I realized at one point that I had mistakenly given the name of a composer instead of the performer. I cursed mildly, saying, "HELL! I made a mistake!" This is definitely not the thing to do in front of a restless crowd of classical music listeners. The official announcer almost killed me because he had jeopardized his job by letting me replace him!

Back to 1995. I paid another emotional visit to my past by taking the Cog Railway in Buda up the Schwab Mountain to revisit five important years of my past. The apartment building Agnes and I used to live in was in a totally dilapidated condition. I don't think it had been repaired since the Second World War ended, fifty years ago. Bad enough people and myself should age, but brick and mortar, too?

I even revisited the little grocery store where we used to shop, and the little coffee shop near our station Then I walked up to the Golf Hotel, located at the final station of the cog railway. My wife and I used to visit their restaurant and enjoy their bone-marrow soup. A couple of years earlier, I had taken my two daughters on a guided tour of my past, and we even had bone-marrow soup there.

A few days before my concert, the National Philharmonic Society approached me and asked if I could take over a concert in Pecs the following week. The program would be Beethoven's Symphony Number Eight, and Berlioz's Harold in Italy. I was very happy to accept the invitation for several reasons. Pecs is one of my favourite cities, with some wonderful old buildings, including a Turkish mosque, which now serves as a Catholic Church. And lately, a McDonald's is located in the beautiful City Hall below the clock tower. I welcomed the opportunity to conduct another Hungarian orchestra while I was in Hungary.

I will jump ahead now a few days. After my concert at the Academy, Annie Fischer, the great Hungarian pianist, invited me to visit her. She had a prior obligation and could not come to my concert, but heard very good reports from people whose judgment she trusted. I knew Annie Fischer from my previous life in Hungary and had also seen Annie after a concert she gave for the Ladies' Morning Musical Society in Montreal in the Sixties. I was looking forward to seeing her. She had very aristocratic, almost ascetic looks and she was a chain smoker.

When I arrived at her apartment I was very warmly received. There were beautiful miniature sandwiches prepared. Her butler-cum-driver served us espresso coffees and we embarked on a wide-ranging discussion about many different topics. At one point she sat down at the piano and played a movement of a Beethoven sonata for me. When she finished, I congratulated her warmly. She complained about occasional pains in the palms of her hands, which had small arthritic growths which were painful sometimes. Thank Goodness they had not interfered with her playing yet. I told her that my father had had similar problems which a simple operation could solve.

Annie had begun to have problems with her eyesight and was reading music with a huge magnifying glass. She told me that when she was lecturing, because she didn't see the length of cigarette ash, her students had acquired the habit of warning her with a hissed, "Hosszu" ("Long"), so she would not drop ashes over the floor or her desk.

Les Préludes

Annie hadn't performed in Budapest for more than twenty years. She was performing only on her international tours, in recording sessions and in some cities outside of Budapest. I tried to convince her to perform the following season in Budapest with me. Finally, she told me to call her when I come back from Pecs and she would give me a definite answer.

When I returned I called her. "May I speak to Annie Fischer?" I said. "Who is calling?" the woman on the other end of the line said. I told her. "She is dead?!?" You can imagine my emotional reaction. It turned out that she had died the previous night while listening to the B Minor Mass of Johan Sebastian Bach. I think I was the last person to hear her play!

Finally, the time came for my first rehearsal with the MAV Symphony Orchestra. MAV stands for Magyar Allami Vasutak (Hungarian State Railways). During the Communist regime, the State Railway had not just a symphony orchestra, but also an opera company. Besides performing in Budapest, they would travel on their special train to smaller communities which didn't have their own orchestras or opera companies. The MAV Symphony turned out to be a very fine orchestra with high professional standards. On our first meeting I told them how happy I was to work with them, since my last concert with them (more than forty years earlier) had been cancelled.

I started the rehearsal with Les Preludes. According to my normal routine with a new orchestra, I suggested to them that in order to get acquainted a little bit, let's play through the work without stopping. I conducted the piece by memory so I could not only hear, but also watch the various players. When we finished, they gave me a big hand, and I complimented them, saying that I could see that we would have not much to rehearse. Kathy and her boyfriend were in the other room, happy to hear the orchestra's enthusiastic welcome.

The rehearsals went extremely well and so did the concert. We had a full house and a very enthusiastic audience. I must confess that I was prepared for the success. I agreed with the orchestra that we were to play the last section of the

Mephisto Waltz for our encore. At the end of the

VENDÉGMŰVÉSZEK A TENGERENTÚLRÓL

LUCILLE CHUNG
zongoraművésznő
(Kanada)

LASZLO GATI
karmester
(Kanada)

Idén második budapesti fellépése!

1956-óta először Magyarországon!

és a
MÁV SZIMFÓNIKUS ZENEKAR

A LISZT FERENC ZENEAKADÉMIA NAGYTERMÉBEN
(Bp., VI. Liszt Ferenc tér 8.)
1998. MÁRCIUS 25-ÉN, SZOMBATON, ESTE 1/2 8 ÓRAKOR

BEETHOVEN	III. LEONÓRA NYITÁNY
HARRY FREEDMAN (CANADA)	KLEE WYCK, „A NEVETŐ" *
LISZT FERENC	ESZ-DÚR ZONGORAVERSENY
LISZT FERENC	MEFISZTÓ-KERINGŐ
CSAJKOVSZKIJ	RÓMEÓ ÉS JÚLIA NYITÁNYFANTÁZIA
LISZT FERENC	LES PRÉLUDES- SZIMFÓNIKUS KÖLTEMÉNY

* MAGYARORSZÁGI ŐSBEMUTATÓ- A MŰVET LASZLO GATI ÉS A VICTORIA SYMPHONY ORCHESTRA FELKÉRÉSÉRE,
BRITISH COLUMBIA FENNÁLLÁSÁNAK 100 ÉVES JUBILEUMÁRA KOMPONÁLTA HARRY FREEDMAN

**A KONCERT KANADA ÉS A KOREAI KÖZTÁRSASÁG
NAGYKÖVETSÉGEINEK VÉDNÖKSÉGÉVEL JÖTT LÉTRE**

A HANWHA koncert támogatója

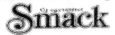

Jegyek kaphatók:

Zeneakadémia	Bp., VI. Liszt Ferenc tér 8. Tel.: 142-0179
Musik Mix 33 Ticket Office	Bp., V. Váci u. 33. Tel.: 138-2237
Publika Jegyiroda (Ibusz)	Bp., V. Ferenciek tere 10. Tel.: 118-3430
Nemzeti Filharmónia jegypénztára	Bp., V. Vörösmarty tér 1. Tel.: 117-6222

So prosaic, this little piece of paper, the concert program of my return to Budapest, where I began my conducting career, and now where I conducted the piece of music which formed in me the ambition to choose this path in life. I do not think very many people visit their past quite so successfully. All in all, it was a wondeful, powerful, moving experience concert, they wouldn't stop clapping. In Hungary, instead of giving a standing ovation they start to clap rhythmically, in unison. While the audience kept clapping, I brought Lucille back on stage several times. She received new bouquets of flowers every time. Finally, after almost ten minutes of clapping we played our encore. When we finished, I grabbed the concertmaster's hand and we led the orchestra offstage.

Personally, the highlight of the concert was the total absorption of the audience in our performances. At the end of each piece, there had been a couple of seconds of silence. This was not due to a lack of familiarity with the works, but because together we had all traveled to a magical realm and it took them some moments to come back to mundane reality.

My feelings conducting the 'fatal' bars of Les Preludes will remain with me for the rest of my life. As the same motif appears practically at the beginning of the composition and it is repeated majestically at the end, most conductors fail to realize that Liszt has a slower tempo marking at the motif at the end of the piece. I took it even slower than marked, in a really Majestic tempo. I had a hard time to let go and end the piece.

Love and hate, success and failure, happiness and unhappiness, hope and despair, marriage and divorce, war and peace, children arriving and parents, grandparents and friends departing and so on. Naturally, I realize that all this is not unique to just me, that millions have gone through similar experiences and have their personal stories to tell. Perhaps my story is a little bit different because I was very fortunate to share it with some of the greatest artists and personalities of the past sixty years. Not to be philosophical at this late stage of my life would be unnatural. Through this autobiography I hope I have shed some light not just on my personal story, but also on some of the universal problems of humanity — depression, war, revolution, hope, and love.

The great Hungarian poet Imre Madacs ends his monumental work The Tragedy of Men, saying,

"Man struggles always and yet hope abides eternal . . ."

Laszlo Gati
September, 2004

Mosaics of a Musician's Life

Laszlo Gati

Laszlo Gati is one of Canada's internationally best-known conductors. He has conducted more than fifty orchestras on four continents. Most of the major contemporary classical artists have appeared under his baton, including Sir Yehudi Menuhin, Dame Moura Lympany, Mstislav Rostropovich, Phillippe Entremont, Jean Pierre Rampal, Van Cliburn, Igor Oistrakh, Janos Starker, and many others.

He was the Music Director of the Victoria and Windsor Symphony Orchestras, l'Orchestre Philharmonic de Montreal, Founder and Artistic Director of the Montreal Chamber Orchestra and the Victoria Summer Festival, Executive Director of the Dollar Concerts of the Pacific, Principal Guest Conductor of the Philharmonic Orchestra of Bogotá, Columbia, the National Symphony Orchestra of Mexico, and many others.

Maestro Gati is also an accomplished violinist and violist. For several years he was a violinist with the Hungarian State Philharmonic Orchestra, and Assistant Solo Violist of the Montreal Symphony Orchestra, where he acted as assistant conductor for Zubin Mehta.

Before leaving Hungary in 1956, he was the Head of the Symphonic and Chamber Music Department of Hungarian Radio in Budapest, where he also established and became Head of the Musical Program Exchange Department. He was also a conductor of the National Philharmonic Society and of the Choir of the University of Economics.

Maestro Gati was one of the founding Directors of the Association of Canadian Orchestras (ACO). In British Columbia, he incorporated Galacon Concerts and presented major attractions in Vancouver, Victoria, and Seattle, including the Canadian Opera Company, The Bach Aria Group, The Royal Winnipeg Ballet, The Romeros, The National Dance Company of Senegal, Andres Segovia, Narciso Yepes, and others.

Les Préludes

During his career Maestro Gati worked with Youth Orchestras in Banff, Budapest, Calgary, Montreal, and Vancouver.

Maestro Gati holds various awards, honorary positions and citations, including a Senior Art Fellowship of the Canada Council, Honorary Professor of the Zoltan Kodaly Academy, Honorary Citizen of the City of Victoria, and holder of the Queen's Jubilee Medal.